D0500275

The Law of the Sea and Australian Off-Shore Areas

The Law of the Sea and Australian Off-Shore Areas

2nd Edition

R. D. Lumb

 University of
Queensland
Press

© University of Queensland Press, St. Lucia, Queensland, 1966, 1978
Second Edition, 1978

Typeset by Academy Press, Pty. Ltd., Brisbane
Printed and bound by Silex Enterprise & Printing Co., Hong Kong

Distributed in the United Kingdom, Europe, the Middle East,
Africa, and the Caribbean by Prentice-Hall International,
International Book Distributors Ltd., 66 Wood Lane End,
Hemel Hempstead, Herts., England

National Library of Australia
Cataloguing-in-Publication data

Lumb, Richard Darrell, 1934–.
  Law of the sea.

  ISBN 0 7022 1147 8.

  1. Territorial water. 2. Maritime law.
  3. Territorial waters–Australia.
  4. Maritime law–Australia. I. Title.

341.448

Contents

Contents

Preface to Second Edition

Since the publication of the first edition of this work in 1966, there have been major developments in the law of the sea, including the convening of a Third Conference on the Law of the Sea. The delay in reaching agreement at the Conference on several vital issues has led a number of nations to take unilateral action, in particular, the adoption of 200 miles (or 320 km) exclusive economic or fisheries zones. On another issue—mining of the manganese nodules in the deep sea-bed area—it is possible that entities operating under national laws will be involved in the exploitation of these resources in the absence of an agreement establishing an International Authority with resource powers.

Two important decisions have been handed down by the International Court of Justice: *The North Sea Continental Shelf Cases* and the *Fisheries Jurisdiction Cases* which have attempted to reconcile national conflicts in the allocation of sea-bed and fishing rights.

In the area of pollution, various conventions have been drawn up to protect the maritime environment from the effects of oil spills and dumping of wastes.

Within Australia, the constitutional conflict between commonwealth and states in relation to sovereignty over the adjacent sea and sea-bed has been resolved by a majority decision of the High Court in 1975 in favour of the commonwealth's claim, embodied in the *Seas and Submerged Lands Act* of 1973.

With respect to Australia's maritime boundaries with other

countries, sea-bed agreements have been negotiated with Indonesia demarcating the division of continental shelf in the northern and northwest areas (apart from the area opposite East Timor) and negotiations are at present being conducted to define the maritime limits of Australia and Papua New Guinea in the Torres Strait area.

The Second Edition takes account of these developments.

Since the completion of the text, the sixth session of the Law of the Sea Conference has come to an end without agreement being reached on a new treaty, although a revised negotiating text has been prepared. A further session of the conference is scheduled for 1978. It appears that a major stumbling block has been the question of the powers of the operating area of the international sea-bed authority to engage in the exploration and exploitation of the resources of the deep sea-bed and the rights of access of national entities to areas of the deep sea-bed.

Unilaterial proclamations of 200 miles resources zones have gathered momentum and it is likely that the concept of a 200 miles exclusive fisheries zone will soon become established in customary international law. At a recent meeting of ministers representing countries of the South Pacific Forum, including Australia, there was a common expression of intention to take measures for the adoption by the individual countries of 200 miles fisheries zones by March 1978.

At a recent meeting of signatories to the Antarctic Treaty of 1959, it was decided to convene a conference in 1978 with the aim of drafting a treaty to govern the exploitation of marine life resources in the Antarctic Region.

The High Court has recently handed down a decision— *Robinson* v. *The Western Australian Museum* (31 August 1977) in which it was held by a statutory authority (the Court being evenly divided, the decision of the Chief Justice prevailed under the provisions of the *Judiciary Act*) that the State of Western Australia did not have the legislative power to control historic wrecks embedded in or lying on the sea-bed adjacent to its coastline. Control of historic wrecks is now regulated by the *Historic Shipwrecks Act* (Commonwealth) the provisions of which are discussed in Chapter 11.

Acknowledgment is made to the Law Book Company Limited,

publishers of the *Australian Law Journal*, for permission to reproduce parts of two articles of mine which have appeared in issues of the *Journal*: "The Off-Shore Petroleum Agreement and Legislation", *A.L.J.*, 41 (1968), p. 453; and "Sovereignty and Jurisdiction over Australian Coastal Waters", *A.L.J.*, 43 (1969), p. 421.

R.D. LUMB
30th September 1977

Table of Statutes
(Commonwealth and United Kingdom)

COMMONWEALTH

UNITED KINGDOM

Table of Cases

PART I

The Position in
International Law

1

Introduction

During the last thirty years the exploitation of the resources of the sea and the sea-bed has opened new legal vistas and posed new problems for solution by lawyers. These problems have arisen not only on the international plane but also in terms of the development of rules within the Australian federal system.

The exploitation of the mineral resources of *terra firma* is, under our federal structure, primarily a matter for regulation by the states. Under the legislative structure of the states pertaining to mining and the extraction of mineral resources, the rights of a landowner are qualified by the recognition of paramount state rights in the mining and minerals areas. These rights are reflected in a variety of ways: in the prerogative right of the Crown, recognized by the common law, to precious metals such as gold and silver; in the statutory vesting of ownership of particular types of minerals in the Crown; in the reservation under state law of rights to minerals, generally when Crown land is granted to a private individual; and in the "mining on private land" legislation under which mining rights may be granted to persons other than the registered proprietor.[1] Under the legislation relating to petroleum, the standard pattern has been for the states to grant to persons (natural or corporate) exploitation and extraction rights under permit, licence or lease, subject to the payment of licence fees and royalties and to compliance with rules relating to methods of operation and safety procedures.[2]

This pattern of law is not, of course, immediately applicable to the resources of the sea-bed because the status of the sea-bed is by its very nature different from that of land. It is true that the Anglo-Saxon legal heritage has taken account of many legal problems associated with the sea. The growth in the Admiral's jurisdiction in England was a response to the profound legal problems associated with maritime commerce and intercourse between European nations. The judgments of the Admiralty Courts which were staffed by some of the most distinguished of British judges have often been referred to as a primary source of knowledge on what was a most complex area of law—a *ius gentium* built up from maritime custom and rules and mercantile practice.[3] But Admiralty law in the main does not contain solutions to the legal issues which have been raised by the modern discoveries of the mineral wealth lying underneath the seas and in the success achieved in devising methods for extracting this wealth. Rather the solution is to be found in the rules of public international law, in particular in the provisions of the Geneva Conventions on the Law of the Sea of 1958.

The proliferation of legislative and executive acts since World War 11 asserting rights of sovereignty or jurisdiction by coastal states over their adjacent continental shelves contributed to the development of an international customary rule which recognizes that continental shelf resource rights inhered in the adjacent state and were not *res communis* (common property) or *res nullius* (ownerless property) open to appropriation by any nation. The formal recognition of the continental shelf doctrine came with the Geneva Convention on the Continental Shelf which, together with three other Conventions, was drawn up at the First United Nations Conference on the Law of the Sea held at Geneva in 1958 following preliminary drafting done by the International Law Commission.[4] There is no doubt that the Conventions which both codified and developed the law of the sea constituted an affirmative recognition by a substantial section of the international community of the legal regime of the sea-bed.[5]

Apart from the Continental Shelf Convention,[6] the other three Conventions were: the Convention on the High Seas, the Convention on the Territorial Sea and the Contiguous Zone, and the Convention on Fishing and the Conservation of the Living Resources of the High Seas. The Convention on the High Seas[7] enshrines the principle of the freedom of the high seas and establishes a code of rights and duties in relation to the uses of the high seas. The Convention on the Territorial Sea and Contiguous Zone[8] defines the manner in which the maritime zones adjacent to a coastline (internal waters, territorial waters and the contiguous zone) are measured[9] (but not the *breadth* of territorial waters)[10] and the rights of navigation in the territorial sea. The Convention on Fishing and the Conservation of the Living Resources[11] of the High Seas deals with procedures for adopting fishing conservation measures on the high seas.

Since the adoption of these Conventions in 1958, the law of the sea has been subjected to pressures from many states claiming increased maritime jurisdiction through concepts such as the 200 miles patrimonial sea or exclusive economic zone.[12] Side by side with this nationalist pressure there has developed a "heritage of mankind" doctrine[13] which has been used to promote an international regime for the future exploitation of the resources of the deep sea-bed area outside the limits of national jurisdiction.

Increased concern directed to the effects of pollution from land-based and vessel-originating sources is reflected in revisions of existing international conventions relating to the pollution of sea by oil and in new conventions relating to pollution as a result of maritime accidents.[14]

During this period the International Court of Justice has handed down decisions in relation to two issues which have generated friction between neighbouring states or in regions of the seas: the *North Sea Continental Shelf Cases* (1969) on the demarcation of sea-bed boundaries between adjacent states,[15] and the *Fisheries Jurisdiction Case* (1974) relating to the regulation of fishing on the high seas by unilateral action of a coastal state.[16]

Since 1973 the nations of the world have been engaged in discussions of a new regime for the seas and sea-bed in the Third United Nations Conference on the Law of the Sea.[17] From a procedural session held in New York in 1973, the Conference has moved through substantive sessions at Caracas in 1974, Geneva in 1975, two sessions at New York in 1976 and to a third session in New York in 1977 (the sixth session of the Conference). The Conference established three main Committees: the first dealing with an international regime for the deep sea-bed beyond national jurisdiction, the second with various questions relating to national zones (exclusive economic zone, etc.), and the third with preservation of the marine environment and scientific research. At the time of writing, no new Convention has emerged from this Conference, although a basis for the Conference deliberations has been a Single Negotiating Text consisting of draft articles which have been revised in the light of the ongoing discussions. As will be seen from a later chapter, the divisions between developed and developing nations over a regime for the deep sea-bed area and the nature of jurisdiction in a two hundred miles exclusive economic zone have constituted the main obstacles to the achievement of a consensus.[18]

In the following chapters I propose to examine first the basic content of the international rules, and secondly, the application of these rules to Australian off-shore areas and the basic content of Australian domestic rules relating to maritime jurisdiction.

There is already a growing literature relating to Australia and the law of the sea and many of the questions to be examined in the work have been analyzed elsewhere.[19] It will be inevitable that I will reconsider some of the basic issues such as jurisdiction over the territorial sea and sea-bed within a federal system. In particular, reference will be made to certain important developments within the last decade, the passage of the complementary *Petroleum (Submerged Lands) Acts* of commonwealth and states in 1967, the declaration of commonwealth sovereignty in the *Seas and Submerged Lands Act* in 1973, and the historic decision of the High Court in the litigation in which this Act was challenged by the states but upheld by the Court: *New South Wales* v. *Commonwealth*.[20]

At the outset it will be of assistance to the reader to give a brief definition of some of the maritime concepts or terms which will be used in the text.[21]

a) *Tidelands* (sea-shore). This is the area of land which is covered by the ebb and flow of the tide, i.e. that area which lies between high-water mark and low-water mark.

b) *Internal* (or *Inland*) *Waters*. These are waters that are either entirely enclosed by land (e.g. lakes) or, which bordering on the open sea, are enclosed within significant indentations of the coastline (gulfs or bays), or as arms of the sea (estuaries, harbours), or are fringed by islands in such a way as to assimilate the waters lying between the coastline and the "fringe" to the regime of internal waters.

c) *Territorial Waters*. This is the area of water which extends from the coastline (accepted generally as the low-water line) to a distance from the shore which is commonly fixed at three nautical miles or one marine league (about 5 km). This breadth or distance from the shore has been rejected by many nations which now claim a twelve mile (about 20 km) limit, although a number of major maritime nations have refused to recognize an extended territorial sea unless the question of transit rights through straits has been determined at an international conference.

d) *Contiguous Zone*. This is an area extending not more than twelve nautical miles from the coastline within which the coastal state may exercise a jurisdiction over foreign vessels in relation to customs, fiscal, immigration or sanitary matters (Convention on the Territorial Seas and Contiguous Zone, Article 24).

Customary international law also recognizes an exclusive fisheries zone of twelve miles in which the coastal state has exclusive fishing rights.

e) *High Seas* (or International Waters). These are the waters of the world's oceans and seas which lie outside territorial waters. They are open to use by all nations and cannot be appropriated by any one nation, although they are subject to certain rules so far as use is concerned.

f) *The Continental Shelf*. The following definition of the continental shelf is derived from Article 1 of the Convention on the Continental Shelf:

> The term "continental shelf" is used as referring (a) to the sea-bed and subsoil of the submarine areas adjacent to the coast but outside the area of the territorial sea, to a depth of 200 metres or, beyond that limit, to where the depth of the superjacent waters admits of the exploitation of the natural resources of the said areas: (b) to the sea-bed and subsoil of similar submarine areas adjacent to the coasts of islands.

g) *Continental Slope*. The zone commencing at the 200-metre line (i.e. the limit of the "physical" continental shelf where there is usually a marked increase in "fall-away") to the edge of the continental rise (which varies between 1200 and 3500 metres in depth).

h) *The Continental Rise*. The area bordering the slope where it "levels out" to a smoother rate of decline (varying between 3500 and 5500 metres in depth) to the deep sea-bed. *Note*: The shelf, slope and rise are often referred to as the "continental margin", the combined shelf and rise as the "continental terrace".

i) *The Deep Sea-Bed Area* (abyssal plain). The area of the sea-bed outside the continental margin which is reputedly rich in manganese nodules. The question of an international regime for this area (which may extend back into the continental margin) is under examination at the Third Law of the Sea Conference.

j) *The Exclusive Economic Zone*. This is a zone extending two hundred miles (about 320 km) from the coastline in which a number of nations have made claims to exercise sovereign rights over both the resources of the sea-bed and also over the living resources of the sea (fish).

2

National Waters and Zones

Prior to the drawing up of the Convention on the Territorial Sea and the Contiguous Zone, it was universally agreed that a coastal state had the right to exercise exclusive control over the waters and sea-bed adjacent to its coastline. There was some difference of opinion over the question whether these rights were rights of sovereignty or merely a bundle of jurisdictional rights, but the matter has been determined by Article 1 of the Convention which affirms a right of sovereignty in the coastal nation over its adjacent territorial waters including the subjacent sea-bed and subjacent air space, subject however to a right of innocent passage of the vessels of foreign states through such territorial sea.[1]

No agreement was reached, however, at the 1958 conference or at a second conference held in 1960 on the breadth (width) of the territorial sea. Under customary international law and practice as reflected in the writings of international jurists (Galiani, Bynkershoek) in the eighteenth century who formulated the "cannon shot" principle, the distance had been recognized as three nautical miles from the coastline. There were proposals before both conferences for wider limits, one of which was based on the "six-plus-six" formula under which two separate zones— a territorial sea and an exclusive fisheries zone, each of six miles, would be recognized.[2] But this proposal although it had widespread support did not achieve the necessary majority for approval (failing by one vote to achieve the required two-thirds majority at the 1960 conference).[3]

Since 1960 a number of nations have by legislative or administrative action claimed a twelve-mile exclusive fisheries zone in some cases qualified by "phasing out" agreements with foreign countries which have traditionally fished in the nine-mile zone outside the three-mile area of territorial waters. Other nations have claimed a full territorial sea of twelve miles. Some nations (mainly South American) have claimed a two hundred-mile territorial sea (or its equivalent).[4]

Although the twelve miles exclusive fisheries zone must now be regarded as established in customary international law[5] it cannot be said that a twelve-mile territorial sea is so established. At the Third Law of the Sea Conference, major maritime powers have expressed their concern that over one hundred straits used for international navigation would become subject to the regime of territorial waters if the wider belt were recognized.[6] While it is true that a right of innocent passage exists through territorial waters, and it is also established under Article 16(4) of the Convention on the Territorial Sea and Contiguous Zone that there can be no suspension of innocent passage through international straits, nevertheless the doctrine of innocent passage is subject to vagueness in interpretation, particularly in its application to the passage of warships or vessels which may pose an environmental hazard. Consequently major maritime nations have proposed a right of free transit through straits, which would not be subject to such doubts or vagueness in interpretation that attach to the doctrine of innocent passage.[7]

THE BASELINE OF THE TERRITORIAL SEA: INTERNAL WATERS

The territorial sea is ordinarily to be measured from the baseline which follows the sinuousities of the coastline, that baseline following the low-water (not the high-water) line.[8] Where, however, the coastline is deeply indented or cut into, or there is a fringe of islands in its immediate vicinity, straight baselines joining appropriate points may be drawn.[9] However, the drawing of such baselines must not depart to any appreciable extent from the general direction of the coast, and the sea areas lying within the line must be sufficiently closely linked to the land domain to be subject to the regime of internal waters.[10] The coastal state must clearly indicate straight baselines on charts to which due publicity must be given.[11] Although Article 4(3) of the Convention provides that straight baselines cannot be drawn to and from low-tide elevations (e.g. rocks or reefs covered at high-tide but dry at low-tide) unless lighthouses or similar installations are built on them, this provision must be considered with Article 11(1) which allows low-tide elevations situated within the territorial sea to be used as a baseline for measuring the breadth of that territorial sea.[12] In determining particular baselines account may be taken of economic interests "peculiar to the region concerned, the reality and the importance of which are clearly evidenced by a long usage".[13]

The waters on the landward side of the baselines are deemed to be part of the internal waters of the coastal state.[14] It is expressly provided, however, that where straight baselines have been drawn so as to cut off waters which previously have been considered part of the territorial sea or the high seas, a right of innocent passage through such waters is preserved.[15] The outer limit of the territorial sea is a line which runs parallel to the baseline.[16]

Article 4 of the Convention is in accordance with the decision of the International Court of Justice in the *Anglo-Norwegian Fisheries Case*[17] where the straight baseline method was accepted by the Court as an appropriate way of demarcating the breadth of Norway's territorial sea. The outer line of the *skjaergaard* (the myriad of rocks, islands, inlets and promontories) had been adopted by the Norwegian authorities for the purpose of drawing the baseline of the territorial sea. The Court recognized not only the relevance of these peculiar geographical features but also the validity of regional economic interests (Norwegian fishery interests) in upholding the validity of the method.

But it must not be forgotten that the straight baseline method is in exception to the general rule according to which the drawing of the baselines follows the sinuosities of the coast. It therefore should not be used as a justification for an inordinate projection of baselines into ocean areas.[18]

11

BAYS

In the case of bays which belong to a single state, the Convention provides that a closing line may be drawn across the natural entrance points where the distance between these points does not exceed twenty-four miles.[19] Where the distance between these points exceeds twenty-four miles a closing line of twenty-four miles *within* the bay may be drawn.[20]

To qualify as a "bay" under the provisions, an indentation must possess a certain geographical configuration and the area of water must have a sufficient penetration into the land mass and not merely be a curvature of the coast; its area must be at least "as large as, or larger than, that of the semi-circle whose diameter is a line drawn across the mouth of the indentation".[21] However, it expressly provided that these requirements do not apply to situations where a straight baseline system is adopted nor to "historic bays".[22]

It is clear therefore that the geographical or ordinary use of the word "bay" to describe an indentation of the coastline is not necessarily equivalent to its juristic meaning as laid down in Article 7.[23] In geographic and cartographic use the words "bay" or "gulf" may be used to describe indentations irrespective of depth of penetration. More often than not the word "gulf" is used to denote a wider and/or deeper water penetration into the land mass.[24] Under Article 7, this geographical usage does not itself determine whether the prescribed closing line may be drawn. The intention of Article 7 in requiring a certain depth of penetration is to prevent coastal states from enclosing minor curvatures of the coast—a practice which would depart from the normal requirement that the low-water line of the coast must be used as a baseline.

Where a bay is regarded in international law as an "historic bay",[25] the twenty four miles closing line restriction does not apply, and a closing line of greater length may be drawn. The criteria for proving "historic title" would appear to be onerous, the requisite elements being an exercise of sovereign rights by a coastal state over a period of time which is acquiesced in by other nations. It would appear that the number of such claims are few and that the burden of proof cast on a claimant state is a difficult one. On the other hand the criteria resting as they do on customary practice are undefined and there would appear to be a need to codify them.[26]

ISLANDS AND LOW-TIDE ELEVATIONS

Article 10(1) of the Convention on the Territorial Sea and Contiguous Zone defines an island as a naturally formed area of land, surrounded by water, which is above water at high-tide. The territorial sea of an island is to be measured in accordance with the provisions of the Convention.

However, an "island" must be distinguished from a "low-tide elevation". A low-tide elevation is a "naturally-formed area of land which is surrounded by and above water at low-tide but submerged at high-tide".[27] Where a low-tide elevation is situated wholly or partly at a distance not exceeding the breadth of the territorial sea from the mainland or an island, the low-water line on that elevation may be used as the baseline for measuring the breadth of the territorial sea.[28] However, where a low-tide elevation is wholly situated at a distance exceeding the breadth of the territorial sea from the mainland or an island, it has no territorial sea of its own.[29] Reference may also be made to the provision contained in Article 4 relating to the drawing of a straight baseline system under which such baselines may be drawn joining islands constituting a "fringe" in the immediate vicinity of a mainland coastline although they may not be drawn to and from low-tide elevations unless lighthouses or similar installations which are permanently above sea level have been built on them.[30] Finally, Article 7(3) deals with islands in and across the mouths of bays. Under the provisions of this Article, in determining the configuration of the area of the bay, the semi-circle "shall be drawn on a line as long as the sum total of the lengths of the lines across the different mouths". Islands within an indentation are to be treated as if they were part of the water areas of the indentation.[31]

The presence of islands off an indentation must also be considered in determining the applicability of a straight baseline method under Article 4 of the Convention, and it has been suggested that even though a closing line may not be drawn across an indentation under Article 7, nevertheless a straight baseline may be drawn so as to enclose a bay wider than twenty-four miles where there are islands which "fringe" the entrance.

It is clear from the Convention that islands may be considered under two classifications, either as fringing islands—in which case they may be used to delimit a mainland coastline, or as separate geographic entities—in which case the ordinary rules relating to the measurement of the territorial sea will apply.

Article 10(1) defines an island as a naturally formed area of land surrounded by water, which is above water at high tide. There has been some dispute in the past as to the legal requirements for the existence of an island. According to one usage an island was an area of land which could be effectively occupied and used.[32] According to another usage an island was any naturally formed area which showed above the sea. This would include areas of land with vegetation and sand as well as smaller reefs and mere rocks or bounders (provided that they were above water).[33] It now seems to be recognized that the effect of Article 10 is that effective occupation is not necessary but that (a) the area must be a naturally formed area of land (rock, sand, etc.): this means that artificial structures such as lighthouses or "floating islands" are not included: and (b) such a naturally formed area of land must be above water permanently, i.e., at both low and high tides. Capacity for use is not embodied in this definition of an island;[34] consequently uninhabited cays, rock outcrops, and boulders above water at high tide qualify as islands and therefore have a territorial sea surrounding them. At the Third Law of the Sea Conference proposals have been put forward to redefine the meaning of an "island" to include some reference to capacity for "habitation" or "use".[35] This in fact arises from difficulties involved in determining the applicability of two-hundred-mile economic resources zones to all areas of land or rock.

There are also low-tide elevations, i.e. areas which are at some part of the day covered by the waters of the ocean. As we have seen, where a low-tide elevation is situated outside the territorial sea of an island or the mainland, it does not have a territorial sea of its own. However, where a low-tide elevation is situated wholly or partly at a distance not exceeding the breadth of the territorial sea from the mainland or an island, the low-water line in that elevation may be used as the baseline for measuring the breadth of the territorial sea.[36]

The exact effect of this provision is a matter of some doubt. On one view it could be regarded as an exception to article 4, paragraph 3, which states that "baselines shall not be drawn from low-tide elevations unless lighthouses or similar installations which are permanently above sea-level are built on them". That is to say, Article 11(1) could be interpreted as authorizing the use of a straight baseline system where such low-tide elevations are within the territorial sea of the mainland or an island. On the other hand, however, the article could be interpreted not as authorizing the use of the low-tide elevation as a terminal point for a straight baseline drawn from the mainland or from an island, but as a factor to be taken into account in determining the extension of the territorial sea of the mainland or an island outwards, that is to say it would merely affect the *breadth* of the territorial sea. It would not therefore be used as a basis for claiming the area of waters lying between it and the mainland or island as internal waters but would only extend the territorial sea of these land areas measured from their own low-water lines. Its legal status was described as follows at a meeting of the International Law Commission which discussed the nature of low-tide elevations: "The basic principle is that drying rocks and drying shoals are not points of departure for measuring the territorial sea. However, if a drying rock or a drying shoal were to be found within the territorial sea (such territorial sea being measured as if the drying rock were not there at all), then the drying rock or shoal in question could be used in order to extend the territorial sea and project seaward its limit."[37] McDougal and Burke support this second interpretation of Article 11,[38] but the question must be regarded as an open one.[39]

It has been suggested that there are one or two gaps in the Convention, i.e. in the case of enclaves[40] and non-adjacent archipelagos.[41] Where a question arises as to the application of a straight baseline method to a coastline which is surrounded by a number of islands, but not a sufficient number to warrant the adoption of this method, the drawing of areas of territorial sea

15

around each island will lead to the existence of small pockets of high seas surrounded by territorial waters. McDougal and Burke refer to the opinion expressed at the 1930 Codification Conference of the International Law Commission that such enclaves if not more than two miles in breadth and entirely surrounded by territorial seas may be included within the latter but, in the case where the waters are open at both ends, the "pockets" should be regarded as part of the high seas.[42]

As far as non-adjacent archipelagos[43] are concerned, it is suggested that the Convention is restricted to individual islands and groups of islands fringing a coastline. There are, however, examples of groups of islands which are not so close to the coastline as to exhibit an affinity with it but yet are so inter-connected with each other as to suggest the application of a joining line of more than six miles (which would be the width of an "island joining" line if measured in the ordinary manner). At the 1930 conference there was some dispute as to the method to be adopted in this case. Some delegates spoke in favour of the ordinary three-mile line principle being applied, while others favoured treating the group as a whole on condition that the distance between islands did not exceed ten miles.[44] The report of the International Law Commission which was made to the 1958 Conference did not contain any recommendation on this question. As McDougal and Burke point out, a compelling argument against any differential treatment for non-adjacent archipelagos which often straddle the sea lanes of the oceans is the principle of the freedom of the high seas, and this may militate against any extension of the ordinary rule in the case of these archipelagos.[45] But there are also strong arguments which support a unitary treatment of archipelagic waters.[46] The matter is under examination at the Third Law of the Sea Conference and various proposals have been made for the unitary treatment of archipelagos.[47]

ADJACENT FUNCTIONAL ZONES

(a) Contiguous zone

Article 24(1) of the Convention on the Territorial Sea and Contiguous Zone provides that in a zone of the high seas contiguous to the territorial sea, the coastal state may exercise the control necessary to (a) prevent infringement of its customs, fiscal, immigration or sanitary regulations within its territory or territorial sea; (b) punish infringement of the above regulations committed within its territory or territorial sea.[48]

The effect of this provision is that the coastal state may control acts of foreign nationals and foreign vessels in a zone extending twelve miles from the territorial sea baselines, but only for defined purposes: i.e., for the application and enforcement of its laws relating to customs, revenue, immigration, health and quarantine, although punitive measures (e.g., arrest and judicial proceedings) may be taken only in respect of infringements committed within the territorial sea.[49] The effect of the action of many states in extending their territorial seas to the twelve miles has meant that the boundaries of their claimed territorial sea and the contiguous zone have become co-terminous.

(b) Exclusive fishing zone

International customary law may now be regarded as recognizing an exclusive fisheries zone which extends from the territorial sea baseline to a distance of twelve miles from that baseline.[50] The international customary law which has generated the recognition of such zone in the years following the failure of the 1960 Conference to define such a limit, was recognized by the International Court of Justice in the *Fisheries Jurisdiction Case*,[51] where the Court referred to "the area in which a State may claim exclusive fishing jurisdiction independently of its territorial sea; the extension of that fishing zone up to a 12 miles limit from the baselines appears now to be generally accepted".[52] Within this zone a coastal state may therefore validly prohibit activities of fishing (and related activities such as transfer of fish catches to "mother vessels").

3

The Continental Shelf

The doctrine of the continental shelf as a legal regime applying to the exploration and exploitation of off-shore mineral resources may be said to have begun in 1945 with the Truman Proclamation by which the United States declared that it had sovereign rights over the exploration and exploitation of the resources of the continental shelf adjacent to the American coastline extending beyond the three-mile limit.[1] Other national assertions of authority followed during the next decade and by 1958 there was substantial evidence of the existence of a principle of customary international law to the effect that rights of exclusive control over continental shelf resources were vested in the coastal state.[2] The Convention on the Continental Shelf, signed at Geneva in 1958, set at rest any doubts about the international community's recognition of the exclusive rights of the coastal state, by recognizing that such rights rested on the basis of adjacency or contiguity and that the existence of such rights did not depend on occupation (notional or effective) or on a proclamation of sovereignty.[3]

In the *North Sea Continental Shelf Cases*[4] the International Court of Justice, referring to the acceptance by the international community of coastal state jurisdiction, stated: "the rights of the coastal state in respect of the area of the continental shelf that constitutes a natural prolongation of its land territory into and under the sea exist *ipso facto* and *ab initio*, by virtue of its sovereignty over the land, and as an extension of its sovereign

18

rights for the purpose of exploring the seabed and exploiting its natural resources. In short, there is an inherent right. In order to exercise it, no special process has to be gone through, nor have any special legal acts to be performed."[5]

The limits of the continental shelf are set out in Article 1 of the Convention which provides:

> For the purposes of these articles, the term "continental shelf" is used as referring (a) to the seabed and subsoil of the submarine areas adjacent to the coast but outside the area of the territorial sea, to a depth of 200 metres or beyond that limit, to where the depth of the superjacent waters admits of the exploitation of the natural resources of the said areas; (b) to the seabed and subsoil of similar submarine areas adjacent to the coasts of islands.

It is to be noted that the definition is open-ended in the sense that it contains both a fixed geographical criterion based on the water depth and also an economic or physical criterion which permits of extension of coastal state jurisdiction beyond that depth. Physically, the continental shelf comprises the sea-bed extending from the low-water mark[6] to a depth at which there is a marked declivity on the slope of the bed. The drafters of the Convention selected the two hundred metre isobath as the uniform limit although the marked declivity (which indicates the beginning of the continental *slope*) may occur at lower or greater depths.[7]

However, the two hundred metre isobath does not mark the limits of coastal shelf jurisdiction, because the "exploitability" criterion in Article 1 would allow extension of the coastal state jurisdiction to the slope.[8]

There are two possible definitions of "exploitability". The term may mean that the resources are physically exploitable, that is to say, that they may be extracted from the sea-bed or subsoil. According to this meaning, as engineering techniques enable a particular mineral resource to be taken from the sea-bed at a particular depth (whether by sub-marine or surface techniques), then such a resource is exploitable, and consequently sovereign rights of the coastal state are extended to that depth, at least in relation to that resource.[9] The alternative test would be an economic one. This would require a mineral to be recoverable in sufficient amounts and at reasonable costs so as to allow it to be processed and sold on a commercial basis. The difficulty with this latter criterion is that it is dependent on economic theory and practice which is contentious: economists differ among themselves on the methods and standards, to be used in assessing such factors as market value, particularly where there is a fundamental disequilibrium as between a state-controlled and a free enterprise economic system.[10] Physical exploitability is therefore more subject to assessment and determination by scientific and engineering techniques and practice, although it must be recognized that it is a concept which is tied to the particular mineral which is the subject of exploitation: the methods used for extracting hydrocarbons from the subsoil would differ from those used in extracting manganese nodules from the sea floor.

Whatever the test to be applied, it is generally admitted that Article 1 allows the coastal state to extend its jurisdiction over the exploitation of resources beyond the two hundred metre line.[11] There are suggestions, however, that the exploitability criterion may be rendered superfluous as a test for determining a coastal state's rights by the statement of the International Court in the *North Sea Continental Shelf Cases*: "the rights of the coastal state in respect of the area of the continental shelf that constitutes a natural prolongation of its land territory into and under the sea exist *ipso facto* and *ab initio*, by virtue of its sovereignty over the land, and as an extension of it is an exercise of sovereign rights for the purpose of exploring the sea-bed and exploiting its natural resources."[12] Some see this statement as tending to support rights of the coastal state over the continental slope as being an appurtenant area according to this definition.[13] On the other hand, others point that Article 1 does not permit of such a vast extension of coastal state jurisdiction,[14] and point to the incorporation of a geographical limitation of "adjacency"[15] in Article 1 as requiring a more restrictive interpretation of the outer limits of the shelf. However, it is also argued that the criterion of "adjacency" allows a coastal state to exercise jurisdiction over "shelf" areas up to two hundred metres in depth, which were separated from its main area of continental shelf by channels or troughs. A lack of continuity would therefore not present the coastal state from claiming this jurisdiction over what are in reality continental borderlands.[16]

The Convention on the Continental Shelf also applies the

provisions of Article 1 to islands, although strictly speaking the shelves around islands are *insular* shelves.[17] This raises questions about the area of shelf pertaining to small islands, islets and rocks which are subject to a different political soverignty from that of a coastal state whose shelf "encompasses" such islands, or where islands straddle a common continental shelf shared by two coastal states.[18]

At the Third United Nations Conference on the Law of the Sea, many nations have supported a two hundred-mile economic zone (covering both living resources of the sea and mineral resources of the sea-bed).[19] This concept is based on a "distance from shore" criterion rather than depth of waters. If adopted it would render superfluous much of the legal doctrine of the continental shelf. It would also create uncertainty on the nature of jurisdiction that might be exercised over that part of a continental shelf which extends beyond the two hundred mile limit, i.e. whether it should continue to remain within coastal state authority or be subject to an international authority, or be subject to some type of mixed regime. It is clear that coastal states with shelves or margins extending beyond a two-hundred-mile limit would be disinclined to give up any rights which they now have under existing international law to the resources of the area.

NATURE OF JURISDICTION OVER THE CONTINENTAL SHELF

In the deliberations of the International Law Commission which preceded the drawing up of the Convention, there was extensive debate about the degree of control which was permissible. In the outcome, the concept of sovereignty was not selected as the criterion of jurisdiction but the less potent concept of "sovereign rights for the purpose of exploring and exploiting the natural resources of the shelf".[20] The concept of sovereignty was rejected because of the fear that it might encourage a coastal nation to claim exclusive control over the high seas above the shelf—a claim which would be antithetic to the freedom of the high seas enshrined in the Convention on the High Seas.[21] The phrase "sovereign rights" therefore was intended to indicate that paramount control over the resources of the sea-bed is vested in the coastal nation. But the rights are not at large, as it were. They may be exercised for the specific purpose of exploring and exploiting the natural resources of the shelf. It can thus be said that the concept of control which is implicit in the Convention is one of exclusive political control directed to commercial ends.[22] The concept is not one of ownership of the sea-bed, although of course a coastal nation may provide by its laws for the vesting of rights in the resources extracted either in itself or in persons or corporations to which these rights of extraction and utilization have been granted. Nor is the concept one of political sovereignty, because the sea-bed is not considered a legal entity in the same way as is land or a vessel.

The sovereign rights of a coastal nation are not dependent on occupation of the shelf nor are they dependent on any proclamation of jurisdiction.[23] They are confirmed by force of the Convention on the basis of contiguity. Consequently if a coastal national declines to take advantage of the rights of exploration and exploitation conferred upon it and leaves its shelf "idle", no other nation or person may come in and utilize the resources of the shelf.[24]

The conferment of sovereign rights over the sea-bed is, however, qualified by certain other rules which protect various interests of other nations with respect to the shelf and superjacent waters. Thus protection is afforded to the laying and maintenance of submarine cables on the shelf[25] and it is provided that acts of exploration and exploitation must not cause any unjustifiable interference with marine resources.[26] As well, the escape of harmful substances must be guarded against.[27] Obviously physical apparatus must be brought in for exploration and exploitation work and for this purpose the Convention recognizes that installations may be erected over the shelf; that safety zones, not exceeding five hundred metres in width, may be established around these installations; and that these zones must be respected by all ships.[28] However, such zones may not be established in recognized sea lanes essential to international navigation,[29] and due warning must be given of the installations within the zones.[30] These installations do not have the status of islands, they have no territorial sea of their own, and they cannot be taken into account in measuring the territorial sea of the coastal state.[31]

Oceanography research may be carried out on the shelf with the consent of the coastal nation,[32] but this consent must not normally be withheld.

RESOURCES OF THE CONTINENTAL SHELF

The resources of the sea-bed which are subject to the sovereign rights of exploration and exploitation are defined by the Convention as the "mineral and other non-living resources of the sea-bed and subsoil together with living organisms belonging to sedentary species, that is to say organisms which, at the harvestable state, either are immobile on or under the sea-bed or are unable to move except in constant physical contact with the sea-bed or the subsoil." The primary mineral resources are of course hydrocarbons (petroleum and natural gas) which have already been discovered in a number of areas of the world's continental shelves, but there are others such as phosphate and sulphur which are to be found beneath the sea-bed. The petroleum resources are today exploited by means of drilling platforms and vessels (whether attached by "legs" to the sea-floor or kept in position by attachment to navigational buoys on the surface), but technological developments may allow submarine methods of exploitation to be used.

Besides the mineral resources there are the living species which dwell on or burrow into the sea-bed. The characterization of these marine species as sedentary by the Convention is based on a physical and biological relationship to the sea-bed; immobility on the sea-bed (at the harvestable stage) or mobility consisting of constant physical contact with the bed.[33] Involved here are difficult questions of classification. Marine biologists and scientists classify under various headings the marine animals which dwell in the depths of the ocean. One classification is the nectonic species, i.e. the bottom fish which could not come within the definition because they do not depend for their locomotion on constant physcial contact with the sea-bed. Another is the benthonic species, which do depend for their physical existence on contact with the sea-bed.[34] The benthonic species are classified as the sessile group,[35] which merely sit on or are affixed to the bottom or move only

23

a few feet during their lifetime (e.g., oysters, coral); the creeping group[36] such as crabs and lobsters, and the burrowing group such as the bêche-de-mer. The definition of sedentary fisheries in the Convention is applicable to many, but not all, animals within the benthonic species. There are some species which both move on the sea-bed and swim in the waters above (e.g. some species of crabs). The Convention would seem to subject to sovereign rights of exploitation only those species which depend for their movement on constant physical contact with the sea-bed. Whether certain forms of crustacea come within the definition is a matter for more particular analysis.[37]

INTER-NATION SHELF DELIMITATION

The Convention also makes provision for the demarcation of the continental shelf where the boundary thereof pertains to more than one state. Such a boundary is to be determined by agreement between these states; where this is not forthcoming, then in the case of opposite states a median line is to be drawn, every point of which is equidistant from the nearest points of the baselines from which the breadth of the territorial sea of each state is measured. The qualification to this general rule is that the median line principle may be departed from where special circumstances exist.[38] Likewise, where a shelf is adjacent to two states the boundary is to be determined by agreement. In the absence of such agreement the boundary (again, if no special circumstances are present) is to be determined according to the principle of equidistance.[39]

The question of the status of the equidistant line was considered by the International Court in the *North Sea Continental Shelf Cases*[40] which dealt with a dispute between Denmark and the Netherlands on the one hand, and West Germany on the other hand (which had been referred to the Court by agreement between the parties), on the demarcation of that part of the continental shelf of the North Sea which was adjacent to the land territories of these states. Denmark and the Netherlands argued that the delimitation should be made in accordance with Article 6(2), viz. that an equidistant line should be adopted, while West Germany argued that the delimitation should be governed by a more general principle that each state was entitled to a just and equitable share. The Court held that the equidistant line was not enshrined in customary international law. The basic principle adopted by the Court was expressed in this way:

> Delimitation is to be effected by agreement in accordance with equitable principles and taking account of all the relevant circumstances, in such a way as to leave as much as possible to each Party all those parts of the Continental Shelf that constitute a natural prolongation of its land territory into and under the sea without encroachment on the natural prolongation of the land territory of the other.
>
> If on the application of the preceding, the delimitation leaves to the parties areas that overlap, they are to be decided between them in agreed proportions or, failing agreement, equally, unless they decide on a regime of joint jurisdiction, user, or exploitation for the zones of overlap or any part of them.[41]

In the negotiations the factors to be taken into account were:

1. The general configuration of the coasts of the Parties, as well as the presence of any special or unusual features;

2. So far as known or readily ascertainable, the physical and geological structure, and natural resources, of the continental shelf areas involved;

3. The element of a reasonable degree of proportionality, which a delimitation carried out in accordance with equitable principles ought to bring about between the extent of the continental shelf areas appertaining to the coastal state and the length of its coast measured in the general direction of the coastline, account being taken for this purpose of the effects, actual or prospective, of any other continental shelf delimitations between adjacent states in the same region.[42]

The application of this method was to give West Germany which had a concave coastline more shelf area than it would have received if the equidistant method had been adopted.[43]

Where two states are *opposite* each other the principle of delimiting the boundary by agreement is contained in Article 6(1) of the Convention. Failing agreement and in the absence of special circumstances, the median line principle is to be applied. In the *North Sea Continental Shelf Cases* the International Court of Justice considered that the median line principle in relation to opposite states was of a different order to that of the equidistant line and was itself a principle (leaving aside special circumstances) demanded by equity.[44]

What are the special circumstances which would justify departure from the median line principle? At a meeting of the International Law Commission to discuss the draft articles of the Convention it was stated: "As in the case of the boundaries of the territorial sea, provision must be made for departures necessitated by any exceptional configuration of the coast, as well as by the presence of islands or of navigable channels."[45] McDougal and Burke's conclusion is that the median line principle is not necessarily the most equitable method of demarcation and that it cannot be imposed unilaterally by a state without consideration of the value of other lines which would take into account all the circumstances involved.[46] However, it could be said that, failing agreement on a common boundary between opposite states, the median line may be adopted as a *modus vivendi* pending a solution by an international organ such as the International Court of Justice.

The principles of equity and proportionality will obviously have a major role to play in the allocation of continental shelf area to islands, and in the effect which islands will have on the delimitation of the continental shelves of opposite states. In certain circumstances such islands, especially if they are large and have an autonomous government, will be recognized as having large shelf areas. At the other extreme, if the islands are small and uninhabited, i.e. are rocks or islets, they may be disregarded in determining the dividing line between opposite states. In the middle situation would be islands which, because of size, population, location, and relationship with metropolitan state, should be given a partial effect in the determination of a dividing boundary.[47]

4

The High Seas

The various rights or liberties comprised within the freedom of the high seas are set out in Article 2 of the Geneva Convention on the High Seas[1] which gives effect to pre-existing customary international law. Article 2 provides:

> The high seas being open to all nations, no State may validly purport to subject any part of them to its sovereignty. Freedom of the high seas is exercised under the conditions laid down by these Articles and by the other rules of international law. It comprises, *inter alia*, both for coastal and non-coastal states:
> 1. Freedom of navigation;
> 2. Freedom of fishing;
> 3. Freedom to lay submarine cables and pipelines;
> 4. Freedom to fly over the high seas.
> These freedoms, and others which are recognized by the general principles of international law, shall be exercised by all states with reasonable regard to the interests of other states in their exercise of the freedom of the high seas.

These freedoms, which vest in individual states and their nationals, are therefore balanced by duties to respect the freedom of other states and their nationals, relating to the uses of the seas.

In relation to navigation, the flag state, save in exceptional cases expressly provided for in international treaties or in the Convention, has exclusive jurisdiction over ships which sail under its flag.[2]

However, there is a requirement that there must be a genuine link between the state and the ship;[3] in particular, the state must exercise jurisdiction in relation to those matters (administrative, social and technical) affecting the ship.[4] It must ensure that its ships observe safety at sea in matters such as the navigation of ships and the use of signals, the manning of ships and their construction and seaworthiness (conforming to accepted international standards).[5] The humanitarian doctrine of assistance to shipwrecked persons and those in danger is recognized in the requirement that masters of ships shall render assistance to such persons and to other ships after a collision.[6] Coastal states must also institute effective search and rescue services.[7]

The exclusive jurisdiction of a flag state over its ships is qualified by the doctrine of hot pursuit under which the naval or government ships of a coastal state may pursue foreign ships from its coastal zone (internal waters, territorial sea or contiguous zone) to the high seas where that state has "good reason" to believe that the foreign ship has violated its laws and regulations. However, such pursuit must be commenced when the foreign ship is in the internal waters, the territorial waters or (in respect of violations of the purposes for which the zone is established) the contiguous zone of the state undertaking the pursuit and the pursuit must not be interrupted.[8] The right of hot pursuit ceases when the pursued ship enters the territorial sea of its own country or of a foreign state.[9]

POLLUTION ON THE HIGH SEAS

Duties to prevent pollution in the sea environment are contained in Articles 24 and 25 of the Convention. Under Article 24, states must draw up regulations to prevent the discharge of oil from ships or pipelines, or resulting from the exploration and exploitation of the sea-bed, taking into account standards contained in existing treaties. Article 24 prohibits a state from contaminating the seas by the dumping of radioactive waste (taking account of standards formulated by international organizations) or as a result of activities associated with radioactive materials.[10]

Pollution of the sea by oil[11]

The 1954 Convention for the Prevention of Pollution of the Sea by Oil (as amended in 1962)[12] prohibits the discharge of oil and oily mixtures from ships within certain zones specified in an Annex. Under amendments made in 1969,[13] the earlier rules were amended. Under these amendments, discharges from tankers are prohibited except when the tanker is proceeding en route and is more than fifty miles from the nearest land.[14] The 1969 Convention also regulates the rate of discharge and (in the case of ballast voyages) the total amounts which may be discharged.[15] With respect to ships other than tankers, discharges are prohibited except when the ship is en route and the discharge is made as far as practicable from land. There are also controls on the rate of discharge and the oil content of the discharge.

In 1973 a new convention was signed—The Convention for the Prevention of Pollution from Ships.[16] This Convention has a more comprehensive operation than the earlier Convention as it applies to a number of ship-borne substances (including oil, noxious liquid substances, garbage and sewage). However, the basic controls in the earlier convention with respect to oil are continued, although new provisions have been inserted in the system in relation to the retention of unwanted oils on board oil-carrying ships and on the construction of tankers. Provision is also made in the Convention for special maritime areas in which discharges of oil are prohibited (subject to minor exceptions). There is also provision for new administrative methods relating to certificates of compliance with the Convention and for investigation procedures to determine whether the Convention has been breached.[17]

Discharge of oil as a result of maritime accidents

The International Convention relating to Intervention on the High Seas in Cases of Oil Pollution Casualties (1969)[18] was the product of international concern over damage to coastline from oil spillage of the *Torrey Canyon* kind. It enables a coastal state to take preventive and defensive measures on the high seas against a foreign vessel following upon a maritime casualty,[19] or acts related to such a casualty, to prevent the danger of pollution to its coastline. Such measures must be proportionate to the danger (actual or threatened).[20]

The International Convention on Civil Liability for Oil Pollution Damage (1969)[21] imposes a liability on the owner of a ship involved in an accident (described as an occurrence or series of occurrences having the same origin) causing pollution damage to pay compensation for the damage caused by oil which has escaped from or been discharged from a ship as a result of the incident, subject to certain exceptions (e.g. act of war).[22] The liability is limited to 210 million francs in respect of any one incident ($US15 million).[23] This limitation on recoverable damages does not apply where the incident occurred as a result of the actual fault or privity of the owner.[24]

Oil escaping as a result of drilling for oil on the sea-bed

Under Article 5(7) of the Convention on the Continental Shelf the coastal state is obliged to undertake in the safety zones established around installations used in the exploration or exploitation of the resources of the sea-bed appropriate measures for the protection of the living resources of the seas from harmful agents.

Dumping of wastes

The Convention on the Prevention of Marine Pollution by the Dumping of Wastes and Other Matter[25] controls the dumping of wastes in ocean areas. The Convention operates by way of various procedures depending on the nature of the waste. Dumping of such toxic materials as mercury, cadmium and radioactive wastes, and wastes such as plastics and crude oil which do not easily dissolve is prohibited. Dumping of wastes listed in Annex 2 of the Convention (e.g. arsenic, lead, copper, zinc) requires a prior special permit. Dumping of all other wastes requires a prior general permit.[26]

FISHING ON THE HIGH SEAS

There are in existence one general convention and a number of regional conventions which permit regulation of fisheries in high seas areas.[27] The Convention on Fishing and Conservation of Living Resources of the High Seas[28] was the last of the four Geneva Conventions to come into force. It imposes a duty of co-operation on states whose nationals fish in the same area of the high seas to adopt measures for the conservation of the living resources of those seas. Conservation in this context is defined as "the aggregate of measures rendering possible the optimum sustainable yield from these resources so as to secure a maximum supply of food and other marine resources".[29] Steps towards the adoption of conservation measures are initiated when a request is made by one state to another to enter into negotiations.[30] If agreement is not reached within twelve months on the measures to be adopted, an arbitration procedure laid down in the Convention may be invoked.[31] But the significant feature of the Convention is its recognition of the special interest of the coastal state in the maintenance of the stocks of fish in areas of the high seas adjacent to its territorial sea.[32] Article 6 of the Convention imposes a duty on other states whose nationals fish in these areas to enter into negotiations with the coastal state at its request, with a view to adopting conservation measures. Failing agreement within twelve months, the prescribed arbitration procedure may be invoked. However, in one situation, the Convention permits the coastal state to adopt unilateral conservation measures if negotiations have not led to agreement within six months. Under Article 7, this may be done where the coastal state can demonstrate:

(a) that there is a need for urgent application of conservation measures in the light of the existing knowledge of the fishery;
(b) that the measures adopted are based on appropriate scientific findings;
(c) that they do not discriminate in form or in fact[33] against foreign fishermen.

If, however, the other states do not agree with these measures, they may challenge them under the prescribed arbitration procedure.

The arbitration procedure consists of a determination of the validity of the measures by a special Commission of five members, unless the parties agree to such a solution by another method of peaceful settlement as provided for in Article 33 of the United

31

Nations Charter. If the parties cannot agree on the composition of the Commission, the members shall be chosen by the Secretary-General of the United Nations in consultation with the President of the International Court of Justice and the Director-General of the Food and Agriculture Organization from among persons qualified in the matters forming the basis of the dispute.[34]

The criteria to be adopted by the Commission in settling disputes under Article 7 where there is a challenge to the unilateral measures of a coastal state are set out above: they depend primarily on the coastal state showing that there is an urgent need for the application of the measures. The criteria to be adopted by the Commission in settling the other disputes are that:

(a) scientific findings demonstrate the necessity of conservation measures;

(b) that the specific measures are based on scientific grounds and are practicable;[35] and

(c) that the measures do not discriminate in form or in fact against fishermen of other states.

It can be seen therefore that a more difficult onus of proof is cast on the coastal state to prove the validity of unilateral measures. In any case, the measures may not discriminate against foreign fishermen. Thus the Convention is incompatible with any unilateral extensions of jurisdiction which *ex facie* discriminate in favour of the coastal state.

Unfortunately, the Convention has not gained the support given to the other Geneva Conventions. Some of the reasons for this lack of enthusiasm for the Convention are an unwillingness on the part of a number of countries to accept the arbitration procedure and its failure to provide for criteria on the basis of which a preferential share in off-shore resources could be allocated to the coastal state in the light of its "special interests".[36] On the other hand, its positive merits are recognized in its affirmation of the goal of conservation and its imposition of a duty of co-operation on fishing states to achieve this goal.[37]

As far as regional fishing conventions are concerned, there are in existence a number of these conventions controlling the exploitation of fisheries in various regions of the world's oceans. Among the most important are the North-East Atlantic Fisheries

Convention (1959),[38] the International Convention for the North West Atlantic Fisheries (1949)[39] and the International Convention for the High Seas Fisheries of the North Pacific Ocean (1952).[40] The main value of these Conventions is that they establish international forums for the resolution of conflicts of interests according to standards of conservation backed up by scientific research. Reference may also be made to the Convention on Whaling.[41]

Regional fisheries conventions may create commissions to institute and oversee the carrying out of conservation measures. In some cases these agencies have merely recommendatory powers, in some cases they have power to adopt measures by regulation. As far as enforcement is concerned,[42] under some conventions this may be vested in the flag state; in other cases an international "control system" may be established whereby authorized officers of a Contracting Party may board a vessel of another Party to see if there has been an infringement of the prescribed measures, but the conferment of a right of seizure has been rare.[43]

The concept of "optimum sustainable yield" has long been recognized as a basic standard to be applied in international fisheries negotiations. Its appeal lies in the fact that it is a scientific concept which can be subject to experimental analysis. It takes account, *inter alia*, of the movement of species of fish in various areas of the world's oceans, their breeding habits, the effects of fishing activity and the use of various types of gear. When such observations reveal that the present or imminent level of fishing activity in a particular stock will lead to a decline in that stock, then the standard of maximum sustainable yield may be invoked to impose some check on the activity. The measures which may be adopted achieve this end have been classified as follows:

A. *REGULATIONS AFFECTING MINIMUM AGE AND SIZE*, among which may be noted control of gear (particularly the mesh of nets and catching apparatus) and the imposition of size limits and the preservation of nursery areas which are designed to assist the younger species to maturity.

B. *REGULATIONS AFFECTING FISHING MORTALITY*. Some of the measures falling within this category are: closed areas, closed seasons, efficiency reduction, control of the number of vessels, and quotas.[44] All of these measures are designed to achieve a reduction in fishing intensity in order to preserve stock.

A criticism, however, directed against most of these methods is that, tied as they are to the concept of maximum biological yield, they ignore important economic aspects of fishing, e.g. profitability of the operations in the light of the measures adopted. For example, it is pointed out that area closures may be effective in reducing mortality but they have the effect of forcing fishing vessels to go greater distances, thus increasing the cost of fishing operations. Likewise, restrictions on the use of certain types of gear may conduce to inefficiency.[45]

However, one particular method which has been suggested as giving adequate protection to the biological goal as well as ensuring that fishing nations can derive economic benefit from the adoption of conservation policies is an overall catch limit coupled with national quotas, which permits overall regulation of the catching of a stock combined with a system of allocating the catch among individual states.[46]

The Anglo-Icelandic Fisheries Case

The concept of a preferential right of the coastal state in the allocation of fishery resources in waters adjacent to its coastline but outside the twelve mile limit was endorsed by the International Court of Justice in 1974 in a decision on a dispute between the United Kingdom and Iceland.[47] The proceedings arose out of the proclamation by Iceland of a fifty mile exclusive fishing zone. The decision of the Court was that this extension of jurisdiction was not "opposable" to the United Kingdom, the vessels of which had traditionally fished in the area.[48] The Court considered, however, that the two countries were under an obligation to undertake negotiations in good faith for the equitable solution of their differences concerning their respective fishing rights in areas adjacent to the Icelandic coastline. In these negotiations the Parties were to take into account, *inter alia*:

(a) that in the distribution of the fishing resources in the areas specified ... Iceland is entitled to a preferential share to the extent of the special dependence of its people upon the fisheries in the seas around its coasts for their livelihood and economic development;

(b) that by reason of its fishing activities in the areas specified ... the United Kingdom also has established rights in the fishery resources of the said areas on which elements of its people depend for their livelihood and economic well-being;

(c) the obligation to pay due regard to the interests of other states in the conservation and equitable exploitation of these resources;

(d) that the above-mentioned rights of Iceland and the United Kingdom should each be given effect to the extent compatible with the conservation and development of the fishery resources in the areas specified ... and with the interests of other states in their conservation and equitable exploitation;

(e) their obligation to keep under review those resources and to examine together, in the light of scientific and other available information, such measures as may be required for the conservation and development, and equitable exploitation, of those resources, making use of the machinery established by the North-East Atlantic Fisheries Convention or such other means as may be agreed upon as a result of international negotiations.[49]

In the course of its judgment the Court in effect considered that the absolute right to fishing in the high seas conferred by the Convention on the High Seas had been affected by the growth of two concepts which had crystallized as customary international law in recent years. One was the twelve miles exclusive fishing zone. The other was the concept of "a preferential right of fishing in adjacent waters in favour of the coastal state in a situation of special dependence on its coastal fisheries, this preference operating in regard to other states concerned in the exploitation of the same fisheries and to be implemented as indicated".[50]

The growth of the practice was stated to have originated in the proposal put forward at the Second Geneva Conference on the Law of the Sea under which the faculty of claiming preferential rights in adjacent waters (outside territorial waters or an exclusive fishing belt) was said to be derived from those special circumstances where a coastal state was greatly dependent on the living resources for feeding its population or for its economic development and when it was shown to be necessary to limit the total catch of a stock or stocks of fish in the area.[51] But other states affected could require that the claim made by a coastal state should be tested and determined by a special commission on the basis of scientific criteria and of evidence presented by the coastal state and other states.[52]

35

Exclusive economic zone

The *Fisheries Jurisdiction Case* application of a doctrine of preferential rights must be inserted in the framework of the discussions which have been taken at the Third Law of the Sea Conference.[53] The concept of the exclusive economic zone which has been supported by many nations at the Conference is based on the recognition of the jurisdiction of the coastal state over the living resources of the high seas and the resources of the sea-bed within a two-hundred-mile limit. If this concept receives ultimate endorsement the concept of preferential rights (which rests on a doctrinal foundation of shared rights) would be superseded. The exclusive economic zone principle would enable the coastal state to take the whole of the total allowable catch of a species of fish subject to its jurisdiction or to license foreign fishing vessels engaged in fishing operations in the zone in respect of the portion of the allowable catch which could not be taken by the coastal state.

Agreement has not at the time of writing been forthcoming at the Conference on the zone and the rights exercisable within it. A number of nations have decided to take unilateral action to proclaim exclusive economic or fishing zones.[54] If such a practice became widespread, the exclusive economic zone might emerge as a principle of customary international law, just as the doctrine of the continental shelf developed in this manner.

However, some states, particularly those which are land-locked or have narrow coastlines,[55] have opposed the exclusive zone concept on the ground that it would limit their access to the living resources of the seas. There is also division among states on the question of the operation of a disputes settlement procedure where the interests of coastal states and other states come into conflict.

It is clear that the economic zone concept will also affect their activities besides fishing. In so far as control of ship-originating pollution whould be one of the management rights vested in the coastal state, questions have arisen as to the standards to be applied to vessel construction and therefore as to the right of passage under coastal state regulation.[56] Scientific research appears also to be affected: the division here appears to be between those who would require coastal state consent for all research (whether pure or resource-orientated) in the economic zone and those who recognize the right of access without consent except in those circumstances where the research is resource-orientated or requires drilling of the sea-bed.[57]

Finally, the status of the economic zone itself is a matter of debate: some states view it as a functional zone *within* the high seas, others would see it as a coastal state zone, with the high seas only beginning at the two-hundred-mile limit. Until the question is resolved by international convention, or a firm practice by a number of states has generated a new rule of customary international law, the nature of fishing rights in the two-hundred-mile zone (apart from the twelve-mile exclusive fishing zone) must rest in the formulation of the doctrine of coastal state preferential rights expressed in the *Fisheries Jurisdiction Case* and on bilateral and regional agreements.[58]

5

The Deep Sea-bed Area

The search for a regime to govern the exploitation of the resources of the sea-bed outside national jurisdiction may be said to have begun in 1967 with the introduction in the United Nations General Assembly of a draft resolution by Ambassador Pardo of Malta.[1] This resolution emphasized the concept that the resources of the sea-bed outside national jurisdiction should not be subject to national appropriation but should be brought under the control of an international authority.[2] Although the resolution was not passed by the General Assembly it generated much discussion in that body which constituted a Seabed Committee to further explore the matter. In 1969, with discussions on a possible regime still unresolved, the General Assembly passed a resolution which has become known as the Moratorium Resolution which enjoined states and persons to refrain from all activities of exploiting the resources of the bed until an international regime had been established.[3]

In 1970 a Declaration of Principles was adopted by the Assembly, the first three paragraphs of which were as follows:

1. The sea-bed and ocean floor, and the subsoil thereof, beyond the limits of national jurisdiction (hereinafter referred to as the area), as well as the resources of the area, are the common heritage of mankind.
2. The area shall not be subject to appropriation by any means by States or persons natural or juridical, and no State shall claim or exercise sovereignty or sovereign rights over any part thereof.
3. No State or person, natural or juridical, shall claim, exercise or

acquire rights with respect to the area or its resources incompatible with the international regime to be established and the principles of this Declaration.[4]

The Declaration later outlined the goal of an international regime, to "provide for the orderly and safe development and rational management of the area and its resources and for expanding opportunities in the use thereof, and to ensure the equitable sharing by States in the benefits derived therefrom, taking into particular consideration the interests and needs of the developing countries whether land locked or coastal".[5]

In an associated resolution, the Assembly decided to convene a Third Law of the Sea Conference which would deal with the establishment of the international regime and also a broad range of related matters. The preparation for the Conference would be undertaken by the Seabed Committee.[6]

The first session of the Conference opened in New York in 1973 and this was followed by sessions in Caracas (1974), Geneva (1975) and New York (two sessions in 1976 and a session in 1977). Two major questions which have generated controversy at the Conference have been the question of the area subject to the international regime and the nature and powers of the international body which will exercise control over the resources of the area.[7]

AREA

As outlined in an earlier chapter, the sea-bed adjacent to a country's coastline consists of the continental *shelf* (ending at a depth of 200 metres), the continental *slope* (extending from the edge of the shelf to depths ranging between 1200 and 3500 metres) and the continental *rise* bordering the bottom of the slope and the deep ocean floor and extending to depths between 3500 and 5500 metres. This area is referred to as the continental margin but is geologically different from the ocean floor which has a structure different from that of the continental margin.[8] Outside the continental margin is to be found the abyssal plain or deep sea-bed.

It appears that the major resources of the abyssal plain are the manganese nodules which lie in globular form on the bed, forming a "carpet" which in certain places is highly concentrated. These nodules contain not only manganese but also nickel, cobalt, copper and other minerals.[9] It is clear, therefore, that an international regime which commenced at the bottom of the international rise would be mainly concerned with the "hard" minerals as distinct from the hydrocarbons (oil, natural gas).

The outer limits of the continental shelf have not yet, however, been defined and controversy continues on the method of demarcating the commencement of the deep sea-bed area. This question was examined in Chapter 3[10] where reference was made to the difference of opinion between those who would see the reasoning in the *North Sea Continental Shelf Cases*[11] as rendering superfluous the "exploitability" criterion specified in Article 1 of the Convention on the Continental Shelf,[12] and those who would see the "adjacency" criterion in that Article as preventing an inordinate expansion of coastal state jurisdiction beyond the two hundred metres line.[13] The former position would select the edge of the continental margin (i.e. bottom of slope or slope plus rise) as the existing limits of national jurisdiction. The latter position would argue that the limits of national jurisdiction on the slope are still determined by the exploitability criterion. These limits might reflect present technological expertise in relation to the drilling of hydrocarbons, which suggests a terminating line somewhere on the continental slope but not at the great depths to which the slope falls, although not denying that at some future time technological expertise may permit exploration at such depths. If the "narrow shelf" concept is accepted, the area of the sea floor subject to the international regime would be increased. However, the very vagueness of "exploitability" may weaken the foundation of the narrow shelf approach, for it could be argued that it is not tied to one type of mineral exploitation (hydrocarbons) and that the exploitation of the resources of the abyssal plain will, at least as far as hard minerals are concerned, show that the exploitability criterion also covers the continental margin where such minerals may also be found.[14]

However, in the light of the discussions at the Third Law of the Sea Conference, this particular question has been relegated to a less important status, for now the two-hundred-mile economic resources zone (covering the resources of the sea and sea-bed) has introduced a "distance from shore" criterion (and not depth of waters) as the basis for delineating the area of national jurisdiction.[15] Such a method of demarcation might absorb many continental margins. In certain cases, however, the area of continental shelf and margin extends beyond two hundred miles. It has been estimated that the revenue derived from the continental margin resources *outside* the two-hundred-mile limit will in the foreseeable future generate more revenue than the exploitation of the resources of the deep sea-bed. But it is difficult to imagine that those states which have under existing international law a right to exploit the sea-bed area outside the 200 miles limit, whatever the distance from the shore may be, will be prepared to sacrifice their interests in this area to an international regime, even if some mixed regime recognizing coastal state jurisdiction over the margin outside the 200 miles limit but associated with a duty to contribute[16] to an international fund, received majority support.

TYPES OF REGIME

In the discussions of the type of regime which might be established, a usual method of classification is between the regime which vests greater power in the international authority and that which would recognize greater authority in states and their national enterprises.[17] Although earlier discussions showed some support for an international registration system, with the authority registering claims "staked out" by states or their nationals,[18] the discussion at the Third Law of the Sea Conference has moved towards a strong International Authority with powers to license activities in the deep sea-bed area. More than that, the developing nations have argued that the International Authority should itself have the major role in exploitation activities through an Enterprise or operating arm which would be part of the structure, and that states or their nationals should only come in on a "contractor" basis and with a duty to pay a proportion of royalties to the Authority. This naturally has created a cleavage between these nations and the industrialized nations which see their state enterprises or private corporations having a major role to play—a role justified by the economic and technological expertise which they possess.[19]

The structure of the International Seabed Authority would be a body with a number of arms or component divisions. Thus, there would be an Assembly with the authority to lay down general rules, a Council to determine executive policy, a Tribunal to determine disputes relating to the uses of the area, a Secretariat, and finally the operating arm or Enterprise. It is this entity which under the developing nations' proposal would have the lion's share of exploitation with state and private enterprise coming in on a "contract" basis with the Enterprise. The proposals for agreement are therefore not bright, although some would see that the best changes of reconciling conflicting positions reside in the concept of the "joint venture".[20]

If agreement is not forthcoming on the structure and powers of the International Authority, the question will arise about what powers states and their enterprises have under existing international law to mine the resources of the sea-bed outside national jurisdiction. The General Assembly Resolutions of 1969 and 1970 do not have legally binding force because they have not yet generated sufficient acceptance as a norm of customary international law. The concept of "common heritage" which points to an ideal to be realized does not contain sufficient content to inhibit existing exercises of international rights.

Consequently, it has been argued[21] that the right of mining the resources of the sea-bed outside national jurisdiction is an existing freedom or right pertaining to the high seas, although not specified in the Convention on the High Seas, and that states may themselves or through their private enterprises or nationals engage in such activities, pending the establishment of an international regime, on the basis that these minerals are *res nullius* or *res communis* as are the fish of the oceans.

PART II

The Position under the Australian Constitutional Structure

6

The Law of the Sea
and Australian Law

The 1958 Geneva Conventions on the Law of the Sea constitute a recognition by a substantial section of the international community of the legal regime applicable to off-shore waters and the uses of the oceans. However, the extent to which they have become, individually and with respect to all their parts, customary international law—either as reflecting customary international law of the late 1950s or as generating a consensus among states which has crystallized into such law in the 1970s—has not been formally determined. This affects the question whether states which have not ratified or acceded to the Conventions will be bound by provisions contained therein.

The four Conventions entered into force in the 1960s,[1] after obtaining the twenty-two ratifications as laid down in their concluding Articles. All were ratified by Australia in 1963.[2] Although no one Convention has been ratified by fifty per cent of the total number of states represented in the United Nations, the number and geographical spread of the ratifications indicate a general acceptance of the basic provisions of the Conventions.[3]

However, the Conventions differ among themselves in their expressed relationship with existing international law and as to reservations, or the right of "opting out" of specific provisions.[4] The Convention on the High Seas in its preamble recognizes the provisions of the Convention as generally declaratory of established principles of international law and makes no provision for reservations. The Convention on the Territorial Sea and

Contiguous Zone contains no reference to its conformity with customary international law but is generally accepted as reflecting customary international law. It has no provision for reservations. The Convention on the Continental Shelf permits reservations other than to Articles 1, 2 and 3 of the Convention.[5] These Articles establish the basic doctrine of coastal state sovereign rights over the shelf. The Convention on Fishing and Conservation of the Living Resources of the High Seas allows reservations other than to six Articles.[6] These again are Articles which recognize basis principles, viz. the special interest of the coastal state in the maintenance of productivity of the living resources of the high seas adjacent to its coastal waters, and the arbitration procedure for resolving disputes between parties over conservation measures.[7] It is generally accepted, however, that at the time of its signing this Convention was not a formulation of customary international law.[8]

It can therefore be said that the basic structure of the three Conventions relating to the exercise of rights by a coastal state over and in relation to its adjacent maritime zones (off-shore waters and continental shelf), and the code of freedoms and duties which relate to the uses of the high seas, reflect customary international law today, but the more detailed elaboration of rules contained in some of these Conventions, particularly in relation to those areas where reservations are allowed, has not achieved this status.[9] Indeed this seems to accord with the opinion of the International Court of Justice in the *North Sea Continental Shelf Cases* which made a distinction between Articles 1–3 of the Convention on the Continental Shelf, which recognize coastal state sovereign rights, held to be part of customary international law,[10] and Article 6(2) of the Convention relating to the method of demarcating the continental shelf between two adjacent states, which was held not to incorporate or reflect customary international law.[11]

As to the Convention on Fishing and Conservation of the Living Resources of the High Seas, international practice appears to have developed in the 1970s which recognizes a special interest of the coastal state in the maintenance of the productivity of fisheries in adjacent areas of the high seas (Article 6) and a duty on the part of other states which fish in such areas to negotiate with a view to implementing conservation measures.[12] But this special interest of the coastal states, as recognized in customary international law of the 1970s, goes beyond conservation measures and entails a preferential right in the exploitation or allocation of the fishery resources[13] where management measures have been adopted (as by means of a catch limitation); therefore discrimination in favour of the coastal state against foreign fishing activities has been effected.

In the light of the various factors mentioned in the preceding discussion, viz. the international participation in their formation and subsequent ratification, and their reflection of existing or subsequent practice, the three major Conventions—High Seas, Territorial Sea and Contiguous Zone, and Continental Shelf—may be relied upon by Australian governments as expressing an international consensus on the law of the sea which is relevant to the determination of Australia's national policies, even without implementing legislation.

This is not to say, however, that they will automatically affect the rights and duties of Australian citizens within the Australian legal structure. The United States concept of "self-executing" treaties[14] is not part of our legal structure. The rule expressed in cases such as *Walker* v. *Baird*[15] is that before a citizen's private rights may be affected by a treaty, legislation "incorporating" the rights and duties arising from that treaty must be enacted by the Legislature.[16] Starke considers that the principle is that treaties which affect the private rights of subjects, or involve the modification of common law or statute law by virtue of their provisions or otherwise, or require the vesting of additional powers in the Crown, or impose additional financial burdens on the Crown, must receive parliamentary assent.[17]

Nevertheless, it is said that no direct legislative enactment is necessary in order to incorporate *customary* international law into the law of the land, provided that such law is not inconsistent with common or statute law.[18] The precise operation of this part of international law has been the subject of discussion in a number of cases. The traditional doctrine formulated by Blackstone, that international customary law is automatically incorporated into the common law, suffered a severe setback at the hands of the majority of the judges in *R.* v. *Keyn*,[19] who seemed to require some specific act of adoption before international law would be applied by a common law court. According to the views of Latham, C.J., and Dixon J., in *Chow Hung Ching* v. *R.*,[20] international law is to be considered a "source" of the common law and not part of it —a view in line with the "specific adoption" theory[21]—but this view was contested in the same case by Starke, J. who seemed to favour the Blackstonian doctrine.[22] The conflict between the "incorporation" and "specific adoption" theories often seems to occur when there is debate about the existence of the rule of international law which is invoked in a particular case, and this is true of cases such as *West Rand Central Gold Mining Company Limited* v. *The King*[23] where the tendency seems to be in favour of the "specific adoption" theory, i.e. the judges seem to incline to this theory where the alleged rule of international law is uncertain or there is doubt whether it has reached the stage of a binding rule.[24] But as Starke points out, courts concerned with the application of international law often have a creative role to play and their position may be "more than purely declaratory; while not actually creating new customary rules, the Court may feel constrained to carry to a final stage the process of evolution of usages so generally recognised as to suggest that by an inevitable course of development they will crystallise into custom. To use Mr. Justice Cardozo's words, by its imprimatur the Court will attest the 'jural quality' of the custom".[25] In any case the differences between the two theories may not turn out to be so great as to dictate different solutions in the context of particular problems arising for determination by the courts.[26]

The dividing line between customary international law and treaties is not a hard and fast one. This is true of law-making treaties which codify pre-existing rules of customary law.[27] Therefore, a law-making treaty of this nature may be looked at as a first source of international law, or, to put it in terms of British constitutional law and practice, it may be like the Statute of Westminster which could be regarded as a crystallization of the pre-existing norms relating to the equality of Commonwealth membership and yet attested to in a written declaration which at the same time "advances" he relations of the parties concerned.

In the international arena, the adherence of Australia to the Law of the Sea treaties would be considered a valid basis for action in accordance with them which is taken against foreign powers or subjects. Thus, the arrest of a foreign fishing vessel which had violated territorial limits or the exclusion of an unlicensed foreign drilling rig which was being used for operations in the continental shelf area, would seem to be actions which the commonwealth executive could take and which, falling within the limits of the treaties mentioned, would accord with international law. Such action would be characterized as Acts of State[28] having their effect in the international arena.[29]

But could action, without such legislative support, be taken against Australian citizens who breached the provisions of these treaties or who performed acts within the areas covered by the treaties which were not sanctioned by the commonwealth? In *Walker* v. *Baird*[30] the plea of Act of State as a justification for the interference with private rights by the Crown was rejected. In that case it was held that the signing of a treaty between Britain and France which related to fisheries was not a sufficient justification for action of the Crown purporting to control the acts of British citizens in areas which came within the operation of the treaty. It seems to be accepted that the case is authority for the broad proposition that private rights of British subjects cannot be infringed by executive action in accordance with a treaty which has not received legislative approval or sanction.[31] It is clear therefore that an effective programme for carrying out those provisions of the Conventions which affect private rights or the public revenue or involve enforcement of rights recognized by the Conventions by Australian Courts, as distinct from diplomatic action taken in foreign or international relations, must be sanctioned by parliament.

In the period to 1973 a number of the principles of the Geneva Conventions had been implemented by federal legislation in a piecemeal fashion, in relation to petroleum and fisheries resources, in response to a perceived need to regulate such activities.[32]

The control of the sedentary living resources of the continental shelf had been a matter of special interest to Australia, even before federation when foreign involvement in sedentary resources fishing had led to the enactment of the *Queensland Pearl Shell and Bêche-de-mer Fisheries (Extra-Territorial) Act* in 1888 and the *Western Australian Pearl Shell and Bêche-de-mer Fisheries*

(Extra-Territorial) Act in 1889.[33] This legislation had been repealed in 1952 by the *Pearl Fisheries Act*[34] which itself was repealed by the *Continental Shelf (Living Natural Resources) Act* of 1968.[35] The purpose of this latter legislation was to establish the basis for regulating the takings of the many types of sedentary resources coming within the definition contained in the Article 2(4) of the Convention on the Continental Shelf.

In 1967 amendments[36] were made to the commonwealth *Fisheries Act* 1952 to take advantage of the growth in customary international law of the twelve mile exclusive fishing zone concept.

The *Navigation Act* 1912 has also been amended to update the provisions relating to Safety of Life at Sea[37] and to implement the International Convention relating to maritime casualties on the high seas.[38] Pollution arising from ship-discharged oil and similar substances is regulated by the *Pollution of the Sea by Oil Act* which has been updated to give effect to the amendments of the 1954 Convention.[39] Concern for the sea environment adjacent to the Australian coastline is reflected in the *National Parks and Wildlife Conservation Act* 1975[40] under which marine national parks may be proclaimed, and a special regime has been established for the Great Barrier Reef by the *Great Barrier Reef Marine Park Act* 1975.[41]

Exploration and exploitation of the petroleum resources of the territorial sea and continental shelf are regulated by the *Petroleum (Submerged Lands) Act* 1967 as amended, which reflects a co-operative constitutional scheme involving commonwealth and states "mirroring" legislation.[42] All these enactments will be examined in later chapters.

THE SEAS AND SUBMERGED LANDS ACT, 1973

In 1973 the federal government decided to enact legislation which would declare generally Australia's sovereignty and sovereign rights as recognized in the Territorial Sea and Continental Shelf Conventions and which would also vest such rights in the Crown in right of the commonwealth. It was envisaged that this would lead to a challenge by the state governments to a "test case" in the High Court which would determine where internal sovereignty resided, viz. whether in the Crown in right of the commonwealth or the Crown in right of the states.

The *Seas and Submerged Lands Act*[43] contains sixteen sections.[44] The operative part of the Act is Part II, Division I of which relates to the territorial sea and Division II to the continental shelf. The crucial section in Division I is s.6: "It is by this Act declared and enacted that the sovereignty in respect of the territorial sea, and in respect of the air space over it and in respect of its bed and subsoil, is vested in and exerciseable by the Crown in right of the Commonwealth." Section 10 of the Act vests sovereignty in respect of internal waters (including air space and sea-bed) in the Crown in right of the commonwealth but this section must be read with s.14 which excludes from that declaration of sovereignty waters which were internal waters of a state at federation. Such waters would include the waters of inlets, etc. Section 7 empowers the governor-general to proclaim the breadth of the territorial sea and the baseline from which the territorial sea is measured, not inconsistently with the provisions of the Convention on the Territorial Sea. (This baseline would designate the outer limit of internal waters.) Section 8 empowers the governor-general to declare bays as "historic" or waters as "historic".

Section 11 of Division II provides: "It is by this Act declared and enacted that the sovereign rights of Australia as a coastal State in respect of the Continental Shelf of Australia, for the purpose of exploring it and exploiting its natural resources, are vested in and exercisable by the Crown in right of the Commonwealth." Under section 12 the governor-general may by Proclamation declare, not inconsistently with the Convention on the Continental Shelf or any relevant agreement to which Australia is a party, the limits of the continental shelf. Finally, section 16 continues any state law which applies in an adjacent maritime area "except in so far as the law is expressed to vest or make exercisable any sovereignty or sovereign rights otherwise than as provided by the preceding provisions of the Act".

Both the Convention on the Territorial Sea and Contiguous Zone and the Convention on the Continental Shelf are set out in Schedules to the Act.

The effect of the Act is therefore to implement the sovereign and sovereign rights of articles of the two Conventions (which in respect of particular areas had already been implemented in earlier legislation) and to empower the Executive to determine maritime boundaries. However, the legislation also has the effect of determining the distribution of *internal* sovereignty within the Australian federal system.

NEW SOUTH WALES v. COMMONWEALTH OF AUSTRALIA[45]

In these proceedings which were brought by the state of New South Wales and the five other state governments, the High Court upheld the provisions relating to sovereignty over the territorial sea (by a 5–2 majority)[46] and (unanimously) the provisions relating to the continental shelf. Two strands of thought are to be found in the reasons of the majority judges, first, that the external affairs power of the Commonwealth Constitution (s.51 [xxix]) is a basis for the exercise of the legislative power of the Commonwealth in relation to the territorial sea, either on the basis that it deals with matters and areas geographically external to Australia or as implementing international conventions relating to such areas; and second, as related to the first proposition, that the area of territorial waters, three miles in breadth, was not within the territorial limits of the colonies at federation and therefore not within the limits of the newly established states after federation. Consequently the legislation was not in derogation of any territorial or proprietary rights held by the states or protected by the Constitution.[47]

The minority judges considered that rights in the territorial sea were vested in the Crown in right of the colonies before federation. Such rights had been acquired by the colonies at the time they had attained responsible government. The colonial legislatures therefore had legislative jurisdiction over the adjacent sea and sea-bed which were properly described as being within "territorial limits". The Commonwealth could under its external affairs power give effect to international conventions dealing with such areas but the *Seas and Submerged Lands Act* went beyond the implementation of the Convention on the Territorial Sea because it purported to deal with the question of "internal" sovereignty by vesting that sovereignty in the Crown in right of the commonwealth.[48]

The effect of the decision has been that within the Australian federal system the sovereignty or paramount rights over the territorial sea and sea-bed are vested in the national government, and the national legislature—the commonwealth parliament— may legislate to regulate activities and matters within the area of that sovereignty (e.g. mining, fishing). However, in the absence of such legislation, the state legislatures may still exercise a legislative jurisdiction with respect to activities in the adjacent area (e.g. mining, fishing) provided that such legislation does not amount to a claim of sovereign rights and provided that the legislation has a sufficient nexus with the state to make it a law for the "peace, welfare and good government to the State".[49]

The decision will be examined in more detail in later chapters.

7

Australian Maritime Zones: Territorial Waters

INTRODUCTION

The national maritime zones which will be treated in this and the following chapters comprise internal waters, territorial waters and fisheries zones. The fisheries zones are, under present legislation, of two types: an exclusive fishing zone extending twelve miles from the baseline of the territorial sea, which applies to foreign nationals and foreign fishing vessels, and a domestic fishing zone which extends in distance from the shore about two hundred miles in most areas.

It is to be noted that in accordance with the English common law principles, ownership of the tidelands or foreshore (the area between high tide and low tide)[1] is vested in the Crown. Traditionally, the Crown's right of ownership of the foreshore has been considered to be a prerogative right.[2] As such it may be considered to be part of the legal inheritance to which the Australian colonies succeeded in the nineteenth century and which were retained by the states on federation. The states therefore may legislate to provide for the control of the foreshore (e.g. by vesting administrative powers in a local government body) and may control mining and fishing activities in the area.[3]

Besides the tidelands, there are internal waters bordering the sea which may be described as bays, estuaries, navigable rivers and creeks, as well as harbours and ports. These areas have been

54

traditionally considered as internal and not territorial waters. Such waters have been referred to as the "narrow seas" in English legal parlance or as *inter fauces terrae*.[4] The cases indicate that such areas of water are to be considered as part of the county and nation for the purposes of territorial sovereignty and jurisdiction, and the Crown was considered as having the prerogative right or title to the sea-bed (including the resources) of these areas subject to public rights of navigation and fishing.[5] Here again this prerogative right would be regarded as having been inherited by the Australian colonies and on federation to have been retained by the states or, if one uses the language of Crown divisibility, by the Crown in right of the states.[6]

The various legal acts of a legislative and executive nature issuing in the eighteenth and nineteenth centuries and to which recourse must be made for an understanding of state boundaries, do not contain a definition of water boundaries, apart from the South Australian Letters Patent which include within the definition of the borders of South Australia "bays and gulfs".[7] The absence of such a definition in the constitutional instruments of the other Australian colonies does not mean that they are deprived of their rights of ownership of the sea-bed in inland waters, for, as we have seen, this was a prerogative right which must be regarded as implicit in the constitutional structure of the colonies and as such to be subject to the colonial legislative jurisdiction to make laws for the "peace, welfare, and good government" of the colony.[8] This jurisdiction still remained with the states on federation and therefore such internal waters must be considered as part of their territory and as subject to their legislative jurisdiction today.

However, developments in international law in the twentieth century, as reflected in Articles 4 and 7 of the Convention on the Territorial Sea and Contiguous Zone, permit greater enclosures of internal waters than were allowed by the nineteenth-century rules. Sovereignty over such internal waters which were not recognized as such at federation has now been claimed by the commonwealth.[9]

The outer limit of internal waters, which may be treated as a notional (but not necessarily a geographical) coastline[10] by the drawing of closing lines across indentations, marks the beginning

of territorial waters. Traditionally these waters have been regarded as extending three miles in breadth from the coastline.[11]
It is with respect to territorial waters that the major constitutional
discussion in the Australian context has taken place.

TERRITORIAL WATERS: COMMONWEALTH OR STATE?

Before and as a result of the declaration of commonwealth
sovereignty over the territorial sea in 1973 in the *Seas and
Submerged Lands Act* of that year, there had been great dispute
whether rights in the territorial sea and sea-bed were vested in
the commonwealth or states. Various arguments were marshalled
in favour of commonwealth or state control.

Territorial Waters As Subject To Commonwealth Sovereignty

Basically it has been argued that if the nineteenth-century
doctrine of English law denied to the Crown ownership of the
sea and sea-bed beneath territorial waters and if the same doctrine
applied to the Australian colonies in the nineteenth century, then
the states do not possess these rights (there having been no grant
of such rights to them at the time of or after federation) although
they do possess a general legislative jurisdiction over territorial
waters or at least over the acts of their residents occurring therein.

The English doctrine, it was argued, was derived from the
decision of the Court of Crown Cases Reserved in *R.* v. *Keyn*[12]
where a slender majority (7–6) held that English courts were not
competent to try a German national who had committed an
offence relating to the navigation of a foreign vessel of which he
was the captain, while passing through waters within three miles
of the British coastline. The exact ratio of the case has been
disputed. While some commentators have preferred to confine it to
the facts of the case which were centred on the exercise of English
criminal jurisdiction in relation to a foreign vessel,[13] others have
considered it to be authority for the proposition that the limit of
the realm of Britain and of the colonies is the low-water mark.[14]

It is therefore said that the waters adjacent to Australia are
outside the territory of the federated colonies—the states. Consequently the sea and sea-bed are open to appropriation only by

that unit of the federal structure which is responsible for external affairs—and that power is reposed in the commonwealth. In so far as the Convention on the Territorial Sea and Contiguous Zone vests sovereignty over the sea-bed in the coastal nation, the commonwealth had by adhering to the Convention become entitled (if it had not already become entitled to such rights on the acquisition of international personality) to rights of sovereignty (which include rights of ownership) over the sea and sea-bed within territorial waters.[15] The argument was taken a step further by reference to certain other powers which were vested in the commonwealth by the Constitution, in particular the power to make laws for fisheries in Australian waters beyond territorial limits.[16] If the phrase "territorial limits" were synonymous with the land geographical boundaries of the states, the power over fisheries outside those limits, i.e. in territorial waters and beyond, belonged to the commonwealth. *A fortiori* the power to control the sea-bed and its wealth outside territorial limits rested with the commonwealth.[17] Finally, it was said, comparative constitutional jurisprudence, in particular the decisions of the Canadian and United States Supreme Courts on the questions relevant to their federal structures, pointed to national sovereignty over these areas.[18]

Territorial Waters As Being Within State Limits

The opposite arguments agreed with the propositions that as none of the original Constitutions of the Australian colonies (apart from the South Australian Letters Patent) defined territorial limits or boundaries so as to include water areas, it was necessary to have recourse to English law to determine whether it was implicit in the concept of territorial sovereignty in the nineteenth century that the territorial sea and the bed beneath the sea were subject to the political control and ownership of the Crown and therefore whether similar rights were held by the Crown in right of the colonies.[19] The proponents of state power favoured the narrower ratio of *R. v. Keyn*.[20] However, if the wider ratio were accepted the following points were put forward.

In the first place, there was weighty ancient authority according to which the Crown had the right to exploit the sea-bed in waters adjacent to the English coastline.[21] Second, there were later authorities such as *Chelikani's Case*[22] which were contrary to the proposition expressed in *R. v. Keyn*, while in the relevant Australian case of *D. v. Commissioner of Taxes*[23] there was a strong expression of opinion tending to support the later English authority.[24] Third, the swift passage of *Territorial Waters Jurisdiction Act*[25] through the British parliament after the decision in *R. v. Keyn* was evidence of governmental non-acceptance of the ratio and embodied adherence to the three mile limit concept of jurisdiction which had been traditionally English executive policy.[26] In the fourth place, whatever the view in 1876 may have been, by the turn of the century (which was the crucial date for the determination of the Australian position) a doctrine of Crown ownership of the sea-bed lying beneath territorial waters would seem to have been recognized in English law.[27] In the fifth place, the conflict of views as to whether there were rights of sovereignty over the sea-bed as well as jurisdictional rights over the superjacent waters seemed to have been affected by the proposition that a state could not be said to have sovereignty over its territorial waters if there existed a right of innocent passage over them.[28] But the determination of this international law question in the Convention on the Territorial Sea in favour of the recognition of sovereignty would seem to have removed, as a matter of English and Australian law, this irritating confusion of the international and internal legal positions. Finally, the relevance of the Canadian and American decisions was denied on the ground that they dealt with different constitutional provisions and that the "critical" dates for determination of state or provincial control preceded that applicable in Australia (1900).[29]

If there were in existence in 1900 a common law doctrine according to which rights of ownership in the sea-bed were vested in the Crown as a concomitant of British "sovereignty" over territorial waters, it was then necessary to determine whether these rights were held by the Crown in right of the Australian colonies at the time of federation. The common law doctrine of the prerogative would seem to have been applicable to the circumstances of the colonies and therefore to have become part of the *corpus* of Australian law.[30] Moreover, the exercise of jurisdictional rights over territorial waters, as well as in certain cases over the sea-bed thereof by Australian colonial legislatures in the latter part of the century, was strong evidence to support the view that colonial sovereignty extended to the three-mile limit.[31] But the major question was whether on federation these prerogative rights were retained by the Crown in right of the states or were acquired by or vested in the commonwealth Crown.

In *Federal Commissioner of Taxation* v. *E.O. Farley Ltd*[32] Evatt J. analysed the nature of the executive or prerogative rights of the Crown in so far as they were affected by the Commonwealth Constitution. He distinguished three classes of prerogative rights:

a)   The royal prerogative by virtue of which the King engaged in foreign relations (e.g., the making of peace, the declaration of war):

b)   The common law prerogatives which conferred superior rights of the Crown *vis-à-vis* the subject (e.g. certain privileges in the matter of litigation and the right to priority in payment of debts in a winding-up):

c)   The prerogative rights of a proprietary nature. Within this third class, Evatt J. listed the rights to escheats, royal metals, and the ownership of the foreshore and the bed of the ocean *within territorial limits.*[33]

With regard to these three classes, Evatt, J. stated, "it was plain, as a general rule, that those prerogatives which, prior to federation, were exercisable by the King's representative in the area of a colony are, so far as they partake of the nature of *proprietary* right, still exercisable by the various states and for the benefit thereof".[34] This conclusion seemed to be compelled by ss. 106 and 107 of the Commonwealth Constitution which confirmed and continued pre-existing state constitutions and powers except where they were affected by the Commonwealth Constitution. Evatt, J. conceded, however, that these prerogatives of a state might be affected by commonwealth legislation.[35]

In the light of the analysis the proponents of state ownership were willing to accept that commonwealth legislation with respect to external affairs and interstate and overseas navigation could affect (though it could not destroy) the prerogative rights of the states to the sea-bed beneath territorial waters, but general legislative power over the sea-bed and the waters above would be vested in the state legislatures, as being within their power

to make laws for the peace, welfare, and good government of
the territorial areas which were subject to their jurisdiction.
There would exist a complementary legislative structure, with
"sovereignty" over the territorial sea and sea-bed being broken up
into legislative and executive powers, some of which are exercisable by the commonwealth and others by the state.[36]

THE AMERICAN "TIDELANDS" CONTROVERSY

The United States "Tidelands"[37] controversy may be considered
in six parts:
a) The original decisions in which the United States government
    challenged the right of the states of California, Texas, and
    Louisiana to legislate with respect to the mineral deposits
    of the sea-bed within territorial limits. The United States
    Supreme Court decided this case in favour of the federal
    government.[38]
b) The legislation of Congress in 1953 which restored to the
    states rights over the sea-bed within their maritime bound-
    aries (the *Submerged Lands Act*) and made provision for
    federal jurisdiction over the continental shelf outside these
    boundaries (the *Outer Continental Shelf Lands Act*).[39]
c) The challenge of the states of Alabama and Rhode Island
    to the *Submerged Lands Act* on the ground that it was
    outside Congressional power in that, *inter alia*, it involved
    a discrimination between the states of the Union by disposing
    of a national asset to the maritime states. This challenge was
    rejected by the Supreme Court.[40]
d) The litigation involving the Gulf states over the determina-
    tion of inland waters and the maritime boundaries of the
    states.[41]
e) The claim by the state of Alaska to Cook Inlet, on the ground
    that it was an "historic bay" (rejected by the Court).[42]
f) The re-affirmation by the Supreme Court, in litigation
    involving the Atlantic seaboard states, of the principles
    embodied in the original decisions in relation to the continen-
    tal shelf.[43]

In the original cases of *U.S.* v. *California*, *U.S.* v. *Louisiana* and *U.S.* v. *Texas*, the Supreme Court decided that the United States possessed paramount rights in the submerged lands lying beneath the Pacific Ocean adjacent to California and in the Gulf of Mexico adjacent to the Gulf states. Such rights, being an attribute of national rather than state sovereignty, were not dependent on the nature or extent of state maritime boundaries. In an earlier case decided in the nineteenth century[44] it had been held that the ownership of minerals beneath the navigable waters of the states was vested in the states; these areas comprised the tidelands as well as the beds of inland waters. But the Court in the instant cases refused to extend this principle to ownership of the sea-bed within the marginal sea (i.e. within the three mile limit of territorial waters). It rejected the argument put forward by the states that at the time of separation from England in 1776 international law recognized that a country had sovereignty over its maritime belt, on the ground that at that time the doctrine was not established in international law. Therefore the original thirteen colonies could not be considered as having such rights over the marginal sea. Those states which later became states of the Union which were admitted on an equal footing with the original states did not therefore hold any superior rights, whatever may have been the international law doctrine in the nineteenth century. The assertion of the United States in the proceedings before the Court of *imperium* over the sea-bed within the three-mile limit was held to be binding on the Court even though no legislation had been passed claiming such sovereignty.[45]

Following these decisions, the *Submerged Lands Act* was enacted by Congress in 1953 and this Act restored to the states ownership of submerged lands in the marginal seas within their maritime boundaries. These submerged lands were defined as comprising, *inter alia*, land extending from the coastline of each state to a line three geographical miles distant or, in the case where the boundary line of a state as it existed at the time it became a member of the Union (or as subsequently approved by Congress) extended beyond three miles, to that boundary line.[46] The term "boundary" was defined as the seaward boundary of a state or its boundary in the Gulf of Mexico as it existed at the time of entry into the Union, or as previously approved by Congress or as extended or approved pursuant to the *Submerged Lands Act*, with the proviso that no such boundary was to be interpreted as extending beyond three geographical miles in the Atlantic or Pacific Oceans or more than three marine leagues in the Gulf of Mexico.[47] The seaward boundaries of the original states were approved and confirmed as "a line three geographical miles distant from the coastline", and states admitted subsequent to the formation of the Union were permitted, if they had not already done so, to extend their boundaries seaward to the three-mile line. However it was expressly provided that this would not prejudice a state's claim to a boundary line more distant than three geographical miles if such a boundary were provided for in its law or constitution at the time of admission to the Union, or if such a boundary was subsequently approved by Congress.[48] It was thus open to the Gulf states to prove an historical boundary extending further than three geographical miles but not exceeding three marine leagues.

The next stage in the Tidelands controversy was the challenge of certain states to this legislation, on the ground that Congress could not dispose of these rights as they were paramount rights vested in the United States and not rights of property. These rights, it was further argued, were held by the United States as trustee for the people of all the states and to cede them to individual states would deprive the people as a whole of the benefit due to them and would be detrimental to the interests of the peoples of the states to which no cession was made. The Supreme Court held that under the clause in the United States Constitution empowering the United States to dispose of property, Congress had the authority to dispose of the submerged lands in the manner effected: such a power could be exercised subject to any conditions.[49] In a concurring opinion Reed J. considered that Congress had the right to cede property to one state without ceding it to another state. In his view, the requirement of "equal footing" did not demand that economic diversities be wiped out.[50]

The next stage in the Tidelands controversy occurred in 1960 when the United States met its first reverse in the litigation with the states. In these cases[51] it sought a declaration that it was entitled as against the Gulf States (Louisiana, Texas, Mississippi, Alabama, and Florida) to all property in submerged lands *more* than three geographical miles from the coastline. The United

States, relying on the foreign relations or paramount rights argument which had been accepted in the original cases, claimed that the recognition of a seaward boundary for the Gulf states beyond three miles would conflict with its policy of adhering to the three-mile limit in international relations. The *Submerged Lands Act*, it was said, did not establish a seaward boundary for the Gulf states beyond three miles, and it was argued that in any action relating to such a boundary, a claim to a three-mile limit as in accordance with United States policy should be respected by the Court. But the Supreme Court did not accept this line of reasoning. It held that the effect of the *Submerged Lands Act*, in basing claims to the sea-bed on the existence and extent of state maritime boundaries, was to separate the domestic issues dealt with by the Act from the executive policy of the United States in the international arena.[52] It was the task of the Court to examine the historical documents which established an admission boundary or a subsequently approved Congressional boundary, in order to determine whether a boundary line beyond the three mile limit could be claimed by a particular coastal state. The power on the part of Congress to establish boundaries for the Gulf states—land and maritime—flowed from its power to admit new states.[53] In the case of two states, Texas and Florida, the Court upheld a three-marine-league boundary on the basis of the historical documents existing at admission (or re-admission) and subsequent Congressional action with respect to them.[54] In the case of the other states,[55] however, the Court held that a boundary exceeding the three miles had not been established.

To return to the major issue, it is clear that the Court recognized that the question of maritime boundaries was a domestic matter between the United States and the states and that the federal adherence to the international three-mile limit could not affect the issue as resolved in the *Submerged Lands Act*. The proof of a three-marine-league boundary by Texas and Florida was therefore upheld.[56] It was held by the Court that the United States claim to a three-mile limit only established a national boundary in a limited sense, presumably as marking the extent to which international authority would be exercised by the United States in maritime areas. It is difficult, however, to reconcile this opinion with the previous decisions which emphasized "paramountcy" of the United States in the maritime arena, although one cannot deny that the Court was correct in stating that Congress had separated the national limit from the domestic limit in making provision for proof of a wider maritime boundary in the case of the Gulf states.

The Court also held that a state boundary fixed by Congress can determine the extent of inland waters as well as the extent of the marginal sea within this boundary. Consequently the *Submerged Lands Act*, in defining the area of state jurisdiction as extending from the "coastline", was authority for the determination of a baseline from which the marginal sea was to be measured.[57] This opinion is important, for it is clear that the determination of such a baseline affects the internal limit of the marginal sea as well as the commencing line of the outer continental shelf which is subject exclusively to United States jurisdiction.

In the case of Louisiana, it had been argued that the admission boundaries extended beyond the three-mile limit because its boundaries included islands within a number of leagues from the coast. But the Court held that inclusion of adjacent islands within a state's boundary did not *ipso facto* bring within state boundaries the marginal sea lying between the coastline and the islands.[58] Finally, it was the opinion of the Court that the exercise by states of jurisdiction over fishing and other allied matters in the marginal sea did not affect the boundary provisions of an Act of Congress admitting a state to the Union where there was no evidence that the geographical extent of a state's boundary was based on such a jurisdiction.[59]

Definition of the inland waters of the states was taken a step further in *U.S.* v. *California*,[60] where the question for determination was the outer limit of inland waters which were subject to California's control under the *Submerged Lands Act*. Mr Justice Harlan delivered the judgement of the Court, in which it was held that the twenty-four-mile closing line and the semi-circle principle as laid down in Article 7 of the Geneva Convention on the Territorial Sea could be applied to the issue of determining the meaning of the word "coastline" and therefore the outer limit of inland waters as defined in the *Submerged Lands Act*. This meant that Monterey Bay which had a closing line of nineteen miles fell within the definition of inland waters and therefore within the jurisdiction of the state of California, and that the baseline for measuring the territorial sea (which was subject to the jurisdiction of the states under the *Submerged Lands Act*) was the closing line so selected.[61]

The adoption of the principles of the Convention on the Territorial Sea had the effect of establishing a "single *coastline* for both the administration of the *Submerged Lands Act* and the conduct of future international relations (barring an unexpected change in the rules established by the Convention)".[62] It was the view of the Court that Congress had vested in the Court the power of determining the coastlines of the states,[63] and that the international policy of the United States involving a twenty-four-mile closing line, which had been adopted on the ratification of the Convention by the United States in 1961, was the natural test to apply in determining the meaning of the phrase "inland waters" as used in the *Submerged Lands Act*.[64] However, the Court did not accept the validity of a straight baseline method proposed by California to enclose waters between the mainland and certain adjacent islands. In so far as the United States had not chosen to apply the straight baseline system permitted by Article 4, the state could not assume the task of doing so, for this was a matter of foreign relations which were exclusively vested in the United States.[65]

California had also claimed certain bays as being "historic" and the Court examined the question what constituted an "historic" bay. In its opinion a "legislative declaration of jurisdiction (by a state) without evidence of further active and continuous assertion of dominion over the waters is not sufficient to establish the claim".[66] While the Court was not prepared to hold that a disclaimer by the United States that a bay was "historic" was decisive where the historic evidence was clear beyond doubt, it did accept the disclaimer by the United States in respect of certain bays in this case.[67] This would seem to suggest that the paramount right of claiming a bay as "historic" would in most cases be vested in the federal as distinct from the state authorities (in the absence of "continuous and exclusive assertion of dominion" by the states to the contrary). Finally, the Court accepted the ordinary low-water line laid as the baseline from which the territorial waters of California are to be measured.[68]

The principles in California II were followed in *US* v *Louisiana*[69] in which the Supreme Court held that the term "inland waters" as used in the *Submerged Lands Act* was not to be interpreted in the light of a definition contained in Congressional legislation passed in the nineteenth century to regulate navigation on waters adjacent to the Louisiana coastline. It was said that in enacting the *Submerged Lands Act*, Congress had left to the Court the function of defining the line marking the seaward limit of inland waters and it was appropriate that that line should be in accord with the definition contained in the Convention on the Territorial Sea.[70] Consequently, in determining the coastline of the State of Louisiana characterized by numerous indentations, bays and fringing islands, the Court took account of the provisions of Article 7 of the Convention in determining the line from which the three-mile limit of territorial waters was to be measured.[71] Among the criteria were the twenty-four-mile closing line (including the drawing of such a line within a bay where the distance between the entrance points excluded twenty-four miles), the semi-circle test of a bay, the treatment of islands within a bay as part of the water area, the use of low-tide elevations and islands in determining the closing lines of bays and their effect on a mainland coastline. However, as in California II, the Court in Louisiana II held that the adoption of a straight baseline system under Article 4 rested with the federal government and not the states.[72] Likewise the Court re-affirmed the reasoning adopted in the Californian case on claims to bays on "historic" grounds.[73]

In *U.S.* v. *Alaska*[74] the Supreme Court held that the evidence for proof of title to Cook Inlet as an "historic bay" of the state of Alaska was not sufficient. The Court considered that the requirements for proof of historic title had not been satisfied, viz. (1) an exercise of authority over the area, (2) which is continuous and (3) acquiesced in by other states.[75] Such evidence as indicated an exercise of authority over Cook Inlet (dating back to Russian control over the area), including enforcement of fishery regulations, did not show an intention to exclude foreign fishing vessels. Indeed foreign vessels were not treated differently from United States vessels.[76]

Finally, in *United States* v. *Maine*[77] the principles in the original cases were followed by the Court in holding that the United States was entitled to exercise sovereign rights over the sea-bed and subsoil underlying the Atlantic Ocean more than three miles seaward from the low-water mark and extending to the outer edge of the continental shelf for the purpose of exploring it and exploiting its natural resources. The Court also expressed the view that control of the marginal sea was a function of external sovereignty which applied to territorial waters. The transfer to the states of rights within these waters did not infringe on paramount federal power embodied in specific powers for the purposes of commerce, navigation, national defence and external affairs.[78]

CANADA: REFERENCE RE OFF-SHORE MINERAL RIGHTS[79]

The Supreme Court of Canada had before it a reference from the governor-general, viz. a request for an "advisory opinion", concerning the question of ownership and jurisdiction over the resources of the sea-bed and subsoil seaward from the ordinary low-water mark on the coast of the mainland and islands of the province of British Columbia both within the territorial sea and on the continental shelf (i.e. to a depth of two hundred metres or, beyond that depth, to where the depth of the superjacent waters admits of the exploitation of the resources of the said area). The Court held that, as between the governments of Canada and British Columbia, Canada had the right to explore and exploit the "submerged lands" and also the legislative jurisdiction in respect of the said lands.

In relation to the territorial sea, the reasoning of the Court was based on *R. v. Keyn*.[80] The boundaries of the Canadian colonies, it was said, ended at the low-water mark. While the British parliament could by legislation extend the boundaries of British Columbia, it had not done so when that province entered the Canadian Confederation in 1871.[81] After Canada had become a sovereign state (in the period between the signing of the Treaty of Versailles and the adoption of the Statute of Westminster) it attained full power to acquire territory and jurisdictional rights. Under the Geneva Convention on the Territorial Sea and Contiguous Zone, sovereignty over the territorial sea was vested in the coastal state. In 1964 Canada in the *Territorial Sea and Fishery Zones Act* had given legislative recognition to its rights in the territorial sea. The Canadian parliament had the legislative power to regulate the exploration and exploitation of the sea-bed under various provisions of the *British North America Act*.[82]

As to the continental shelf, the Court considered that the rights recognized by international law to exploit the resources of that area were vested in the Canadian and not the provincial government of British Columbia.[83]

AUSTRALIAN LITIGATION

Bonser v. La Macchia (1969)

The issue of sovereignty over territorial waters adjacent to the Australian coastline was referred to but not decided in *Bonser v. La Macchia*[84] which concerned a prosecution of a fisherman for using illegal equipment for fishing at a point some six miles from the New South Wales coastline. Under the commonwealth *Fisheries Act* power was given to the governor-general to proclaim Australian waters beyond territorial limits for the purposes of controlling fishing by Australian fishermen.[85] Proclamations had been made defining areas extending generally to two hundred miles from the coastline.[86] It was held that the waters so proclaimed were waters subject to the legislative power of the commonwealth under s. 51(x) of the Constitution to make laws for fisheries in Australia waters beyond territorial limits, and that therefore the fishermen was guilty of an offence.[87]

The location of the offence meant that, whether one accepted territorial limits as commencing at the low-water mark or at the three-mile limit, the offence had not occurred *within* such limits. Consequently it was not necessary for the Court to determine the question whether the limits were commonwealth or state. However, two judges (Barwick C.J. and Windeyer J.) adverted to the question and came down strongly in favour of commonwealth sovereignty, with the consequence that state limits ended at low-water mark,[88] while another judge (Kitto, J.) considered that "territorial limits" comprised state waters.[89]

The reasoning of Barwick C.J. and Windeyer J. accepts in

general the applicability of the Canadian reasoning to the Australian situation. Pursuant to this line of reasoning, the boundaries of territorial limits of the Australian colonies end at the low-water mark. The passage of the *Territorial Waters Jurisdiction Act* in 1878 was designed to break the jurisdictional shackles inhibiting British courts, including colonial courts, from trying foreign nationals for offences within territorial waters and not to vest general proprietorship of the sea-bed in the Crown in right of the colonies, although international comity recognized that the adjacent nation state had at least plenary jurisdictional rights in the area. Rights in the sea-bed adjacent to the coastlines of the Australian colonies were therefore vested in the Imperial Crown. At some time after the passage of the Statute of Westminster (which recognized the equality and independence of the members of the British Commonwealth of Nations) and the drawing up of the Convention on the Territorial Sea, the sovereign rights of the British Crown passed to the Crown in right of the commonwealth with the attainment by Australia of independent nation status in the eyes of international law.[90]

Seas and Submerged Lands Act: New South Wales and Commonwealth

The opinion expressed by Barwick C.J. and Windeyer J. in *Bonser v. La Macchia* suggested that the commonwealth had acquired sovereignty over the territorial sea by some doctrine of inheritance from the British Crown as a result of a combination of constitutional developments within the British Commonwealth and international law recognition of sovereign rights as a result of multilateral treaty. Although there was no specific discussion of the legislative power which might support the enactment by the commonwealth parliament of legislation proclaiming its sovereignty over the territorial sea, the inference which might be drawn from the judgments of the two judges was that the external affairs power (s. 51 [xxix]) provided the constitutional source for legislation relating to the area on the basis that, in so far as the boundaries of the states ended at the low-water mark, the area was geographically external to the continent of Australia and also had become the subject of an international convention. As against this interpretation it could be argued that the implementation of the Convention by vesting sovereignty in the Crown in right of the commonwealth could not go beyond the terms of the Convention which was not concerned with the location of internal sovereignty in a federal system. On this view, while the commonwealth parliament could enact legislation relating to international aspects of the Convention (e.g. innocent passage) it could not deal with territorial aspects which were already provided for under the Australian constitutional system.[91]

The reliance on American and Canadian decisions was also a factor to be taken into account, for those decisions gave the commonwealth position comparative constitutional support in relation to the recognition of central government paramount rights, despite the differences in the critical dates at which the colonies had come together in federal or confederal association.

In 1973 the Whitlam Labor government revived an earlier Bill[92] which had lapsed because of an opposition within the previous coalition government parties, and the *Seas and Submerged Lands Act* was passed by parliament to implement the commonwealth's claim of sovereignty.

The words used in s. 6 of the Act "declares and enacts" suggest that the commonwealth was both giving effect to the status quo as already recognizing commonwealth sovereignty, and also making full use of any power which might be acquired by giving effect to the Convention on the Territorial Sea and Contiguous Zone.

The subsequent litigation—*New South Wales* v. *Commonwealth*,[93] in the High Court, which as has been seen, resulted in a 5–2 majority in favour of commonwealth sovereignty over the territorial sea, will be considered under a number of headings.

State Boundaries and Territorial Limits. The majority considered that the three-mile area of territorial waters had not been incorporated into the boundaries or limits of the colonies before federation either by way of Imperial action in the nineteenth century or, following *R.* v. *Keyn*, in recognition by the common law.[94] In the view of Barwick C.J. the boundary of the continent of Australia (and the island of Tasmania) was the low-water mark around the land areas. Barwick C.J. cited with approval the dictum of the United States Supreme Court in *U.S.* v. *Texas*[95] to the effect that "once the low-water mark is passed, the international domain is reached".[96]

Mason and Jacobs JJ. examined in some detail the definitions of the littoral boundaries of the colonies in Imperial legislation and letters patent and found that the three-mile limit of territorial waters was not incorporated within such definitions.[97]

As to whether the common law recognized the inclusion of the three-mile limit within territorial boundaries, the majority adopted the ratio of *R.* v. *Keyn*: at common law the boundaries of the United Kingdom and, by necessary implication, the boundaries of its colonies ended at the low-water mark.[98] The decision in *R.* v. *Keyn* had not been undermined by later judicial decisions. Mason J., in examining the later course of judicial decisions, pointed out that three judges of the *minority* in that case considered, in another case decided sometime afterwards, that *R.* v. *Keyn* had determined the low-water mark boundary principle.[99] Dicta in later cases, such as *Lord Advocate* v. *Wemyss*,[100] *Lord Fitzhardinge* v. *Purcell*[101] and *Secretary of State for India* v. *Chelikani Rama Rao*[102] were considered by Mason J. to carry overtones of the ancient doctrine of the narrow seas under which English sovereignty in the expanses of the adjacent seas had received some judicial recognition, but that doctrine had been superseded by nineteenth-century international law developments relating to the breadth of the territorial sea.[103]

The more difficult question was to determine the effect of the Imperial *Territorial Waters Jurisdiction Act* of 1878. The opening section of the Act (s. 2) was designed to overturn the actual holding in *Keyn* that English courts did not have jurisdiction over foreign nationals within territorial matters. It provided:

> An offence committed by a person, whether he is or is not a subject of Her Majesty, in the open sea within the territorial waters of Her Majesty's Dominions, is an offence within the jurisdiction of the Admiral, although it may have been committed on board or by means of a foreign ship, and the person who committed such offence may be arrested, tried and punished accordingly.

The definition of territorial waters of "Her Majesty's Dominions" referred to such part of the sea adjacent to the coast of the United Kingdom, or the coast of some other part of Her Majesty's dominions, as is deemed by international law to be within the territorial sovereignty of Her Majesty; and for the purpose of any offence declared by this Act to be within the jurisdiction of the Admiral, any part of the open sea within one marine league of the coast measured from low-water mark shall be deemed to be open sea within the territorial waters of Her Majesty's Dominions. (s. 7).

Barwick C.J. explained the effect of that Act on the legal status of the territorial sea adjacent to the colony as follows:

When a nation state has dependent territories international law concedes to the nation state the same dominion over an area of the high seas which washes the shores of its territories as it does in relation to the waters which wash the territorial margins of the homeland. Consequently, it would be quite proper in the eyes of the British Empire to regard the Imperial Territorial Seas as including the portions of the high seas which washed the shores of Imperial colonial territories. It was in the sense that the *Territorial Waters Jurisdiction Act* was conceived and enacted.[104]

He continued:

If one had in the eyes of the Empire to describe the Imperial territorial waters which were adjacent to an Imperial Colony, one would not unnaturally speak of the waters as the colonial territorial waters, not in the sense that the Colony itself had dominion over these waters, but in the sense that it was a colony with a littoral, thus attracting to Great Britain as the nation State the international concession of dominion over them; the expression described the location of those territorial waters which washed the shores of the Imperial colonial territory. The dominion over those waters was, in my opinion, exercisable in the case of the British Empire by the Imperial executive or Imperial legislature.[105]

Mason J. considered that the Act had a more limited effect:

The *Territorial Waters Jurisdiction Act* 1878 (Imp.) did not reverse the principle according to which *Keyn's Case* was decided. The Act did not alter the seaward limits of British Territory. It assumed the correctness of that decision and conferred on British and Colonial courts jurisdiction to try offences committed by foreigners on board foreign ships within 3 nautical miles of the low-water mark—the jurisdiction which *Keyn's Case* had held to be wanting in the absence of Imperial action to confer it. The assertion of jurisdiction in the preamble to the Statute over the "open seas adjacent to the coasts of the United Kingdom and of all parts of Her Majesty's dominions to such a distance as is necessary for the defence and security of such dominions" was a declaration of jurisdiction not a declaration that the adjacent seas formed part of British territory.[106]

It can be seen that while Mason J. considered that the Act did not make territorial waters part of the "realm", Barwick C.J., following his reasoning in *Bonser* v. *La Macchia*, was inclined to treat the three miles of water adjacent to the coastline of the Australian colonies as Imperial territorial waters, although it may be that by this he meant that the British parliament and Crown have paramount jurisdiction over them.

The minority view. The opinion of Gibbs J.[107] was that either the narrower or the wider ratio could support the decision in *R.* v. *Keyn.*

> In my opinion it is apparent that the decision in *R.* v. *Keyn* could have been reached without deciding whether the territory in England stopped at the low-water mark. In any case, I find it surprising that it should be thought that a decision as to the jurisdiction of the Central Criminal Court, given by the narrowest of majorities after an extensive conflict of judicial opinion, should be treated as binding by this Court in deciding a question as to the limits of the territory of the Australian States.[108]

Gibbs J. quoted international law authorities to show that by the beginning of the twentieth century the accepted view was that a coastal state had sovereignty over its territorial waters.[109] He also referred to legislation and administrative practice both in the United Kingdom and in Australia in the nineteenth century which proceeded on the basis that the territorial sea formed part of territorial limits.[110] As to whether such limits were Imperial limits or colonial territorial limits, Gibbs J. considered that on the granting of responsible government to the colonies (which occurred in the 1850s) the rights attaching to the Imperial Crown were vested in the Crown in right of the colonies.[111]

Stephen J. favoured the narrow ratio of *R.* v. *Keyn*: it was a case restricted by its facts to the exercise of admiralty jurisdiction over foreigners.[112]

Prerogative or proprietary rights in the sea-bed. In the light of their reasoning on the meaning of the phrase "territorial limits", the majority considered that prerogative rights (including rights to minerals) affecting the sea-bed were vested in the Imperial Crown and not in the Crown in right of the colonies.[113]

The minority considered that such rights had been transferred to the Crown in right of the colonies on the granting of responsible government. The judgment of Stephen J. contains a detailed explanation of this transfer:

> So long as anything less than responsible government applied in the Australian colonies this position remained unaltered: Crown lands were vested in the Imperial Crown, they were the Sovereign's colonial lands. When responsible government was granted to the first four Australian colonies in 1855 this involved no change in the ownership of these Crown lands but rather a change in their control.[114] The Sovereign thenceforth held them in right of the colony and control of them passed to the colonial government—Isaacs J. in *Williams' Case*.[115] The Sovereign, in matters internal to the colony, ceased to be advised by Ministers responsible to the British legislature; instead it was the colonial Ministers responsible to the colonial legislature, which advised upon those matters. The control and disposition of Crown lands was for the first time placed in the hands of the responsible colonial legislatures; all this is dealt with, in its full historical detail in relation to New South Wales, by Isaacs J. in the *Williams Case*. The position was no different in other colonies. With the grant of legislative authority over Crown lands to the local legislatures went also executive control—"as rights of self-government were conferred on each Colony exclusive rights of executive authority over matters within the ambit of the rights conferred became of necessity vested in the executive power of the Colony": O'Connor J. in *South Australia v. Victoria*.[116]
>
> Those proprietary prerogatives of the Crown which related to matters other than the waste lands comprised in the land masses of Britain's colonial possessions also became exercisable, upon self-government, by the Crown in right of the self-governing colony. Long Innes CJ in Eq was concerned, in the *Butterworth Case*,[117] with the proprietary prerogative right of the Crown in the printing of Statutes and said (at 245), that proprietary prerogative rights had come to be "vested in the Crown in right of the Colony of New South Wales immediately prior to the confederation of the Commonwealth of Australia".

Despite this compelling legal analysis, it would appear that the majority were not prepared to recognize any divergence between the definition of territorial limits and the location of the prerogative rights to the sea-bed. This reflects a refusal to distinguish between *imperium* and *dominium*, sovereignty and ownership.

Federation. The majority considered that even if the rights in the territorial sea had been vested in the individual colonies before federation (which they denied) the consequence of federation was to lay the basis for the vesting of such rights in the new polity created by federation: the Crown in right of the commonwealth. As Barwick C.J. put it:

> A consequence of the creation of the Commonwealth under the Constitution and the grant of power with respect to external affairs was, in my opinion, to vest in the Commonwealth any proprietary rights and legislative power which the Colonies might have in or in relation to the territorial sea, sea-bed and airspace and continental shelf and incline. Proprietary rights and legislative powers in these matters of international concern would then coalesce and unite in the nation.[118]

Although in a previous passage in the same judgment, Barwick C.J. speaks of the maturing of the commonwealth personality after the Statute of Westminster and its adoption—a view already expressed in *Bonser* v. *La Macchia*, the cited passage would suggest an earlier acquisition of such power, although it is possible that Barwick C.J. meant that federation created a potential commonwealth power over the territorial sea which was not actualized until later.[119] Mason J. leaves open the date of acquisition:

> When it (the Commonwealth) actually became a member of the community of nations, and accepted as an international *persona*, it is not necessary to decide. Whether it was achieved on federation or at some time before the Balfour Declaration, the *Statute of Westminster* 1931, and the *Statute of Westminster Adoption Act* 1942 is not of great importance ... What is of importance is that it is consistent with the Commonwealth's character as an international person and with the States' lack of that character, that legislative power and jurisdiction over the territorial sea and its sea-bed should reside in the Commonwealth rather than the States.[120]

The judges forming the minority considered that federation had not deprived the states of any territorial or proprietary rights which they possessed at the time when they federated.[121]

The External Affairs Power—s. 51 (xxix). The majority held that the source of legislative power for the enactment of the *Seas and Submerged Lands Act* was to be found in s. 51 (xxix) of the

Constitution. Before analysing their reasons, it will be of assistance to summarize earlier cases and views on the scope of this power.

In the early literature on the nature of the external affairs power there is conflict as to its precise meaning. Harrison Moore suggested that it was intended to confer a general power of enacting extra-territorial legislation (which was deemed to be outside the power of the states).[122] Quick and Garran, on the other hand, considered that its scope was more limited. In so far as other sections of the Constitution expressly referred to extra-territorial competence when this was intended,[123] s. 51 (xxix) could not be regarded as a blanket conferment of extra-territorial competence in all matters. In their opinion, the power was to be restricted to matters "in which political influence may be exercised, or negotiation and intercourse conducted, between the government of the Commonwealth and the governments of countries outside the limits of the Commonwealth". These were matters such as the external representation of the commonwealth in other countries and the extradition of offenders against Australian laws from foreign parts.[124] This more limited view of the power would seem to be more in keeping with the general doctrine of colonial extra-territorial competence which applied at the turn of the century, at least in so far as it emphasized the "relations" aspect of the power; and the specific unshackling of the commonwealth from the operation of this restriction in s. 2 of the Statute of Westminster at a later date would seem to confirm this view.[125]

With the development of the international personality of the commonwealth in this century and its participation in international treaties as a nation in its own right, the political conditions were established for the recognition of the potentialities of the external affairs power, and in the *Burgess Case*[126] the High Court held that under this power the commonwealth could legislate to give effect to the terms of an air navigation treaty entered into at the end of World War I, which affected aerial navigation and ancillary matters within the territories of the participating nations. However, in this case particular commonwealth regulations were declared invalid on the ground that they did not give effect to the terms of the Convention in question but departed from them in certain significant respects.[127] But a decision in a later case dealing with the same treaty showed that a genuine attempt to give effect to the terms of an international convention was within the external affairs power even though in matters of detail the subject-matter regulated did not follow the precise terms of the convention.[128]

These cases dealt with a treaty which had an effect within the geographical limits of the commonwealth, i.e. it affected, *inter alia*, aerodromes in and air space over the territories of the various states. Such an "internal" effect did not deprive the legislation of its quality as being an enactment with respect to an "external affair" of the commonwealth. In the view of Dixon, J. the purpose of the power was "to authorise Parliament to make laws governing the conduct of Australia in and perhaps out of the Commonwealth in reference to matters affecting the external relations of the Commonwealth".[129] Latham, C.J. considered that the regulation of relations between Australia and other countries was the substantial subject of external affairs. It included both negotiations and the making of treaties and empowered the commonwealth to legislate to give effect to international obligations or to protect national rights internationally obtained by the commonwealth whenever legislation was necessary or claimed to be desirable for this purpose.[130] There was some difference of opinion in the *Burgess Case* as to whether the treaty had to deal with matters of an international nature before commonwealth legislative power was attracted to it. Evatt and McTiernan, J.J. considered that the power existed even when the treaty dealt with a "domestic" matter: the mere fact that a treaty had been entered into in such a matter made it an external affair of the commonwealth or, to put it in another way, made it a matter of international concern.[131] On the other hand, Dixon J. was more guarded in his approval and referred to the power as one to give effect to a treaty which dealt with matters "indisputably international in character".[132]

Recognition of the external affairs power as sanctioning legislation giving effect to treaties applying within the geographical limits of the Commonwealth is to be found in the *Airlines Case*, where an international air convention (the Chicago Air Convention) was relied upon by the commonwealth as a source of legislative power under the external affairs placitum for commonwealth control over Australian aerial navigation.[133] Barwick, C.J. said of the convention that "having regard to its subject-matter, the manner of its formation, the extent of international participation in it and the nature of the obligations it enforces upon the parties to it, it unquestionably is, or at any rate brings into existence, an external affair of Australia". The Chief Justice added, however, that the limits of commonwealth power were to be found in the convention. The commonwealth parliament was limited to enacting laws to perform the obligations or to secure the benefits which the treaty imposed or conferred on the commonwealth.[134] McTiernan, J. considered that legislation which was a bona fide attempt to carry out the provisions of a convention would be upheld as an exercise of the external affairs power,[135] and Menzies, J. also thought that the choice of ways and means for carrying out a convention was essentially a matter for parliament.[136]

It therefore seems to be established that the external affairs power would be a source of authority for legislation giving effect to a multilateral treaty to which Australia was a party, which dealt with matters of an international nature, and which conferred rights or imposed obligations on the commonwealth, the choice of the means of implementation resting with the commonwealth parliament. The High Court decisions of course concern treaties which had an effect within Australian geographical limits, but it would also seem to be a logical consequence of the reasoning in the cases that the power would equally extend to treaties having an effect outside those limits or at least relates to areas immediately adjacent to those limits.[137]

In *New South Wales* v. *Commonwealth*, the reasoning of the majority points to two bases for invoking the external affairs power. In the view of three of the judges (Barwick C.J., Mason and Jacobs J.J.)[138] and possibly a fourth judge (Murphy J.)[139] the external affairs power extends to matters and things geographically external to Australia's territorial limits. Thus legislation relating to the territorial sea falls within the power. In the view of four of the judges (Barwick C.J., McTiernan, Mason and Murphy J.J.)[140] the external affairs power would also sustain the legislation on the basis that it has given effect to an international convention, the Convention on the Territorial Sea and Contiguous Zone, s. 2 of which recognizes coastal state sovereignty.

The judges forming the minority disagreed with this interpretation. Both Gibbs and Stephen J.J. considered that the legislation departed from the Convention in a basic manner in that it purported to deal with "internal" and not merely "external" sovereignty, i.e. it purported to vest the sovereignty recognized by the Convention in one of the component units of the federation, viz. the commonwealth Crown.[141] Stephen J. also pointed out that "The subject matter of the Convention calls for little by way of municipal action for its implementation; there is still less which requires implementation by legislation as distinct from executive action; and what little does require legislative action the Act fails to implement."[142] Moreover, in so far as both judges considered that the territorial sea was within the limits of the states at federation, the "external" criterion for invoking s. 51 (xxix) would also not apply.

BREADTH OF TERRITORIAL SEAS

The zone or belt of territorial waters recognized by customary international law is considered to extend to a minimum of three miles from the baselines from which the territorial sea is measured.[143] Prior to the enactment of the *Seas and Submerged Lands Act*, the limit of territorial waters had not been established in commonwealth legislation. The three-mile limit had been derived from imperial and colonial practice in the nineteenth century as well as being based on commonwealth executive policy in the present century.[144] It had also been recognized in pre-federation legislative enactments dealing with particular topics such as fishing and navigation, as well as in a few judicial decisions.[145] The reasons for the absence of any general legislative declaration of a three-mile limit were not difficult to discern. Such a declaration would have been in the light of British and Australian practice otiose; in any case the declaration of the limits of territorial waters had been considered to be an executive or prerogative act,[146] and such a prerogative right would be vested in the commonwealth which is responsible for the control of external affairs.

In *New South Wales* v. *Commonwealth* it was accepted by certain members of the Court that the present breadth of the Australian territorial sea was three miles. This reflected international law practice in the nineteenth century and recognition in Imperial legislation.[147] However, Mason J. referred to the fact that at the present time, a wider territorial sea is being claimed by a number of nations and to the possibility of the commonwealth extending its territorial seas beyond three miles.[148]

In upholding the validity of the *Seas and Submerged Lands Act*, the Court must therefore be taken to have upheld the validity of s. 7 which empowers the governor-general to declare, not inconsistent with section 11 of Part 1 of the Convention of the Territorial Sea, the limits of the whole or any part of the sea adjacent to Australia. Under s. 7(2)(a) such a power may be exercised in relation to the breadth of the territorial sea. This would enable the governor-general either to formally proclaim the three-mile limit and/or to proclaim a wider water limit at some future time when international practice or agreement had recognized such wider limit.[149]

However, there are areas where the breadth of the territorial sea adjacent to Australian territory will merge with the territorial seas of a foreign country. These areas are in the Torres Strait where islands forming part of the state of Queensland are contiguous to Papua New Guinea. The principles for demarcation of the territorial sea in such cases[150] are to be derived from Article 12 of the Convention on the Territorial Sea:

> Where the coasts of two states are opposite or adjacent to each other, neither of the two states is entitled, failing agreement between them to the contrary, to extend its territorial sea beyond the median line every point of which is equidistant from the nearest points on the baselines from which the breadth of the territorial sea of each of the states is measured. The provisions of this paragraph shall not apply, however, where it is necessary by reason of historic title or other special circumstances to delimit the territorial seas of the two states in a way which is at variance with this provision.

Certain islands of the Talbot Group in Torres Strait are separated from the Papuan coastline by a distance of less than six miles. These islands are within the line that is set out in the schedule to the *Coast Islands Act* 1879 (Qld) which confirmed the annexation of the islands to Queensland.[151] The line is not a territorial sea line but a line which separates the territorial land areas of two political entities. Unless it could be agreed that the qualifying part of Article 12 "by reason of historic title" would support a claim to all waters within the line as Australian territorial waters on historic grounds (which is doubtful), the general median line principle enshrined in Article 12 could appear to require that a dividing line equidistant from the Papuan shoreline and the shoreline of the islands be drawn. It is conceivable, however, that Papua New Guinea may invoke the "special circumstances" qualification to claim a territorial sea extending beyond the median line.[152] This matter and the question of a continental shelf boundary is at the time of writing the subject of negotiations between the Papua New Guinea and Australian Governments.[153]

LEGISLATIVE JURISDICTION OF THE STATES OVER THE TERRITORIAL SEA

What effect does the commonwealth claim of sovereignty have on the exercise of legislative jurisdiction by the states over the territorial sea? It appears that the *Seas and Submerged Lands Act* was drafted in a way to ensure that state legislative jurisdiction over persons, things and events on the territorial sea was not intended to be affected, because section 16(b) provides that "the provisions of the Act do not limit or exclude the operation of any law of a State in force at the date of commencement of the Act or coming into force after that date, except in so far as the law is expressed to vest or make exercisable any sovereignty or sovereign rights otherwise than as provided by the preceding provisions of this Act".

The case of *Pearce* v. *Florenca*[154] establishes that the claim of sovereignty made by the Act, in the absence of commonwealth legislation giving effect to that sovereignty in a particular area, has had little effect on state legislation affecting activities in the territorial sea. The question in that case concerned the *Fisheries Act* 1905–1975 (Western Australia) which made it an offence to possess certain types of undersized fish taken within Western Australian waters[155] or elsewhere. The respondent had been charged with the possession of such fish within two miles from the coastline. The question before the High Court was whether the Western Australian Act could operate consistently with the *Seas and Submerged Lands Act* in relation to possession of fish in the territorial sea. The High Court held that the *Fisheries Act* had a valid operation in the area and did not infringe commonwealth sovereignty.

It would appear that in determining the validity or application of state legislation in relation to the territorial sea, four questions must be asked:

1. Does the legislation apply expressly or by necessary intendment to the territorial sea? This is a question of construction.
2. Does the legislation contain a sufficient nexus with the state to make it a law for the peace, order and good government of the state? This is a question affecting the constitutional power of the state under its state constitution.[156]
3. Does the legislation infringe on commonwealth sovereignty as proclaimed by the *Seas and Submerged Lands Act*.[157]
4. Is it inconsistent with any specific commonwealth legislation applying in the area which has paramountcy under s. 109 of the Commonwealth Constitution?

As to the nexus requirement, two judges in *Pearce* v. *Florenca* applied a liberal test of what constituted a sufficient nexus. Gibbs J. said:

> The very fact that the waters are off shore waters of the State provide the nexus necessary to render valid a law operating within those waters. There is an intimate connection between the land territory of a State and its off-shore waters. These waters have been popularly regarded as the waters of the State, and as vital to its trade. The people of the State have traditionally exploited the resources of the off-shore waters and used them for recreation. The enforcement of laws of the State would be gravely impeded if a person could escape from the reach of the laws and the authority of the State by going below low-water mark.[158]

Jacobs J. considered that the special concern of a state in fishing in waters near its coast was sufficient to provide the nexus.[159] But he based his decision on the wider ground that the legislation operated in Australian waters:

> Because the waters off the coast of Western Australia are Australian waters they are at the same time Western Australian waters, waters

off that part of the community of Australia that is the State of Western Australia. Both before and after the passing of the *Seas and Submerged Lands Act* the fact that the waters are Australian waters and the fact that part of the waters is adjacent to the coast of Western Australia gives the State, as a part of Australia, a relationship or nexus with those waters which is in itself sufficient to support the application of the law of Western Australia to those waters, provided that the law is intended by the Legislature of Western Australia to apply to those waters, and provided that it is not inconsistent with a law of the Commonwealth itself.[160]

It would appear that most state legislation applying to territorial waters does not amount to a claim of sovereignty over those waters. In so far as a state law is usually framed in the form of an exercise of jurisdiction over persons, acts or events, such an exercise of legislative power, as in the case of fisheries, does not amount to an exercise of sovereign powers. However it would be necessary to scrutinize any minerals legislation applying to the territorial sea-bed (or beyond) for if proprietorship rights are vested in the state Crown by such legislation, the legislation would probably fall, on the ground that the reasoning of the High Court in *New South Wales* v. *Commonwealth* supports the view that proprietary rights are an aspect of sovereignty.[161]

The declaration of sovereignty in the *Seas and Submerged Lands Act* therefore stands within the Australian federal system as a declaration of pre-eminent or paramount federal authority over the territorial sea and sea-bed[162] and activities associated with or occurring thereon. It also operates as an investment of the commonwealth with the attributes of sovereignty including prerogative rights. But under this panoply of commonwealth sovereignty, ordinary state laws, so intended to operate and having a sufficient nexus with the state, continue to operate with respect to activities of fishing, etc., in the absence of commonwealth legislation specifically applying to such activities.

8

Internal Waters

A determination of the baseline from which territorial waters are to be measured will also have the effect of determining the outer limits of internal waters and, in so far as the legal regimes applicable to these areas differ, will have important practical consequences. Which governmental unit in the Australian federation is entitled to determine such baselines? In so far as the Convention on the Territorial Sea embodies certain rules as to baselines or closing lines in the cases of bays and island-fringed coastlines, a determination of such lines will have repercussions not only in the domestic but also in the international spheres. The problem therefore is to determine a line or lines which constitute the "coastline" (or the baseline of the territorial sea).

It is, I think, necessary to state at this stage that an application of the baseline principle embodied in the Geneva Convention on the Territorial Sea will involve to a certain extent a departure from the previously accepted methods of demarcation. This is true if we consider that, apart from "historic" bays, the previous Australian policy was to claim as a maximum a ten mile closing line for bays.[1] Would the new policy therefore involve a modification of state boundaries? If such were the case, the boundaries alteration procedure prescribed by s.123 of the Commonwealth Constitution would have to be observed.

The simple answer to this question is that s.123 envisages a change in boundaries which involves extension of land and geographical boundaries such as an addition or diminution in the continental land mass of a state or in the adjacent islands which are subject to its sovereign authority. It would not seem to be in accord with the intention of the drafters of s.123 to hold that a modification of the baseline of territorial waters (even though that involved a modification of the area of inland waters fronting the open sea) would have to be submitted to the tortuous process of boundary alteration prescribed in s.123.[2] This opinion is strengthened by a consideration of the uncertain nature of baseline or closing lines for bays in the era before the Convention on the Territorial Sea came into operation. Such a question was one which English courts approached with timidity, framing their decisions in language which constituted by no means a final determination of the issue and often deferring to a particular statement of the Executive.[3] To hold therefore that the application of the principles of the Convention which involved a clarification of these rules could only be carried out under s.123 would not seem to be a realistic approach to the problem. In any case the application of the baseline procedure laid down in the Convention does not involve a change in the three mile limit but only in the manner of measuring waters within that limit. The area involved was therefore to be regarded as a fluctuating or imprecise area which until recently was not determined in the Australian context according to precise rules.[4]

There are examples of state legislative enactments which have defined maritime areas which are subject to state fisheries control and also harbour and port areas which are subject to marine enactments.[5] This would seem to support the proposition that a state may in particular areas within its constitutional competence define the inland and territorial waters to which its legislation will apply, providing this does not extend beyond the area of control to which the commonwealth has subscribed by participation in an international convention. To claim areas in excess of this would be to commit the commonwealth internationally and to impair the prerogative or executive right in foreign affairs which is exclusively vested in the commonwealth. O'Connell phrases the constitutional competence of the states in this matter as follows:

> It is implicit in any State Constitution that the boundary of the State includes those internal waters which international law permits the State to regard as such and which the State does so regard. The

definition of the boundary could be considered as making explicit what is already implied. The legislative or executive function in this respect is perhaps no different from the judicial.[6]

He points out that, in certain cases decided on the extent of territorial waters, it has been taken for granted that by legislation a state could claim its territorial belt, and it seems possible to conclude that the definition of internal waters would be similarly regarded.[7] Such a determination would fall within a state's power to make laws for its peace, welfare, and good government and would be made in areas within the state's constitutional competence (e.g., fishing within inland and territorial waters.)

But the commonwealth also has a national maritime boundary which of course ought to consist of the individual maritime boundaries of the states as well as of the internal territories of which the commonwealth is composed. Indeed in the light of the obligations case upon the commonwealth by the Convention on the Territorial Sea to mark on large-scale maps straight baselines which are adopted in accordance with Article 4, the determination of the national maritime boundary is pre-eminently a commonwealth responsibility. The commonwealth could of course proceed to do this in the context of particular legislative action (e.g., in defining the areas such as those to which the commonwealth *Fisheries Act*[8] applies) or by executive action which is more flexible. Procedure by way of executive action in determining the national maritime boundary would, in the absence of legislation empowering such procedure, be characterized as a prerogative act. In England the application of the straight baseline procedure permitted by the Convention on the Territorial Sea has been accomplished in this manner.[9] The determination of the national maritime boundary would, on the analogy of such cases as *Joseph* v. *Colonial Treasurer (N.S.W.)*,[10] be a matter for the Commonwealth executive in so far as it would affect international rights of navigation and fishing, but it would also have a domestic operation (i.e., in determining the limits of commonwealth and state competence). In the absence of a general declaration taking the form of a proclamation or order in council, a definition of the national maritime boundary could be accomplished in a piecemeal manner, as for example by the issue of an executive certificate whenever an issue as to maritime jurisdiction arose in the courts. There are dicta in High Court cases such as *Ffrost* v. *Stevenson*[11] and *Chow Hung Ching* v. *R*.[12] which indicate that such a certificate in relation to territorial jurisdiction would be accepted as binding by an Australian court but opinions expressed by members of the Court in *Bonser* v. *La Macchia* indicate that the Court has an overriding jurisdiction to determine whether a declaration of maritime limits falls within constitutional power.[13]

The *Seas and Submerged Lands Act* contains a provision which enables the governor-general to proclaim baselines and therefore it is no longer necessary to rely on the prerogative for this purpose. Under Article 7 the governor-general may from time to time by Proclamation declare not inconsistently with section II of Part I of the Convention on the Territorial Sea and Contigous Zone the limits of the whole or any part of the territorial sea including the baseline from which the breadth of the territorial sea or any part of the territorial sea is to be measured.

But the Act also distinguishes between internal waters which were within the limits of a state at federation and another category of internal waters which is not specified but which presumably comprises waters which may be claimed as internal waters under the provisions of Articles 4 and 7 of the Convention on the Territorial Sea. Thus, s.10 of the Act vests sovereignty over internal waters in the commonwealth but this section is qualified by s.14 which provides:

> Nothing in the act affects sovereignty or sovereign rights in respect of any waters of the sea that are waters of or within any bay, gulf, estuary, river, creek, inlet, port or harbour and
> (a) were, on the 1st January, 1901 within the limits of a State; and
> (b) remain within the limits of the State, or in respect of the airspace over, or in respect of the sea-bed or subsoil beneath, any such waters.

Presumably, if the commonwealth exercises its power to proclaim baselines allowed for by the Convention and the internal waters so enclosed are greater than the area of internal waters as defined by Imperial act, colonial act or under the rules of the common law,[14] the status of the enclosed areas which extend beyond the areas recognized as internal waters at federation become commonwealth internal waters[15] and the other portions state internal waters.

In so far as section 7 prescribes that the drawing of baselines should be consistent with the articles of the Convention on this matter, I proposed to examine the nature of the criteria to be used and the extent to which they may differ from pre-existing practice.

APPLICATION OF THE CONVENTION TO THE AUSTRALIAN COASTLINE

This topic may be considered in three parts:
a) Bays.
b) Complex areas of coastline (consisting of deep indentations and for fringing islands).
c) Islands and low-tide elevations.

Bays

Article 7 of the Convention on the Territorial Sea allows a state to draw closing lines across the entrances or within the entrances of bays which have a certain geographic configuration, although "historic" bays are not subject to the operation of this Article. We have seen[16] that to qualify as a juridical bay a water area must have a sufficient penetration into the land area and not merely be a curvature of the coast. The depth of the penetration must be at least equal to the radius of an area marked out by a semi-circle the diameter of which is based on the distance between the entrance points. The intention of Article 7 in requiring a certain depth of penetration is to prevent coastal states from enclosing small curvatures of the coast—a practice which would detract from the normal requirement that the low-water line of the coast must be followed in determining the baseline of territorial waters.

Along the Australian coast there are a number of indentations which are called bays but which clearly do not come within the juristic definition of a bay, for example Discovery Bay in Victoria, Lacepede Bay in South Australia, and Flinders Bay in Western Australia. The depth of penetration of these bays in proportion to the width of the opening does not seem to be sufficient to bring them within Article 7.

Where a bay does fulfil the geographic requirements laid down in Article 7 it is provided that a closing line of twenty-four miles may be drawn across the natural entrance points or, where they are more than twenty-four miles apart, a line of twenty-four miles may be drawn within the waters of the bay so as to enclose the maximum area of water permissible with a line of that length.[17]

Australian practice on bays has never been clearly defined but it seems that the maximum length of a closing line was in the past (apart from "historic" bays) restricted to ten miles.[18] In 1929 the commonwealth government stated in a memorandum, in reply to a questionnaire from an international body, that a six-mile baseline should be drawn but that it was prepared to recognize a ten-mile limit if there were general agreement on this among states.[19] Bouchez remarks that it is permissible to suppose that Australia still maintains a limit of six or ten miles for baselines in bays, but this remark was made at a time when the Convention on the Territorial Sea had not come into force.[20]

In another recent work on the law of bays it is indicated that there is a great deal of confusion in the previous Australian position on bays.[21] Strohl refers to a United Nation. Memorandum concerning Historic Bays[22] in which it is mentioned that Australia claims fifteen historic bays. The authority for this statement is said to be a 1936 letter from the Navy Office to Professor Charteris, late Professor of International Law at the University of Sydney, which refers to a list of bays along the Australian coastline. The bays mentioned are Van Diemen's Gulf, Buckingham Bay, Blue Mud Bay (Northern Territory); Coffin Bay, Streaky Bay, Spencer Gulf, Investigator Strait and St Vincent's Gulf (South Australia); Exmouth Gulf, Roebuck Bay and Shark Bay (Western Australia); Broad Sound, Upstart Bay, Moreton Bay, and Hervey Bay (Queensland); and Oyster Bay and Storm Bay (Tasmania). The heading to this list states that it is a list of bays whose width between heads exceeds six miles. Four of these bays were marked with an asterisk: Van Diemen's Gulf, Shark Bay, Exmouth Bay, and Moreton Bay, and a note indicates that the bays so marked were claimed as historic bays.[23] As Strohl points out, the effect of the letter seems to indicate that only four bays were claimed as historic bays and the comment made in the United Nations Memorandum that *all* the bays were claimed as historic seems wrong on this point.[24]

O'Connell also has examined the question. He considers that while the Navy Office recognized the four bays as historic, other bays in the list could be claimed today as internal waters under an application of the closing line rules.[25] A few of these bays appear to have entrances more than twenty-four miles wide: the remainder range between six and twenty-four miles. The impact of the 1936 note would therefore seem to be a singling out of historic bays only from a list of fifteen bays (which was by no means exhaustive) of those over six miles in width which was at that time possibly regarded by the Navy Office as the established limit.

There is no doubt, therefore, that at the present time all bays up to six miles in width are claimed as internal waters by Australia under the normal rule and quite apart from historic grounds. Within this category would fall bays such as Port Phillip Bay (Victoria), Broken Bay (New South Wales), Encounter Bay (South Australia), and numerous inlets along the coastline.

What is the position with respect to these bays whose width falls within the range of six miles to twenty-four miles? It could, I think, be suggested that with the crystallization of the position in the 1940s and 1950s before the Geneva Conventions, a ten-mile limit at least would have been recognized by the Commonwealth of Australia, especially in the light of the 1929 Commonwealth Memorandum; and there seems to be every reason for advocating that as a closing line of twenty-four miles has been prescribed by an international convention as a maximum, this width should now be adopted by the commonwealth as a firm rule, thus obviating the need to justify a claim to bays falling within the ten miles to twenty-four miles category as historic.

With respect to bays which exceed twenty-four miles in width, the only claim recognized by international law is on historic grounds. It is not proposed to examine the elements of such a claim in this work except to point out that an exercise of sovereign rights by the coastal nation and acquiescence by other nations are necessary elements of such a title.[26] While most writers consider that Shark Bay may be claimed as an historic bay, there are also suggestions that St Vincent's Gulf and Spencer Gulf in South Australia could be claimed on this ground.[27] Strohl has even speculated that the Gulf of Carpentaria, the entrance of which is three-hundred-and-fifty miles wide, could be claimed as historic.[28] In the case of the South Australian gulfs, O'Connell refers to a decision of the Supreme Court of South Australia in 1875 which suggests that St Vincent's Gulf is part of the internal waters of South Australia.[29] O'Connell also considers that the application of state fisheries legislation to various reaches of the gulf may be evidence of state appropriation of the whole area.[30] Moreover, the original Letters Patent defining the boundaries of the province included within these boundaries "gulf and bays".[31] Even if such evidence is not sufficient to constitute a claim based on historic grounds, it must be remembered that Article 7 allows for a twenty-four mile closing line to be drawn inside the bay. Applied to the South Australian gulfs this would mean substantial parts thereof could be claimed according to the ordinary rule, and the same would be true of those bays, whose width between entrances exceeds twenty-four miles, which are to be found along the Australian coastline.

Article 7, paragraph 3, relates to islands along the mouth of, and within, bays. It provides: "Where because of the presence of islands, an indentation has more than one mouth, the semi-circle (whose diameter is a line drawn across the mouths) shall be drawn on a line as long as the sum total of the lengths of the lines across the different mouths. Islands within an indentation shall be included as if they were part of the water area of the indentation." One writer has described this provision as being so difficult to apply in practice that it is impossible to appreciate either its value or purpose.[32] However, its application would appear to be called for where there is an island or a small number of islands located either in the mouth of or within a bay which falls within Article 7. The effect of this paragraph is twofold: (a) in respect of the islands in the mouth, the twenty-four mile crossing line may be discontinuous, it may be broken by the intervening areas of land; (b) in respect of islands within the bay, the depth of penetration is determined by including these islands as part of the water area, i.e. the area comprised by these islands is discounted as "land" in determining the depth of penetration.[33]

The presence of islands off an indentation must also be considered in determining the applicability of a straight baseline method under Article 4 of the Convention, and it has been suggested that even though a closing line may not be drawn across an indentation under Article 7, nevertheless a straight baseline may be drawn so as to enclose a bay wider than twenty-four miles where there are islands which "fringe" the entrance.[34] This straight baseline method, however, is dependent on considerations different from those comprised in Article 7 and will be considered in the next section.

It remains to be pointed out that "historic bays" would in the light of s.14 of the *Seas and Submerged Lands Act* be treated as within state limits, on the assumption that such an historic title has come to fruition before federation.

Complex areas of coastline

As we have seen, Article 4 of the Convention provides that in localities where the coastline is deeply indented, or if there is a fringe of islands near to the coast, straight baselines joining appropriate points may be used. These baselines may not depart to any appreciable extent from the general direction of the coast, and the sea areas lying within them must be sufficiently closely related to the land domain to be subject to the regime of internal waters. In determining particular baselines, economic interests peculiar to the region may be taken into consideration but the existence of these interests must be evidenced by long usage.[35] Baselines are not to be drawn from low-tide elevations unless lighthouses or similar installations which are permanently above sea level have been built on them.[36]

The purpose of this Article is to provide for an exception to the general rule on the drawing of the baselines of territorial waters, where the configuration of a coastline requires it. As such, Article 4 ought to be strictly interpreted and should not be used as a justification for an inordinate projection of the baseline into ocean areas.[37]

Article 5 provides that the waters on the landward side of a straight baseline are internal waters of the coastal nation, although this is not to affect the right of innocent passage through such waters if they were previously considered as part of the territorial sea or of the high seas.

The adoption of a straight baseline method under Article 4 will therefore lead to an increase in a state's area of sovereignty over inland waters as well as projecting the baseline of the territorial sea outwards. Strictly interpreted, the requirements of Article 4 are as follows:

a) The existence of *localities* (and not merely points where the coastline conforms to the geographical description outlines).

b) Either *deep* penetrations of the coastline or a fringe of islands, or both.

c) A sufficient physical connection between the enclosed sea areas and the land domain so that those areas may be treated as inland waters.

d) A prohibition against drawing straight baselines to low-tide elevations unless lighthouses or other installations which are above water permanently have been built on them. This prohibition must, however, be considered in the light of Article 11 of the Convention.[38] It is also permissible in determining particular straight baselines to take into account economic interests which are based on long usage (e.g. a particular community may have depended for its economic existence on fishing in the waters in question for a long period in history).

It will be recalled that in the *Anglo-Norwegian Fisheries Case*[39] the method of drawing straight baselines was approved by the International Court of Justice as an appropriate way of determining the width of territorial sea along the Norwegian coastline, where the outer line of the *skjaergaard* (the myriad of rocks, islands, and promontories) fronting the coastline was adopted by the Norwegian authorities as the baseline. The Court recognized not only the relevance of these peculiar geographical features but also the validity of economic interests (Norwegian dependence on fishing). Moreover, the length of the baselines which were approved was not restricted to a mathematical measurement such as ten miles (put forward by Britain in its plaint).[40]

The Norwegian coastline is characterized by the twin features of deep indentations and fringing islands and elevations. These features characterize most coastlines to which Article 4 would be applicable. It has been asked whether Article 4 applies to a small number of or even one fringing island or whether there has to be a substantial number before it can be invoked. McDougal and Burke consider that it may have been the consensus of the International Law Commission in its deliberations on the draft article that while the straight baseline system was directed to geographical situations in which the immediately adjacent islands were relatively numerous, the presence of a few islands was adequately provided for by a recognition of a belt of territorial waters for each island.[41] But they later qualify this remark when they say that "it would nevertheless be a grave error to assume on this account that future tribunals will necessarily refuse to honour a claim to treat a few adjacent islands as a unit for delimitation purposes, thereby extending the sea and creating new areas of internal waters".[42] The suggested reconciliation of these views is to be found in the statement that claims of this nature "should preferably be limited to those exceptional circumstances in which the presence of a few islands creates a very intense concentration of coastal interest in the waters adjacent to them and the mainland".[43]

The application of Article 4 to the Australian coastline is a question of some difficulty.[44] There is at least one major section of the coastline to which it would apply and that is the northern coastline of Western Australia between fourteen and sixteen degrees south latitude where the islands of the Bonaparte Archipelago front the coastline. This area is characterized by a number of deep penetrations fringed by numerous islands and reefs; a system of straight baselines would seem to be the only practicable method of delimiting the coastal waters of this region. There are certain areas in other parts of the Australian coastline to which the straight baseline method would be properly applied because of the presence of fringing islands, for instance the Barrier Reef areas of the Queensland coastline, such as the coast near Proserpine which is fringed by the Whitsunday group of islands and the coast north of Cairns.[45]

It could also be argued that a claim to a "bay" on historic grounds would be reinforced by the presence of fringing islands adjacent to its mouth, e.g. as in the case of Van Diemen's Gulf which is fringed by a number of islands.[46] It could also be suggested that the straight baseline method may be adopted where there are a number of islands adjacent to a bay which fails to measure up to the requirements of Article 7,[47] but such a suggestion ought to be looked at with caution as it could be used as a covert means of extending the juridical concept of a bay where the complete requirements of Article 7 are not present. However, the suggestion has immediate relevance to the status of St. Vincent's Gulf in South Australia, the entrance of which is adjacent to a very large island, Kangaroo Island. If no claim can be made to the whole area of this bay on historic ground grounds, it has been suggested by O'Connell,[48] with sympathetic agreement on the part of others,[49] that the presence of this island might justify the application of a straight baseline which, drawn from the headlands of the gulf and crossing to Kangaroo Island, would have the effect of enclosing the whole area of the "gulf" as internal waters.

One point which must again be noted is that coastal states which adopt the straight baseline method are obliged to mark the baselines which they have adopted on large-scale maps so that other countries may become aware of such a claim to a wider area of internal waters (which will of course also affect the location of the territorial sea).

Islands and low-tide elevations

It is clear from the Convention that islands may be considered under two classifications, either as fringing islands in which case they may be used to delimit a mainland coastline or as separate geographic entities in which case the ordinary rules relating to the measurement of the territorial sea will apply. Article 10(1) defines an island as a naturally formed area of land surrounded by water, which is above water at high tide. We have seen that capacity for use does not determine the status of an island.[50] Rocks and uninhabited cays are within the definition.[51] This provision is of great importance so far as the Great Barrier Reef areas of Queensland are concerned and also to the "reef" areas off the Western Australian and Northern Territory coastlines. There are hundreds of reefs (coral and otherwise) and rocks in these areas which are above water at high tide and which therefore are surrounded by belts of territorial waters.

But there are also a number of low-tide elevations, i.e. areas which are at some part of the day covered by the waters of the ocean. Article 11 of the convention refers to these areas as "naturally formed areas of land which are surrounded by and above water low tide but submerged at high tide". A low-tide elevation does not have a territorial sea of its own. However, where a low-tide elevation is situated wholly or partly at a distance not exceeding the breadth of the territorial sea from the mainland or an island the low-water line on that elevation may be used as the baseline for measuring the breadth of the territorial sea.[52]

The differing interpretations of Article 11 are of course of most importance so far as the Great Barrier Reef area off Queensland is concerned. There is a myriad of islands and rocks in this area which are surrounded by rocks and reefs which are covered at high tide but exposed at low tide. The adoption of the former interpretation would have the effect of increasing the area of water lying between the islands and low-tide elevations and projecting outwards the baselines from which the belts of territorial sea are to be measured. The latter method would have the effect of merely extending the outer limit of territorial waters and of not therefore converting the intervening waters into internal waters.

It remains finally to refer to our previous discussion of enclaves and non-adjacent archipelagos.[53] The application of the foregoing principles would mean that there are considerable small pockets of high seas surrounded by territorial waters adjacent to both the Queensland and Western Australian coastlines, and also that further out there are groups of islands having a close inter-relationship but not sufficiently adjacent to the mainland coastline to permit the application of Article 4. It may be that enclaves should be enclosed to preserve some geographical symmetry in the demarcation of territorial waters.[54] Moreover, where islands form a cluster of their own a straight baseline method of some sort may be used.[55]

It will be a painstaking and arduous task to delimit the territorial waters off the Queensland and Western Australian coastline because of their physical configuration and structure. The maritime charts show a great variety of "islands" and low-tide elevations in these areas. They comprise reefs which are entirely covered at high tide but exposed at low tide and likewise reefs which are partially exposed at high tide (in both cases with great variations in length and breadth). There are also rocks which are entirely covered at high tide and exposed at low tide, or only partially covered at high tide. There are numerous sand cays above water at high tide but surrounded by fringing reefs which are submerged at this tide. All these features must be taken into account in delimiting the internal and territorial waters of the Australian coastline and its adjacent islands, a task which must be accomplished in order that such waters may be distinguished from the high seas surrounding this continent.

9

Fishery Zones

The commonwealth *Fisheries Act* 1952–1975 which regulates acts of fishing and associated matters (e.g. the carrying of equipment) within Australian waters in effect establishes two different areas for the purpose of the exercise of fisheries jurisdiction: an "exclusive fisheries zone" of twelve miles which applies to foreign fishing[1] and a domestic fisheries zone the boundaries of which are set out in proclamations[2] made under the *Fisheries Act* and which are generally about two hundred miles from the low-water mark of the mainland coast line, except in parts of the Northern region (Arafura Sea) where the distance is less than two hundred miles (to take account of Indonesian jurisdiction), and in areas of the Pacific Ocean where outlying islands are involved and where the distance extends beyond two hundred miles.

EXCLUSIVE FISHING ZONE

The phrase used in the *Fisheries Act* to describe this zone is the "declared fishing zone" (s.4). Read with s.5 of the Act the controls applicable to this zone apply to foreign fishing vessels and foreign fishermen. The area of the zone is defined as:

> (a) the waters adjacent to Australia and having as their inner limits the baselines by reference to which the territorial limits of Australia are defined for the purposes of international law and as their outer limits lines seaward from those inner limits every point of each of which is distant 12 international nautical miles from the point on one

of those baselines that is nearest to the first-mentioned point; and (b) the waters adjacent to each external Territory and having as their inner limits the baselines by reference to which the territorial limits of that Territory are defined for the purposes of international law and as their outer limits lines seward from those inner limits every point of each of which is distant 12 international nautical miles from the point on one of these baselines that is nearest to the first-mentioned point, but does not include any waters that are not proclaimed waters.

Under s.7 of the Act the governor-general may by Proclamation declare any Australian waters to be proclaimed waters for the purposes of the Act. Australian waters are defined by s.4 to mean (a) Australian waters beyond territorial limits; (b) waters adjacent to territory and within territorial limits;[3] and (c) waters adjacent to an external territory and beyond territorial limits.

The phrase "territorial limits" are used in the *Fisheries Act*, which was enacted under the power granted by s.51(x) of the Constitution to make laws with respect to fisheries in Australian waters beyond territorial limits, came under examination in *Bonser* v. *La Macchia*[4] where five members of the Court considered that it had reference to the three mile limit.[5] Consequently, the *fisheries power* of the commonwealth commences at that limit, with the states exercising a fisheries jurisdiction *within* that limit.

Barwick C.J. considered that at federation the phrase "territorial limits" referred to the limit of *Imperial* territorial waters. Consequently, the meaning to be attributed to s.15(x) was that the geographical scope of the commonwealth fisheries power extended to waters beyond the three mile limit.[6] However, he accepted that there was a conception abroad in the nineteenth century that the limits were in some way *colonial* territorial limits and that the power conferred on the Federal Council of Australasia with respect to "fisheries in Australian waters beyond territorial limits" which was exercised in the *Queensland Pearl Shell and Bêche-de-mer Fisheries Act (Extra-territorial) Act* of 1888 was based on this "misconception".[7] All this pointed to a construction of s.51(x) as covering an area outside the three-mile limit. But apart from the fisheries power, Barwick C.J. took the view that at the present time the commonwealth had, by inheritance from the British Crown acquired sovereignty over territorial waters, i.e. waters within three-miles of the coastline.

The effect of the decision in *New South Wales* v. *Commonwealth*[8] upholding the vesting of sovereignty over the territorial sea in the commonwealth is that the Commonwealth parliament has plenary legislative power over any activity associated with the sea including fishing; and that power is derived from s.51(xxix). However, in the absence of commonwealth legislation, state fisheries legislation continues to operate within the three-mile limit.[9]

To return to the definition of the phrase "declared fishing zone" in s.4 of the *Fisheries Act*, the effect of s.4 read with s.7 is that the declared fishing zone extends a distance of nine miles from what may be described as "fishery territorial limits" viz., the limits referred to in s.51(x).[10] This interpretation may appear to conflict with the specific words of s.4 that the declared fishing zone means the waters adjacent to Australia and having as their inner limits the baselines by reference to which the territorial limits are defined *for the purposes of international law*, i.e. the coastline,[11] but reference must be made to the concluding words of the definition section which state that the waters do not include any waters that are not proclaimed waters. Under s.7 only Australian waters beyond territorial limits may be so proclaimed, namely waters from the three-mile limit outwards.

Section 5(2) of the *Fisheries Act* provides that in relation to proclaimed waters comprised in the declared fishing zone, the Act applies to all persons, including foreigners, and to all persons, including foreign boats. The major sections of the Act, ss. 8 and 9, operate by way of a regulation of fishing (including prohibition) and licensing of activities. The effect therefore of the amendment of the *Fisheries Act* introducing the concept of the declared fishing zone has been to make provision for a nine-mile exclusive fishing zone additional to a three-mile zone of territorial waters.

The recognition of a "phasing-out" period for foreign vessels with traditional fishing rights in the nine-mile zone which reflected international practice in the 1960s was contained in an Agreement between Australia and Japan and Fisheries signed in 1969 which was expressed to operate for a period of five years.[12] Under the Agreement, Japanese vessels engaged in tuna fishing were permitted to engage in such fishing in specified areas of the declared fishing zone in the Tasman and Coral Seas and off the Papuan coastline. There was also provision for the vessels to use Australian ports for provisioning. On the expiry of the period, the port access rights were continued in operation and have been recently extended for a further period.

DOMESTIC FISHING LIMITS

The outer limit of Australian waters for the purpose of the imposition of fishing controls on Australian nationals is not specified either in s.51 (x) of the Constitution or in the *Fisheries Act* but by way of proclamation (made under that Act) of lines joining co-ordinates of points of longitude and latitude in the seas around Australia. The proclaimed waters cover considerable expanses of ocean.[13]

In *Bonser* v. *La Macchia* several members of the Court considered that the meaning of the expression "Australian waters" in the Constitution was a matter for the Court and not for the Executive to determine, although the opinion of the Executive as expressed in the Proclamation was a relevant matter for the Court to consider.[14] They were of the opinion that the waters as specified in the Proclamation could properly be described as Australian waters even though they extended a vast distance from the coastline. It would appear that the outer limit is to be determined by geographical and geo-political considerations, particularly the relationship of the waters with the waters adjacent to foreign countries. As Kitto J. put it:

> When the lines described in the governor-general's proclamation of the 30th November, 1954, are traced upon a map of the world, and it is seen how close and distinctive is the physical relation of the enclosed waters to the Australian coastline and Tasmania, to the islands off the coast which are politically Australia, to the Territory of Papua and New Guinea and to the Territory of Ashmore and Cartier Islands, and how carefully the area is delineated to exclude all waters which, in a context referring to the self-government of countries in regard to fisheries, may fairly be thought to be Indonesian rather than Australian, the conclusion seems to me to admit of no doubt that in such a context every part of the area is naturally to be subsumed under the heading either of "Australian waters" or "waters adjacent (in a corresponding sense) to a Territory.[15]

When Australia adopts for international purposes a two hundred miles fisheries zone then it is probable that the declared fishing zone of twelve miles and the domestic fisheries zone would coalesce, thus extending commonwealth jurisdiction to both Australian nationals and foreigners within two hundred miles of the Australian coastline or within zones whose boundaries would be proclaimed pursuant to amending legislation.[16]

10

The Continental Shelf

INTRODUCTION

The continental shelf adjacent to the coastline of Australia and its territories is an extensive zone. The hundred fathom or two hundred metres line which is marked on most maps varies in distance from the shore, and off some states this distance is much greater than off others.[1] The shelf is rather narrow off the coast of New South Wales but very extensive off the coast of the Northern Territory. Off the Queensland coastline it varies in width between ten and two hundred miles, following the outer line of the Barrier reef, but outside the Reef there are smaller insular and reef shelves in the west Coral Sea. Off the South Australian coast it extends to a great distance in the Bight, while off Western Australia it is at its most extensive off the northern coastline. As far as Victoria and Tasmania are concerned, the shelf extends over the whole of Bass Strait and joins both coastlines. Off the north Queensland coastline the shelf also extends across Torres Strait to the Papua New Guinea and West Irian coastlines. The demarcation of these continental shelf boundaries, where the physical features of adjacency or contiguity are present, calls for the application of the median line principle (in the absence of agreement), subject to the qualification that the existence of islands straddling Torres Strait (which are part of Queensland) may call for a modification of this principle.

Under the Convention, sovereign rights over these areas are recognized as being vested in the Commonwealth of Australia irrespective of any proclamation or acts of jurisdiction over the area. In fact, however, Australia and other nations had, before the signing of the Convention, already taken steps to declare their rights over the shelf. In 1953 the governor-general proclaimed sovereign rights over the shelf adjacent to the Australian coastline and the Territories of Papua and New Guinea for the purpose of exploring and exploiting the natural resources thereof.[2] These prerogative acts are a clear indication of Australia's claim as far back as 1953. But the Convention makes it clear that they are not the basis of Australia's title which is based on contiguity.

Prior to this proclamation, the Commonwealth had enacted a *Pearl Fisheries Act*[3] to make provision for the regulation of the pearl fisheries on the shelf. This enactment, which replaced legislation of the Federal Council passed in the nineteenth century,[4] and the regulations and proclamations made under it, constituted a framework of legal control relevant to the interpretation of the scope of the legislative framework for the regulation of the mineral resources of the shelf. The Act empowered the governor-general to proclaim certain waters or parts thereof as Australian waters to which the Act could be applicable.[5] These waters were defined as being (a) Australian waters beyond territorial limits; (b) waters adjacent to a territory and within territorial limits; and (c) waters adjacent to a territory not being part of the commonwealth, beyond territorial limits, *being waters which were above the continental shelf.*[6] The continental shelf was defined as the sea-bed and subsoil contiguous to the coasts of Australia and its territories to a depth of one hundred fathoms.[7] Of particular significance was s. 5(5) of the Act:

> If the Governor-General is of opinion that it is reasonable that the sea-bed and subsoil of a submarine area, being an area that—
> (a) is not more than one hundred fathoms below the surface of the sea; and
> (b) is adjacent to any part of the coasts of Australia or of a Territory, but is separated from the part of the continental shelf that is contiguous to that part of those coasts by an area that is more than one hundred fathoms below the surface of the sea,
> should be deemed to be part of the continental shelf the Governor-General may, by Proclamation, declare that the sea-bed and

subsoil is part of the continental shelf for the purposes of this Act. ...

This provision was evidently intended to apply to small insular shoals and reef shelves off the Western Australian and Queensland coastlines, which were separated from the immediately contiguous parts of the shelf by channels of more than a hundred fathoms depth.[8]

It has been suggested that these shelves are subject to Australian jurisdiction and control and that the second part of the definition of the shelf in the Convention would support Australia's claim to them.[9] It seems to the writer, however, that the more important basis of the claim is that they are contiguous to islands which are subject to Australian sovereignty and they could therefore be claimed on the insular shelf principle and not merely on the ground of adjacency to the mainland.[10]

The 1958 Convention on the Continental Shelf provides the international basis for a claim to the resources of the shelf to the two hundred metre line or, beyond that depth, to where the resources were exploitable. Division II of the *Seas and Submerged Lands Act* (to be discussed later) provides the internal legislative basis for Australia's exercise of rights over the continental shelf.[11] The resources of the shelf comprise both non-living (mineral) resources and living resources.

SEDENTARY SPECIES OF FISH

Article 2(4) of the Convention of the Continental Shelf provides: "The natural resources referred to in these articles consist of the mineral and other non-living resources of the sea bed and subsoil together with living organisms belonging to sedentary species, that is to say, *organisms which at the harvestable stage, either are immobile or on under the sea bed or are unable to move except in constant physical contact with the sea bed or sub-soil.*" It is appropriate to note that this article was the basis for the enactment of legislation in 1968—the *Continental Shelf (Living Natural Resources) Act*—which therefore derives its validity from s. 51(xxix) of the Constitution, although in the pre-Convention years (that is before 1958) the claim to the living resources, expressed in relation to specified resources in the *Pearl Fisheries Act* 1952, was based on the fisheries power.[12] The following points may be made about the meaning and operation of article 2(4):

a) The provision applies to living organisms which are described as those that belong to the sedentary species. These include, for want of a better expression, both vegetable matter (that is, seaweed, sea-plants) and animal species (for example, those ranging from minute organisms such as anemones to large shellfish such as clams). A number of these sedentary species would be described as shellfish but not all of them are properly described as such; indeed some of them, such as sea-slugs, are without shells. Therefore, the Convention chooses the more inclusive phrase "living organisms" to describe the entities which are within its compass.

b) The definition is based on the movement characteristics (or absence thereof) of the organisms; it covers those which are immobile under the surface of the sea-bed or on top of it (that is the sessile species) *or* are unable to move except by constant physical contact with the sea-bed or subsoil. We will return to this part of the definition later.[13]

c) The criterion of mobility or immobility is determined at the time of harvestability, that is, when the fish or living organisms are of such an age and size that they may be caught for human consumption or other use. This part of the article indicates that the resources are subject to classification at the time of maturity, not at the previous stage such as the larval or post-larval stage when some of them may go through a swimming or floating existence.

By far the greatest difficulty attaches to the classification of living resources as sedentary and much depends in this context on the classification made by marine biologists. It was pointed out in a preliminary document placed before the Geneva Conference on the Law of the Sea in 1958 that the continental shelf is not merely a passive platform *vis-à-vis* these resources but contributes to particular physical and chemical conditions that are of considerable significance to the living organisms. Conversely, the organisms exercise some influence on the characteristics of the shelf and help create a milieu for the marine life of the shelf. The living resources, therefore, may be characterized in the way which they live on, live within, or feed on or reproduce in the continental shelf environs. So far as living space is concerned, there are those (a) which bury into bottom material, that is sand or mud, through which they move or inhabit holes or even tubes which they have constructed (coral); (b) those that are fastened to the sea bottom (that is mussels); (c) those that dwell on the surface of the sea-bed but may move in waters immediately above it; (d) bottom-dwelling fish which move in the waters above the sea-bed.

Among representative organisms are: (i) *Sponges*, which are anemones that usually attach themselves to rock and have a filtration system by which they draw in their nutriment. (ii) *Corals*: sea-worms that build tubes in which they live, these tubes being attached to the sea-bed. Corals usually form a colony and give rise, because of their multitudinous colours, to a brilliant environment in the sea bed. The Great Barrier Reef to an extent consists of the skeletons of these animals. (iii) *Molluscs*, which are shell-fish, snails and slugs that are either fixed, in the case of the bivalves (hinged double shells) such as oysters, mussels, or are capable of some movement, such as sea-snails. Among the molluscs are the pearl oyster, prized both for the pearl which it contains as well as in certain species (mother-of-pearl) its outer shell; the edible oyster, trochus, bêche-de-mer, turban shell (green snail), abalone, scallop, cockle, mussel and clam. (iv) *Crustaceans*. In this group are included crayfish and lobsters, crabs and prawns.

It is with respect to the crustacean group that the greatest difficulty of classification has arisen.[14] There is no doubt that most of the species of the other groups fall within the definition of sedentary species in article 2(4) of the Convention. Among the crustaceans, the prawn is the most valuable to Australia from an economic point of view, large prawning areas having been discovered in the Gulf of Carpentaria in recent years. The prawns include various types, the most well-known in the Gulf being the banana, king and tiger prawns. Biological evidence reveals that the banana prawns spend their early life in rivers and coastal waters in the Gulf area but move out during their adult life into the waters of the Gulf. They spend much of their time lying buried in the sand and come out at night to feed. The diurnal cycle, however, may be affected by their reproductive habits and it is at this stage that they school and may be caught in large numbers even during the day. The usual method of catching them is by trawling. Crayfish, of course, are caught off the West Australian, Tasmanian and South Australian coasts, and crabs are found in plentiful supply around the Australian coastline particularly in Queensland waters.

Crustaceans

We have said that some uncertainty has arisen as to the status of crustaceans under article 2(4) of the Convention on the Continental Shelf. There is no doubt that some of these would fall within the classification of sedentary species in terms of constant physical contact with the sea-bed, for example the mud-crabs which bury into the mud or crawl along the bed. Other species of crabs as well as crayfish may burrow into the sea-bed or have their habitat under rocks and in crevices of the sea-bed, but nevertheless may at certain times propel themselves in the waters above it. Prawns, too, may settle on the sea-bed for a considerable part of the day but may venture out to feed during the night.

At the Geneva Conference a clause containing the words "but crustacea and swimming species are not included" had been attached to the end of article 2(4) to indicate that crustacea were not to be treated as sedentary species. However, at the plenary session when the committee report containing this additional clause was considered, there was a majority vote against inclusion and therefore it did not appear in the final form of article 2(4).[15] Oda, the Japanese fisheries law expert, comments on this omission as follows:

> Some states may take the view that the fact that [these words were] rejected mean that crustacea and swimming fish are included in the natural resources referred to. On the other hand, a different view is possible that there is no provision incorporating these resources into the regime of the continental shelf. The author submits that the latter interpretation reflects the view of the majority and is more realistic, although the less advanced coastal states would undoubtedly support the former. There still remains another difficult question. Are some species of crustacea which are unable to move except in constant physical contact with the sea bed to be treated in the same way as the continental shelf? In line with the statement by the sponsors of

the original proposal of the provision an affirmative answer is obviously not acceptable. The Convention however, contains no explicit provision on this point, thus leaving the situation uncertain. The author has stated elsewhere that it would be difficult to reject this possibility.[16]

The view that crustaceans are excluded is also shared by Garcia-Amada[17] and others.[18] However, in the light of recent disputes over the classification of sedentary resources, it appears that certain crustaceans do come within the category of sedentary resources and the question as to the exact status of certain species is one that will have to be settled by particular negotiations between countries concerned. A dispute between the United States and Japan over fishing for king crab on the continental shelf off Alaska resulted in an exchange of notes between the two countries, the United States taking the view that the king crab was a natural resource of the continental shelf, the Japanese taking the opposite view.[19] In the light of the fact that Japan has accepted conservation measures in this agreement in relation to the king crab, it must be said that the United States position is a strong one. Similarly, a dispute between France and Brazil over the catching of lobsters on the Brazilian continental shelf ended in an agreement in which French fishermen were allowed to continue fishing for this type of marine resource but were obliged to give tribute in lobsters to Brazilians.[20] Again, this is evidence of a recognition that those crustaceans which spend most of their life either burrowing into or moving along the sea-bed are resources of the continental shelf and therefore subject to control by the coastal nation even though on certain occasions they may move above the shelf. Prawns, however, are known to be mobile at certain stages and therefore they would not seem to fall at the present within the definition.[21] although in the light of the developments as to crabs and lobsters, the possibility is not foreclosed that they could be claimed as sedentary resources, or at least certain species of them which spend most of their existence buried in the sea-bed could be so claimed, either under the Convention or at least as being subject to special conservation measures.

Australian legislation relating to sedentary species

Control over certain species of sedentary fisheries or resources has been exercised for a period that goes back to colonial times. In particular the colonies of Queensland and Western Australia had legislation controlling the search for pearl shell and bêche-de-mer in their territorial waters. However, there was a need to control the taking of these fish in adjacent waters outside "territorial limits" and it was for this reason that, when the Federal Council of Australia was set up, the Imperial parliament conferred on that body a power to make laws with regard to fisheries in Australian waters *outside* territorial limits. Pursuant to this power and at the request of these two colonies, the Federal Council passed the *Queensland Pearl Shell and Bêche-de-mer Fisheries (Extra-Territorial) Act*[22] 1888 and in the following year a similar Act[23] which applied to waters adjacent to Western Australia (that is to Australian waters outside the territorial limits of these colonies). It is to be noted that the legislation was restricted to British vessels[24] and therefore did not amount to a claim to these waters in international law as subject to the exclusive fisheries jurisdiction of the Federal Council. Moreover, the legislation was limited to pearl oysters, pearl oyster-shells, bêche-de-mer and similar fish, that is, it was restricted to what is now called sedentary species and did not apply to swimming fish. The legislation required vessels engaged in the search for or the processing of these resoucres to be licensed. It also imposed controls on the employment of seamen and labourers on these vessels, it being necessary to protect the native and Polynesian labourers from exploitation on the part of their masters, a serious social problem of the previous century.

On federation, the commonwealth parliament was given the power, previously residing in the Federal Council, over fisheries in Australian waters beyond territorial limits. It was not, however, until 1952 that the Federal Council legislation was repealed and the *Pearl Fisheries Act* 1952 was passed. The *Pearl Fisheries Act* (as amended) applied to four types of sedentary resources: pearl shells, trochus, bêche-de-mer and green snails.[25] It provided that the minister might prohibit the taking of these resources from any area of proclaimed waters and imposed the requirement of a licence in respect of the search for and taking of these resources.[26] It was specifically provided that the Act extended to all persons including foreigners and to all ships and boats including foreign ships and boats.[27] Thus, for the first time, Australia made a claim in international law to the exclusive control of these resources.

The *Pearl Fisheries Act* was repealed by the *Continental Shelf (Living Natural Resources)* Act 1968.[28] This Act extends to shelves adjacent to all territories as well as shelves adjacent to the continent of Australia and adjacent islands.[29] It applies to all persons including foreigners and to foreign boats.[30] It establishes an administrative framework by empowering the Executive to specify controlled areas of the shelf,[31] to issue notices relating to sedentary species and the method of taking them,[32] and to license persons and vessels to engage in the taking of organisms.[33] In so far as the *Pearl Fisheries Act* had applied only to four types of sedentary resources, it had become abundantly clear that there were other resources that were not covered by the Act but could be claimed by Australia under Article 2(4) of the Convention on the Continental Shelf. Pursuant to a proclamation made under s. 7 of the Act in 1970[34] the following organisms have been proclaimed as sedentary resources.

Classes of Marine Organisms

1. Corals, of any kind, included in the Phylum *Coelenterata*, Class *Anthozoa* or Class *Hydrozoa*.
2. Lace corals, of any kind, included in the Phylum *Ectoprocta*, Order *Cheilostomata* or Order *Cyclostomata*.
3. Sea anemones included in the Phylum *Coelenterata*, Class *Anthozoa* (other than sea anemones included in the family *Minyadidae*).
4. Sea-pens included in the Phylum *Coelenterata*, Class *Anthozoa*, Order *Pennatulacea*.
5. Sponges of any kind.
6. Sea-urchins included in the Phylum *Echinodermata*, Class *Echinoidea*.
7. Bêche-de-mer (also called sea cucumbers or trepang).
8. Sea lilies or stalked crinoids included in the Phylum *Echinodermata*, Class *Crinoidea*, sub-order *Millercrinida*.
9. Bivalve molluscs (except scallops), including oysters, mother-of-pearl, pearl shell, mussels, clams, pipis, venus shells, cockles and razor fish.

10. Gastropods (except sea-hares, sea-butterflies, sea-slugs of the Order *Opisthobranchiata*, violet snails of the Family *Ianthinidae* and organisms of the Family *Heteropoda*), including abalone, green snail, trochus, triton shells, helmet shells, cone shells, bailer shells, winkles and cowries.
11. Chitons.
12. Seaweed of the Family *Gelidiaceae* of Family *Gracilariaceae*.
13. Kelp of the Genus *Macrocystis*.

MINERAL RESOURCES OF THE SEA-BED

After several years of negotiations between the commonwealth and states, agreement was reached in 1967 on the principles which should govern the exploration and exploitation of the petroleum resources of the sea-bed adjacent to the Australian coastline. This legislation consists of an Act of the commonwealth and legislation of six states which "mirrored" one another.[35] In other words, the provisions of the Acts covering exploitation of petroleum resources —the mining code—are identical.

The underlying principles of the legislation are embodied in an Agreement which was signed by the commonwealth prime minister and the six state premiers on 16 October 1967. The most significant clause in the preamble to the Agreement points to the basis of the legislation: "... the Governments of the Commonwealth and of the States have decided, in the national interest, that without raising questions concerning, and without derogating from, their respective constitutional powers, they should co-operate for the purpose of ensuring the legal effectiveness of authorities to explore or/and to exploit the petroleum resources of these submerged lands. ..."[36] The affirmed intention, therefore, was to avoid constitutional litigation such as that which has occurred in the United States relating to jurisdiction over the resources of the sea-bed—a conflict which had dragged on in that country for over twenty years and which had also occurred in Canada.[37] Both the territorial sea-bed and the continental shelf were made subject to the operation of the legislation.[38]

The Agreement and the legislation make it clear that the actual administration of the mining code, that is, the grant of licences, permits, etc. is in the hands of the states through their mines ministers who are described as "designated authorities". Nevertheless it is provided in the Agreement but not in the legislation that the states will consult the commonwealth in matters affecting exploration and exploitation which under the Commonwealth Constitution are matters of federal responsibility (for example, external affairs, overseas and interstate trade, and commerce, etc.).[39] In the Agreement there is a provision which allows the administering authority to require that any petroleum produced shall be refined in the adjacent state, or any gas discovered shall be used within that state, although there must be consultation between the commonwealth and the state before any action is taken to this end.[40] Again, there is no provision in the legislation which embodies this requirement. There is also an annex to the Agreement which provides that it is "the common intention of the signatories not to discriminate against interstate trade,"[41] although this also is not incorporated in the legislation.

The states participate in the ten per cent royalty payable on petroleum and natural gas discovered in an off-shore area to the extent of sixty per cent in proportion to the commonwealth's share of forty per cent (the value being determined at the well-head).[42] In addition, the states are entitled to the whole of what is called an over-ride royalty[43] (of between one per cent and two-and-a-half per cent). The over-ride royalty operates as follows: When a location (which consists of a number of blocks—not more than nine—including a particular block which is nominated by the permittee as the centre of the location) is created, an application may be made for the grant of a production licence in respect of five of these nine blocks. A standard royalty of ten per cent is payable for the petroleum extracted from these blocks and the other four blocks revert to the Crown. However, as an alternative, the permittee may take a licence for the five blocks and an additional licence for one or more of the remaining blocks. If it exercises this choice then it must pay in addition to the ten per cent an over-ride royalty of between one per cent and two-and-a-half per cent on the petroleum recovered from both licence areas (that is in respect of petroleum extracted from any of the blocks of the location).[44] Consequently in this case the royalty will be between eleven per cent and twelve-and-a-half per cent.

Among the other major sections contained in the legislation are sections which provide that the provisions of the law in force in an adjacent state apply in the adjacent area in respect of acts related to the exploration for and exploitation of petroleum.[45]

As pointed out previously, the commonwealth and state Acts are "mirroring" legislation and, so far as the mining code is concerned, are identical. There are some provisions, however, in the machinery parts and also in Part II of the legislation (which applies the law in force in the adjacent state to the adjacent maritime area) which take account of the differing constitutional position of commonwealth and states: to this extent the Acts of the commonwealth and the states are not completely identical.[46]

The object of this mirroring legislation was to ensure that, if any litigation occurs in a particular area with respect to the exploration or exploitation of petroleum, a court would find that no legal vacuum existed, in other words it would hold that either commonwealth power or state power operated in the area. To ensure, however, that the commonwealth Act is not applied to the exclusion of the state legislation, as a result of s. 109 of the Constitution (the inconsistency provision), s. 150 of the commonwealth Act provides that it is "the intention of the Act" not to affect the operation of any Act of a state or a territory in the adjacent areas.[47]

In 1967 a Senate Select Committee was set up to inquire into various aspects of the legislation, in particular, to determine whether "the constitutional conception underlying the legislation was consistent with the proper constitutional responsibilities of the Commonwealth and the States."[48] In an Interim Report handed down in 1970,[49] the Committee criticized the constitutional conception underlying the legislation. It was particularly worried by the procedure adopted—the drafting of a bill by seven governments which was presented to the parliaments as a *fait accompli* for formal ratification. The Committee concluded that "notwithstanding the advantage to the national interest which the legislation and its underlying conception has produced, the larger national interest is not served by leaving unresolved and uncertain the extent of State and Commonwealth authority in the territorial sea-bed and the continental shelf."[50]

Following the presentation of the Report, the federal government of the time (the Gorton government) in 1970 introduced a Bill to declare commonwealth sovereignty over the sea-bed and sovereign rights over the resources of the shelf for the purpose of exploring it and exploiting its natural resources. Because of opposition within the coalition and from state governments, the Bill was not proceeded with, but after the advent of the Whitlam government the Seas and Submerged Lands Bill was introduced and finally passed by both Houses in 1973 (although the Senate deleted a part relating to an off-shore mining code for minerals other than petroleum).

Division 2 of the *Seas and Submerged Lands Act* deals with the continental shelf. Section 11 provides: "It is by this Act declared and enacted that the sovereign rights of Australia as a coastal State in respect of the continental shelf of Australia, for the purpose of exploring it and exploiting its natural resources, are vested in and exercisable by the Crown in right of the Commonwealth." In *New South Wales* v. *Commonwealth*[51] all the judges considered that the section was valid. In the words of Barwick C.J.

> Sovereign rights at least imply exclusive and paramount rights to exploit together with all the powers necessary to secure the principal rights. But the important thing is that whatsoever the extent of the power or jurisdiction sovereignty or sovereign rights embraces, that power, jurisdiction or authority is conceded internationally to the nation State and depends on international mutuality.
> ... Consequently, the acceptance of the concession and the assertion of the internationally-conceded rights are, in my opinion, pre-eminently external affairs.[52]

Gibbs J. referred to the proposition of the states based on the holding of the International Court of Justice in the *North Sea Continental Shelf Cases* that "the rights of coastal State in the area of the Continental Shelf that constitute a national prolongation of its land territory exist *ipso facto* and *ab initio*, by virtue of its sovereignty over the land, as an extension of it in an exercise of sovereign rights for the purpose of exploring the seabed and exploiting its natural resources". But in answer to the states' argument that the colonies at Federation held these rights, Gibbs J. stated that the operation of sovereign rights over resources *outside* territorial waters reflected a new principle which was not recognized at federation (it was generated by the Truman

Proclamation in the 1940s). Under international law the commonwealth was the international person entitled to assert and exercise rights to the resources of the shelf.[53]

Stephen J. considered that legislation asserting commonwealth sovereign rights over shelf resources was also an exercise of power conferred by s. 51 (xxix). At federation, the continental shelf was *res nullius* not subject to state proprietary rights.[54] Mason J. expressed an opinion to the same effect.[55]

It could therefore be said that as with the territorial sea, so too with regard to the continental shelf, the exercise of legislative power under s. 51 (xxix) has a double basis, (a) as dealing with an area geographically external to Australia, and (b) as giving effect to the Convention on the Continental Shelf in claiming the rights recognized by the Convention. It would also be possible to justify the legislation as an exercise of power under s. 51 (xxxix) as legislation incidental to the exercise of executive power, rights over the continental shelf having been claimed by executive proclamation of the commonwealth in 1953.

The *Seas and Submerged Lands Act* specifically provides that it does not limit or exclude the operation of any law of the commonwealth in force at the date of commencement of the Act or coming into force after that date.[56] This means that the co-operative scheme embodied in the *Petroleum (Submerged Lands) Act* and related legislation still survives, with a common mining code, the application of law in force in the adjacent state, and sharing of royalties, being the major features of that scheme. This legislation operates under the umbrella of sovereignty formally proclaimed in the 1973 legislation.

STATE POWER IN RELATION TO THE CONTINENTAL SHELF

Prior to the enactment of the *Petroleum (Submerged Lands) Act*, each state had extended the operation of its mining or petroleum legislation so as to vest rights in the petroleum resources of the shelf in the state Crown.[57] As this claim of proprietorship would have been inconsistent with the constitutional understanding lying behind the Petroleum (Submerged Lands) Agreement and legislation, each state in enacting its own *Petroleum (Submerged Lands) Act* repealed or amended its earlier legislation in relation to this vesting of rights in petroleum resources in the state Crown. The question arises as to whether, subsequent to the *Seas and Submerged Lands Act*, the individual *State (Petroleum Submerged Lands) Acts* continue to operate so as to regulate together with the commonwealth Act the exploration and exploitation of the petroleum resources of the shelf.

Dicta in certain cases support the proposition that state laws may operate outside the three-mile limit of territorial waters. In *Bonser* v. *La Macchia* Barwick C.J. accepted the proposition that "the colonies were competent to make laws which operated extra-territorially, that is to say, beyond their land margins and in and on the high seas, not limited to the 3 mile belt of the territorial sea."[58] Windeyer J. said, "The power of a State legislature to make laws which operate upon persons, things and events beyond the State is not limited by 3 miles of sea. It depends upon relationship to the State—not distance from it—on whether the persons concerned, or their transactions, are related to the peace, order and good government of the State."[59] In *New South Wales* v. *Commonwealth* Jacobs J. cited with approval the statement of Barwick C.J.[60] In *Pearce* v. *Florenca*, Gibbs J. considered that the legislative power of the states was not restricted to territorial waters[61] although Mason J. considered that the question should be reserved for future consideration.[62]

It would appear, therefore, that similar considerations to those discussed in relation to state legislation applying to the territorial sea apply to the question of state jurisdiction over the continental shelf and its superjacent waters:

1. The state Act must be intended to apply in the area.[63]
2. There must be a sufficient nexus with the state in respect of the subject matter of the Act or its operation.[64]
3. It must not infringe on commonwealth sovereign rights over the shelf.[65]
4. It must not be inconsistent with commonwealth legislation applying to the shelf.[66]

On the nexus requirement certain comments may be made. It seems that the application of state laws in waters outside the shelf could be justified on the basis that the shelf itself is geologically related to the land mass and therefore acts occurring on the waters above it have a nexus with the adjacent state. Alternatively they could be upheld as operating within "Australian waters" as defined in accordance with s. 51 (x) of the Constitution, i.e., within, say, two hundred miles of the coastline: there is a sufficient geographical nexus with the adjacent state at least so far as the acts of residents of the state are concerned.[67]

The final question to be determined is whether the *State Petroleum (Submerged Lands) Acts* continue to operate in the light of the declaration of commonwealth sovereign rights over shelf resources contained in s. 11 of the *Seas and Submerged Lands Act*. It is suggested that the geographical features mentioned above would support the application of state law to drilling operations on the shelf, and the civil and criminal law of the state to activities associated with such drilling or taking place in the course of operations. The *State Petroleum (Submerged Lands) Acts* do not vest ownership of minerals in the state Crown and are therefore not inconsistent with the commonwealth claim of sovereign rights. However, it may be that the ambit of state power is not sufficient to control the activities of non-residents who do not operate from a state base or where those activities do not have a sufficient connection with the State.[68] In such a case the full operation of the petroleum legislation might depend on the commonwealth Act as applying to foreign-based operations or foreign persons (corporate or natural) under the power conferred by s. 51 (xxix) of the Constitution.

In relation to minerals other than petroleum, state enactments which purport to vest ownership or title to those minerals in the sea-bed outside their boundaries in the state Crown would be inconsistent with the claim of sovereignty and sovereign rights contained in the *Seas and Submerged Lands Act*.[69] Consequently, either commonwealth legislation or joint commonwealth-state legislation will be necessary to provide an effective basis for the exploitation of minerals other than petroleum lying on or under the sea-bed of the continental shelf.

CONTINENTAL SHELF BOUNDARIES

A schedule to the commonwealth *Petroleum (Submerged Lands) Act* contains a description of the "internal" and "external"

boundaries of the "adjacent area" contiguous to each state and territory. The first paragraph of Schedule 2 provides: "The adjacent area in respect of a State or a Territory is the area the boundary of which is described in this schedule in relation to that State or Territory, to the extent only that that area includes:
a)   area of territorial waters
b)   area of superjacent waters of the continental shelf."
(Internal waters are therefore not included in the adjacent areas). Then follows a description of the boundaries (in terms of co-ordinates of points of latitude and longitude) of the adjacent areas of the six states, the area adjacent to the Northern Territory, and the area adjacent to the Ashmore and Cartier Islands.[70] These descriptions therefore indicate the area in which the law in force in the adjacent state operates and the area in which the adjacent state will share in royalties arising from successful discoveries of petroleum.

The description of these areas was amended in 1973 to take account of three agreements signed with Indonesia in 1971, 1972 and 1973, relating to the drawing of sea-bed boundaries, namely, the external shelf boundaries separating the continental shelf pertaining to Australia from that pertaining to Indonesia in the northern and northwestern areas. The 1971 Agreement[71] delimited the sea-bed between Australia and Indonesia in the Arafura Sea and between Papua New Guinea and Indonesia off the southern and northern coasts of Papua New Guinea. The 1972 Agreement[72] delimited the sea-bed between Australia and Indonesia in the Arafura Sea and the Timor Sea west of the 1971 line. The 1973 Agreement[73] dealt with the sea-bed boundary immediately south of the border of Papua New Guinea and West Irian. These new boundaries affected the original boundaries as contained in the schedule to the *Petroleum (Submerged Lands) Act* in relation to the Queensland, Northern Territory and Ashmore and Cartier Islands adjacent areas.

The 1972 Agreement, which was the most significant of the group, delimited the sea-bed between West Timor and the area of the continental shelf adjacent to Ashmore and Cartier Islands and the Northern Territory. The geological structure of the sea-bed between West Timor and Australia is characterized by the following features: a broad shelf extending from the Australian coastline, a trough of great depth, and a narrow shelf extending from the island of Timor. *Prima facie* under the interpretation of the continental shelf in Article 1 of the Convention on the Continental Shelf, the trough would mark the end of the geological shelves of both areas (viz. the two hundred metres lines) and therefore divide the continental shelves of both areas so that there would be no common continental shelf. However, the Continental Shelf Convention also incorporates the principle of "adjacency" and there are circumstances in which a trough has been crossed in inter-nation shelf agreements which involve a concession to a more adjacent state of shelf area on the opposite side of a trough.[74] The 1972 Shelf Agreement is based on a line which reserves to Australia the whole of the shelf proper although parts of the continental slope on the southern slope of the Timor Trough are within the Indonesian area.[75]

The *Petroleum (Submerged Lands) Act* has been amended to incorporate the new boundaries as outlined in the Agreements.[76] Similar descriptions of shelf boundaries in relation to living resources under the *Continental Shelf (Living Natural Resources) Act* have been incorporated in regulations made under that Act.[77]

The area of the Continental Shelf opposite to East Timor remains undelineated. Negotiations had taken place with Portugal (the administering power) before the takeover of that territory by Indonesia but diplomatic issues have affected negotiations with Indonesia on the matter.

Specific power is conferred on the governor-general by s. 12 of the *Seas and Submerged Lands Act* to determine, not inconsistently with the Convention on the Continental Shelf or any relevant international agreement to which Australia is a party, the limits of the whole or any part of the continental shelf of Australia. It is therefore clearly within the competence of the commonwealth, taking account of the limitations specified in s. 12 of the Act, to demarcate shelf boundaries.

Torres Strait Border Issue

The article of the Convention on the Continental Shelf which is relevant to the determination of the shelf boundary between Australia and Papua New Guinea is Article 6(1):

Where the same continental shelf is adjacent to the territories of two or more States whose coasts are opposite each other, the boundary of the continental shelf appertaining to such States shall be determined by agreement between them. In the absence of agreement and unless another boundary line is justified by special circumstances, the boundary is the median line, every point of which is equidistant from the nearest points of the baselines from which the breadth of the territorial sea of each State is measured.

Article 6(2) deals with the delimitation of the shelf as between adjacent states (i.e. lateral boundaries) and is to similar effect except that the general line of division is referred to as the equidistant line.

We have seen that in the *North Sea Continental Shelf Cases*[78] the International Court of Justice considered that the equidistant line referred to in Article 6(2) was not a principle of customary international law and therefore did not bind states which were not parties for the Convention.[79] The Court considered that, in determining the shelf boundary between adjacent states, customary international law demands the application of principles of equity, particularly the principle of proportionality by which the area of sea-bed, which was the natural prolongation of a state's land territory, was regarded as subject to its jurisdiction.[80] Comments of the Court did suggest that a median line (as between opposite states) was more demanded by principles of equity than was an equidistant line (as between adjoining states). "... Whereas a median line divides equally between the two opposite countries areas that can be regarded as being the natural prolongation of the territory of each of them, a lateral equidistance line often leaves to one of the States concerned areas that are a natural prolongation of the territory of the other."[81] The Court here is referring to boundaries between mainland territories. It is accepted that the presence of islands on a common continental shelf are special circumstances which might require departure from the general median line principle.[82] The islands of the Torres Strait are subject to Australian sovereignty having been annexed to Queensland by Imperial action in the nineteenth century which was ratified by the *Queensland Coast Islands Act* of 1879. The northernmost islands are located within a few kilometres of the Papuan coastline.[83]

In order that a reasonable area of continental shelf might be allocated to Papua New Guinea under the principle of equity and proportionality referred to previously, it has been suggested that islands in the northern portion of the Torres Strait shelf area should not attract a full continental shelf that deprived Papua New Guinea of the shelf area which is the natural prolongation of its land mass.[84]

Negotiations between Australia and Papua New Guinea over the Torres Strait boundaries have continued since the end of 1972.[85] In June 1976, the foreign affairs ministers of Australia and Papua New Guinea stated jointly that agreement had been reached on a number of points basic to a settlement. The statement was as follows:

> A seabed boundary would be delimited between Australia and Papua New Guinea. It would run through the protected zone which, the two Ministers agreed, would be established in the Torres Strait. Papua New Guinea agreed that the seabed boundary would lie to the north of all Australian inhabited islands except Boigu, Dauan and Saibai. Australia has accepted that the seabed boundary would be drawn in a location more southerly than the line at present applying under Australian legislation for offshore petroleum administration purposes, that this line did not represent the Australian view of the appropriate permanent location of the seabed boundary, that the seabed boundary would run to the south of Boigu, Dauan and Saibai and it would be continuous.
>
> Papua New Guinea, in view of the wishes of the Torres Strait Islanders which Mr. Peacock had stressed, had accepted that Australia would retain all Australian territorial sea around the islands of Boigu, Dauan and Saibai, which would lie to the north of the seabed boundary, would be three miles, and that there would be a line delimiting the territorial seas between these islands and Papua New Guinea.
>
> A zone would be established in the Torres Strait to protect and preserve the traditional way of life and livelihood of the Torres Strait Islanders and the residents of the adjacent coast of Papua New Guinea, including fishing and freedom of movement throughout such a zone, both north and south of the seabed boundary.
>
> The two Ministers expressed satisfaction at progress achieved in their negotiations. They instructed officials to proceed with further negotiations to build on the agreement they had reached on these fundamental points, and to direct their attention jointly to a number of other matters which would need to be included in a final settlement. The Ministers reaffirmed their determination to arrive as soon as

possible at an equitable and stable settlement, in respect of an area which was of great importance to both countries, which would take due account of the humanitarian, environmental and other interests of all concerned.[86]

In December 1976, a Sub-Committee on Territorial Boundaries of the Federal Parliamentary Joint Committee on Foreign Affairs and Defence to which had been referred the question of the boundary between Australia and Papua New Guinea issued its Report[87] which recommended that no charge should be made in the 1879 boundary either with respect to uninhabited islands (on which the June statement had remained silent) or inhabited islands. The Committee concluded that the provisions of s. 123 of the Constitution prevented any boundary alteration which did not follow the procedure laid down in that section.[88] It also recommended that the federal government should take steps to explain the difference, in clear terms, between a sea-bed boundary and a normal international boundary.

In January 1977, the Papua New Guinea foreign minister indicated that agreement with Australia had not been reached on three points: the claim by Australia to eight small uninhabited islands in the area north of the proposed sea-bed line; the claim by Australia to a three miles territorial waters and twelve miles fisheries zone around these islands; and the fact that the proposed line was to be a sea-bed line and not a fisheries management line as well.

Further discussions were held on the matter during a visit by the Australian prime minister to the Papua New Guinea prime minister in February 1977. At this time the Papua New Guinea parliament enacted legislation (to come into effect on a date or dates to be proclaimed) which, *inter alia*, provided for a twelve miles territorial sea and a two hundred miles zone described as "offshore seas", and gave the Executive power to declare its maritime boundaries with other countries.[89] Negotiations were suspended to enable the governments of the two countries to discuss the outstanding issues referred to above.

11

Legislation Applying in Australian Off-shore Waters

INTRODUCTION

The effect of the *Seas and Submerged Lands Act* as we have seen, is not to modify the operation of state legislation which is not inconsistent with the commonwealth's claim of sovereignty but such legislation is subject to being over-ridden by any commonwealth legislation with which it is inconsistent.[1] The commonwealth is not subject to any extra-territorial legislative incapacity as its legislation, falling within a head of power, has full operation outside the geographical area of Australia.[2] Certain Imperial Acts also operate in adjacent maritime areas.

It is proposed to consider the basic features of the legislation operating in this area under the headings: fishing, minerals, pollution, conservation of the maritime environment, navigation and shipping, civil and criminal jurisdiction, and wrecks and salvage. A final note will refer to international agreements affecting the military use of the seas and sea-bed to which Australia is a party.

FISHING

At the present time, state fisheries legislation applies to the area of waters extending to the three-mile limit,[3] The commonwealth *Fisheries Act* 1952 (as amended) applies, as we have seen to the area from the three-mile limit seawards, and operates within a twelve-mile declared fishing zone in relation to foreign fishermen and in a much wider zone in relation to Australian fishermen and vessels.[4]

The *Fisheries Act* defines fish as including turtles, dugong and those species of crustacea and molluscs which are not sedentary organisms for the purpose of the *Continental Shelf (Living Natural Resources) Act*. It does not apply to whales[5] (the taking of which is regulated by the *Whaling Act*).[6]

Section 13B of the Act makes it an offence for a person in an area of proclaimed waters comprised in the declared fishing zone to use a foreign boat for the taking of fish, to use a foreign boat for processing fish that have been taken with the use of that boat, or to have in possession or charge a foreign boat for the taking of fish unless the boat is licensed for that use.

It is also an offence for a person to have in his charge in the zone a foreign boat equipped with nets, traps or other equipment for the taking of fish subject to certain defences (such as that the boat was engaged in transit and the equipment was stowed).[7]

The regulation of fishing, both in the declared fishing zone and outside, operates by way of administrative procedures based on ministerial notices which may prohibit the taking of species of fish or undersized fish, may establish controlled areas and controlled seasons, and may prohibit the use of certain types of equipment to be used in fishing.[8] Fishing in proclaimed waters is controlled by a licensing system which is applicable to persons and/or boats.[9] A licence is subject to any conditions that are specified in the licence and operates for a yearly period.[10] It is subject to cancellation or suspension on grounds specified.[11] Powers of inspection and arrest for breaches of the Act are conferred to Australian officials.[12]

The taking of sedentary organisms is regulated by the *Continental Shelf (Living Natural Resources) Act*. We have already referred to the classes of marine organisms which have been proclaimed as sedentary organisms under that Act.[13]

The administrative system established by that Act operates in respect of the prescription of controlled areas,[14] a notice system which applies in relation to size, use of types of equipment or boats, or controlled periods for taking. It prohibits the searching for sedentary organisms or specified kind except by a licensed person.[15] Licences for searching taking or removing sedentary resources from controlled areas of the shelf are issued under the Act and are subject to conditions specified, which may regulate the use of ships, equipment and methods of taking the resources.[16]

Offences for taking organisms by an unlicensed person are set out in the Act[17] and powers of inspection and arrest are conferred on Australian officials.[18] Special permits are issued for the taking of sedentary organisms for scientific purposes.[19]

MINING

We have seen that the exploration and exploitation of the hydrocarbons (oil and natural gas) is regulated by the *Petroleum (Submerged Lands) Agreement* and legislation.[20] The agreement is based on the adoption of a common mining code to apply in adjacent areas,[21] the law in force in the adjacent state to apply to operations associated with mining activities[22] and a sharing of royalties in the proportion of sixty per cent to the states (plus "over-ride" royalty) and forty per cent to the commonwealth.[23] Administration of the mining code is in the hands of designated authorities who in the case of the areas adjacent to the states and the states mines ministers.[24] They are responsible for issuing permits and licences although the Agreement provides that they will consult the commonwealth before approval is given to the issue, renewal or transfer of a permit or licence.[25] The commonwealth's role in dealing with such matters is limited to the areas of power which it has under the Constitution including external affairs,[26] the ambit of which is, in the light of *New South Wales* v. *Commonwealth*, extensive.[27] But in so far as the Agreement is non-justiciable,[28] such consultation, or the results therefrom, are not enforceable.

The Legislation: Operation of State Laws

Part II of the joint legislation is designed to secure the application of the ordinary law (civil and criminal) in the adjacent areas in respect of petroleum exploration and exploitation. The commonwealth Act provides that the provisions of the laws in force in a state (and these would include common law, state and commonwealth statutes) apply to the adjacent area pertaining to it; and each state Act applies the laws in force within the state to its own adjacent area. This would have the effect of applying for example, the law relating to tort or crime, and workers' compensation legislation, but in every case only in so far as they affect "acts, matters, circumstances and things ... connected with the exploration of the seabed or subsoil of the adjacent area for petroleum and the exploitation of the natural resources, being petroleum, of the sea-bed".[29] This means that the commonwealth and state Acts between them provide a statutory basis for the application of what might be called the rules of the adjacent legal system—an application which otherwise might have fallen outside the territorial competence of the states acting under their own constitutional instruments.

However, in order to prevent duplication of the statutory application of the adjacent legal systems (and, for example, the possibility that a person breaching the legislation may be convicted under both the commonwealth act and a particular state Act) it is provided that where any right has been created or obligation imposed by the commonwealth or state act (whether in respect of the applied adjacent legal system or of the mining code contained in Part III), then to the extent to which there is a discharge of the obligation or the exercise of the right under the one Act, to that extent the right or obligation under the other Act is not exercisable or is extinguished.[30]

Jurisdiction with respect to the legislation is conferred by both the commonwealth and state Acts on state courts within the limits of locality, subject matter, etc. Such jurisdiction extends both to the applied provisions and the mining code and other matters arising under the Acts. The commonwealth Act specifically provides that the jurisdiction conferred on the state courts is federal jurisdiction.[31] The state Acts recognize the probability of the conferred jurisdiction being exclusively federal in providing that the jurisdiction of a magistrates' court shall be exercised by a magistrate.[32]

The Legislation: The Mining Code

The third part of the legislation consists of over one hundred-

and-forty sections which contain what has been called the common mining code to be applied in the adjacent areas. The commonwealth Act makes provision for arrangements to be made between the commonwealth governor-general and the governor of a state with respect to the carrying out of the powers of the Designated Authority[33] under the Acts and its regulations.[34] Under the state Acts the ministers of mines are constituted Designated Authorities. Permits, licences and all other administrative functions are therefore within the administration of these state ministers in respect of their own adjacent areas.[35]

The areas are divided into a particular system of blocks, the size of each block being five minutes of are of latitude by five minutes of are of longitude.[36] This means that in the northern areas the size of blocks will be about thirty square miles (seventy sq. km). The size decreases as one moves southward (because of the convergence of longitudes towards the South Pole) so that south of Tasmania the size would be approximately twenty-three square miles (sixty-two sq km).[37] The legislative code is divided into a number of divisions dealing with exploration permits, exploitation licences, pipeline licences, registration of instruments, general matters and transitional provisions. In the following pages a general outline of these matters will be given.

Exploration Permits ,

The maximum permit area is 400 blocks (between 25,900 and 31,100 sq km) while the minimum area will ordinarily be 16 blocks (about 250 sq km).[38] Such a permit gives the permitee the right not only to conduct general exploration activities in the area but also to carry out test drillings and associated operations.[39] The initial period of permit is six years with renewals for further five-year periods.[40] However, at the end of each period (including the initial period) the permitee must surrender half the permit area.[41] Conditions may be attached to the granting of a permit.[42] If a pool of petroleum is discovered, there is a duty on the part of the permittee to inform the Designated Authority of the discovery and, if required, of various technical details relating to the pool.[43] At this stage the permittee may nominate a block which will become the centre of a location or group of blocks.[44] It is a matter for the Designated Authority to declare a location which will ordinarily be constituted by nine blocks.[45]

Production Licences

When a location has been declared, a permittee may apply for the grant of a licence for production in respect of five of the nine blocks which constitute a location (five blocks would be about 125 square miles or 325 sq km).[46] A standard royalty of ten per cent of the value of the petroleum at the well-head would be payable for the petroleum extracted from these blocks.[47] However, as *an alternative*, the permittee may take a licence for the five blocks and an additional licence for one or more of the remaining four blocks. If he exercises this choice, then he must pay in addition to the ten per cent an "over-ride" royalty of between one and two-and-a-half per cent on the petroleum recovered from both licence areas.[48]

Consequently in this case royalty will be between eleven and twelve-and-a-half per cent. The "over-ride" royalty was agreed upon as an alternative to the original scheme, details of which were released in 1965, under which a permittee would be required to relinquish four blocks of a location. The permittee may now retain these four blocks (which under the original scheme would have been auctioned) but must pay higher royalty over the whole location.

A licence gives the holder the right not only to carry out operations for the recovery of petroleum but to carry out further exploration activities in that area.[49] The term of a licence is twenty-one years with a right of renewal for a further twenty-one years provided that the licensee has complied with the terms of the licence.[50] Further extensions beyond forty-two years are a matter for future parliaments. The rate of royalty for the second twenty-one year period can be varied pursuant to joint federal and state legislative action.[51] Conditions may be attached to licences.[52] Where a licensee is not recovering petroleum to the satisfaction of the Designated Authority directions may be given to carry out steps specified by the Designated Authority.[53] In the case of petroleum pools overlapping the boundaries of licence areas held by different licensees there is provision for unit development by agreement or by direction of the Designated Authority.[54]

Pipeline Licences

The Acts require a licence for the operation of a pipeline carrying petroleum from or through adjacent areas.[55] The production licensee has a preferential right to the grant of a pipeline licence which confers a right to construct the pipeline and pumping stations as well as operating the pipeline.[56] The term of a pipeline licence is twenty-one years, provision being made for renewal of the licence.[57] The Designated Authority has however certain rights over a pipeline. He may request that its route be varied[58] and also may require the licensee to be a common carrier of petroleum (for example, in respect of petroleum extracted from other licence areas).[59]

Registration of Instruments

Provision is made for the Designated Authority to establish a Register of permits, licences, pipeline licences and other instruments which shall set out various details as to the holder, description of area held and other relevant matters.[60] The Designated Authority has the right to approve transfers of permits, licences and pipeline licences and the memorandum of transfer is to be entered in the Register.[61] The Designated Authority is not however concerned with the legal effect of any instrument lodged for registration.[62] Jurisdiction is vested in the Supreme Court of a state to deal with any appeals against the making of entries without sufficient cause or omission of entries.[63]

General Provisions

There are various sections in the legislation designed to secure compliance with the obligations imposed on a coastal nation by Article 5 of the Convention on the Continental Shelf with respect to exploration and exploitation activities.[64] A permittee or licensee is required to carry out such activities in a workmanlike manner and to prevent the excape of petroleum.[65] When exploration or exploitation of an area has been finished, the permittee may be directed to remove any works or property.[66] The permittee of licensee may also be directed by the Designated Authority to conserve the natural resources of the sea-bed.[67] Safety zones (not exceeding five hundred metres) may be established round drilling rigs and wells and the Designated Authority may prohibit vessels from entering these areas.[68] Care must be taken not to interfere unreasonably with navigation, fishing and other activities.[69]

Fees and Royalties

Because of possible constitutional limitations arising from ss. 53, 54 and 55 of the Commonwealth Constitution, the *Commonwealth Petroleum (Submerged Lands) Act* 1976 (Cth), does not contain provisions for the imposition of royalty charges and other fees which are dealt with in separate Acts.[70] The State *Petroleum (Submerged Lands) Acts* however cortain separate divisions dealing with fees and royalties.[71]

The following fees are payable (all of which are retained by the state): *Permits*—five dollars a block per annum with a minimum payment of one hundred dollars; *Licences*—three thousand dollars per block per annum; *Pipeline licences*—twenty dollars per annum for each mile of pipeline; *Registration fees*—one-and-a-half per cent on the value of the consideration for transfer of a title, or the value of the interest in the title transferred whichever is the greater, with a minimum fee of one hundred dollars.

It has already been mentioned that royalty may be determined in two different ways: the ordinary ten per cent, or that ten per cent plus an "over-ride" royalty. The legislation makes provision for the sharing of royalties received. With regard to the ordinary ten per cent rate the sharing is on the basis of forty per cent to the commonwealth and sixty per cent to the states.[72] The states retain in full the over-ride royalty.[73]

MARITIME POLLUTION

Pollution by discharge from vessels

Pollution of the sea from vessel sources is, at present, controlled by state Pollution of the Sea by Oil legislation (which applies within the three-mile limit) and the Commonwealth *Pollution of the Sea by Oil Act* applying outside those waters, which gives effect to the International Convention on Oil Pollution of 1954 as amended in 1962.[74] The Convention imposes an obligation on participating governments to provide for enforcement measures against ships registered in their territories or having their nationality. The Act is expressed to apply to the discharge of oil or an oily mixture into a prohibited area of the sea.[75] Certain defences are provided for in relation to a prosecution under the Act.[76] The Act also gives to Australian officials powers of inspection of ships other than Australian ships to determine whether the provisions of the Convention have been breached.[77]

The *Pollution of the Sea by Oil Act* 1972 gives effect to the 1969 amendments of the Convention.[78] These amendments come into force in 1978.

Maritime casualties leading to pollution

Part VIIA of the *Navigation Act* 1912 gives effect to coastal state rights conferred by the International Convention on Intervention concerning Maritime Casualties on the High Seas (1969).[79] However, Australia had not, at the time of the enactment of Part VIIA in 1971 become a contracting party to this convention or to the associated Civil Liability Convention. Consequently the validity of these provisions of the *Navigation Act* would be dependent on s. 51 (i), s. 98 and the "external scope" of s. 51 (xxix) outlined in *New South Wales* v. *Commonwealth.*[80]

Section 329E (1) of the *Navigation Act* provides:

> Where oil is escaping from, or the Minister is satisfied that oil is likely to escape from, a ship, then, for the purpose of preventing, or reducing the extent of the pollution or likely pollution by the oil of any Australian coastal waters, any part of the Australian coast or any Australian reef, the Minister may, by notice in writing addressed to the owner of the ship and served in accordance with the next succeeding section, do all or any of the following things:—
>
> (a) require such action to be taken in relation to the ship or its cargo, or the ship and its cargo, as is specified in the notice:
>
> (b) prohibit the removal of the ship from a place specified in the notice except with, and in accordance with, the approval of the Minister; or

    (c) prohibit the removal from the ship of any cargo, or any cargo specified in the notice, except with, and in accordance with, the approval of the Minister.

The section does not apply in relation to a ship not registered in Australia unless the ship is in Australian coastal waters.

When a requirement specified in a notice is not complied with, the minister may cause such things to be done as he thinks proper for the carrying out of the action required by the notice to be carried out.[81]

Section 329K specifically applies to ships carrying oil in bulk. Under 329K (2) where oil escapes from a ship to which the section applies (whether in Australian coastal waters or elsewhere) the minister may (whether or not a notice has been served) cause such things to be done as he thinks proper to prevent, or reduce the extent, of the pollution by the oil of any Australian coastal waters, any part of the Australian coast or any Australian reef, or to remove or reduce the effects of the pollution by the oil of any such waters, coast or reef.

Succeeding subsections of s. 329K are designed to give effect to the policies contained in the International Convention on Civil Liability for Oil Pollution Damage.[82] To this extent, where expenses and other liabilities have been incurred in relation to oil that has escaped from a ship as a result of an incident, the moneys so involved are treated as a debt due to the commonwealth and becomes a charge on the ship which may be detained (except where the ship is not a ship registered in Australia or is not in Australian coastal waters) until the amount is paid or satisfactory security provided.[83] Certain defences as allowed by the Convention are provided for in the Act.[84] In accordance with the Convention where oil has escaped without the actual fault or privity of the owner of the ship the total limit is $12,600,000 or an amount calculated by multiplying the tonnage of the vessel by $120, whichever is the less.[85]

Pollution from oil rigs on the continental shelf

Section 124 of the *Petroleum (Submerged Lands) Act* enshrines the requirement contained in the Convention on the Continental Shelf that operations for exploring or exploiting the resources of

133

the shelf must not involve any unreasonable interference with other uses of the sea (such as navigation and shipping) or the conservation of the natural resources of the sea.[86] Such an obligation may be carried out in specific cases by way of directive issued under the authority of the Act.[87]

CONSERVATION OF THE MARITIME ENVIRONMENT AND WILDLIFE

Conservation of the maritime environment is dealt with by two Acts passed in 1975: the *National Parks and Wildlife Conservation Act*[88] and the *Great Barrier Reef Marine Park Act*.[89]

The object of the *National Parks and Wildlife Conservation Act* is to provide for the establishment and management of parks and reserves, *inter alia*, in the Australian coastal sea; for purposes related to the rights (including sovereign rights) and obligations of the commonwealth in relation to the continental shelf of Australia; and for facilitating the carrying out by the commonwealth of obligations under, or the exercise by the Commonwealth of rights under, agreements made between Australia and other countries.[90]

Under s. 7 of the Act the governor-general may by proclamation declare as a park or reserve an area of the Australian coastal sea or an area of sea over part of the Australian continental shelf (in both cases where the sea-bed title or interest is vested in no person other than the commonwealth government) or over an area of land or sea outside Australian coastal waters in respect of which Australia has, under international agreement, obligations relating to wildlife.[91]

The area of the park or reserve is defined to include waters, sea-bed and subsoil below the surface of the sea.[92] Upon a declaration of a park, all right, title and interest held by the commonwealth in respect of the land, but not in respect of minerals, is vested in the director of national parks and wildlife.[93] No operations for the recovery of minerals can be carried out in a park or reserve other than operations that are carried on, with the approval of the governor-general, in accordance with the plan of management relating to that park or reserve.[94] There are more stringent controls on activities which may be carried on in a wilderness zone.[95]

After declaration of a park or reserve, the director must prepare a plan of management in respect of the park or reserve, paying regard to various objects including the encouragement and regulation of the use of the area, the preservation of its special features, and the protection of the park against damage.[96] Such plans must be laid before both Houses of Parliament and are subject to disallowance.[97]

It is to be noted that the *National Parks Act* does not prevent state parliaments from establishing marine parks in the coastal sea but that once a declaration has been made under the Act in respect of a specific area, s. 109 of the Constitution would operate to over-ride inconsistent state controls in or management of that area.

Great Barrier Reef

Special provision for the Great Barrier Reef is contained in the *Great Barrier Reef Marine Park Act*. The object of this Act is to make provision for the establishment, control, care and development of a marine park in the Great Barrier Reef region in accordance with the provisions of the Act, taking account of the commonwealth's powers in relation to the Australian coastal sea, the continental shelf, external affairs, fisheries in Australian waters beyond territorial limits, places acquired by Australia for public purposes, and other purposes.[98] A Great Barrier Reef Authority consisting of a chairman and two other members is established to exercise the functions prescribed by the Act.[99] There is also established a Great Barrier Reef Consultative Committee to advise the Minister or the Authority in respect of matters relating to the operation of the Act and the Marine Park.[100] The major functions of the Authority are to make recommendations to the minister in relation to the care and development of the park including the areas that should be made part of the park and the making of regulations under the Act, to prepare zoning plans for the marine park, and to carry out research. [101]

Part V of the Act establishes the park under the name of the Great Barrier Reef Marine Park.[102] The governor-general may declare an area, within the Great Barrier Reef Region,[103] to be part of the Marine Park.[104] The waters, sea-bed and the air space above the area are treated as a part of the Park.[105] After an area has been declared to be part of the Marine Park, the Authority "shall prepare a zoning plan in respect of that area".[106] Sections 32 and 34 distinguish between a special zone which is to managed in accordance with the *National Parks Act* and a zone, other than a special zone, in respect of which the zoning plan shall make provision with respect to the purposes for which the zone is to be used or entered. Where a special zone is established all right, title and interest in the land including the sea-bed and subsoil other than minerals is vested in the director of national parks and wildlife.[107] In preparing the zoning plan, regard is to be had to various objects including the conservation of the Reef, the regulation of the use of the Park, and the regulation of activities that exploit the resources of the Reef Region so as to minimize the effect of those activities on the Reef, the reservation of some areas of the Reef for its appreciation by the public, and the preservation of some areas of the Reef in their natural state undisturbed by man except for the purposes of scientific research.[108] Zoning plans must be laid before both Houses of parliament and are subject to disallowance.[109]

While a zoning plan is in operation, the Authority is required to perform its functions and exercise its powers in relation to the zone in accordance with the plan, and government departments and statutory authorities are required to observe the plan in relation to the exercise of their powers in the zone.[110]

It is specifically provided that no operations for the recovery of minerals should be carried on in the Marine Park except "for the purpose of research and investigations relevant to the establishment, care and development of the Marine Park or for scientific research".[111]

Reference must also be made to s. 4 of the *Australian Heritage Commission Act* which defines the national estate as consisting of these places being components of the natural environment of Australia (which includes the territorial sea and continental shelf of Australia) that have aesthetic, historic, scientific or social significance or other special value for future generations as well as for the present community.[112] Among the functions of the

Committee are to identify places included in the National Estate and to prepare a register of those places.

NAVIGATION AND SHIPPING

Before *New South Wales* v. *Commonwealth*[113] it had been thought that the power of the Commonwealth parliament over shipping and navigation was controlled by the provisions of s. 51 (i) and s. 98 of the Constitution and by parts of the Imperial *Merchant Shipping Act* (1894) from which, as a legislature of a British possession, it derived certain powers.[114] Consequently, the power was not a complete one over all forms of navigation including all types of intra-state navigation. However, the wide interpretation given to s. 51 (xxix) in that case may suggest a full power over Australian ships while navigating outside state internal waters is derived from that placitum.

The application of commonwealth legislative power to navigation and shipping depends on an interaction between provisions of the Imperial *Merchant Shipping Act*[115] and the Commonwealth *Navigation Act* (1912).[116] Basically, the *Merchant Shipping Act* applies to British ships. All British ships (subject to size exceptions) must be registered.[117] The status of a British ship is determined by ownership whether by British subjects (which expression includes Australian citizens) or by corporations formed under the laws of some part of Her Majesty's Dominions (including ships owned by Australian corporations).[118] The procedure for registering British subjects involves a recognition of registration at ports within Britain and in the Dominions (i.e. in Commonwealth countries including Australia).[119]

Section 6 of the *Navigation Act* recognizes that a British ship includes a ship registered in a Commonwealth country (including Australia) or a ship recognized by the law of a Commonwealth country as a ship belonging to that country. Many provisions of the Act apply only to British ships (e.g. Part II)[120] but others apply to foreign registered ships (e.g. Part IV). As to Australian trade ships, it is provided that the Act does not apply to such types of ship unless the ship (a) is engaged in trade or commerce with other countries or among the states or with or among the territories; or (b) is on the high seas, or in waters which are used by ships engaged in trade or commerce with other countries or among the states; or (c) is in the territorial waters of any territory; or (d) belongs to, or is in the control of, the commonwealth and is included in a prescribed class of ships.

This means that local trade ships (viz. harbour trade ships) are not covered unless they fall within 2 (b) of the Act. This affects the competency of Courts of Marine Enquiry operating under Pary IX of the Act to deal with all types of collisions or casualties affecting ships, and the application of other provisions of the Act.[121]

The *Navigation Act* consists of a number of parts with the following headings: Masters and Seamen, Foreign Seamen, Ships and Shipping, Passengers, the Coasting Trade, Wrecks and Salvage, Prevention of Pollution by Oil of the Australian Coast Waters and Reefs (already referred to),[122] Limitation and Exclusion of Shipowners' Liability, Courts of Marine Enquiry, and Legal Proceedings. Of particular interest are the provisions of Division 1 of Part IV dealing with ships and shipping which gives effect to the provisions of the International Convention for the Safety of Life at Sea (1960) and the International Convention on Load Lines (1966) both of which relate to the seaworthiness of vessels.[123] Powers of inspection of both British and foreign vessels engaged in international voyages are given by the Act and certificates of survey and equipment may be issued by the appropriate authorities.[124] Section 192C enables regulations to be made for ensuring that nuclear ships do not cause unreasonable radiation or other nuclear hazards to the crews or passengers of such ships, or to other persons, or to any waterways or to food or water resources.

Under the *Navigation Act Amendment Bill* 1976, certain amendments are proposed in relation to the duties of masters of ships to report their location in Australian waters[125] and in relation to the liability of shipowners in suits for damages.[126]

CIVIL AND CRIMINAL JURISDICTION

Civil Jurisdiction

The exercise of jurisdiction over vessels and events occurring on the sea is affected by the existence of Imperial legislation which has conferred Admiralty jurisdiction on courts in the British Dominions. This jurisdiction originally vested in the High Court of the Admiral passed to the ordinary courts in the nineteenth century.[127] This Admiralty jurisdiction was conferred on certain courts of the British Dominions by the *Colonial Courts of Admiralty Act* 1890.[128] Under s. 2(1) of that Act the legislature of the British possession may declare a court of law within that possession to be the Court of Admiralty. In the absence of such definition every court of unlimited civil jurisdiction is a Court of Admiralty. Under s. 2(2) the jurisdiction of Colonial Courts of Admiralty shall "subject to the provisions of this Act be over the like places, persons, matters, and things as the Admiralty jurisdiction of the High Court of England, whether existing by virtue of any Statute or otherwise, and the Colonial Courts of Admiralty may exercise such jurisdiction in like manner and to as full an extent as the High Court in England, and shall have the same regard as that Court to international law and the comity of nations".

Admiralty jurisdiction covers matters such as claims for salvage, actions in relation to collisions between vessels, personal actions arising from collisions between vessels and actions for torts occurring on the high seas.[129] In the context of Admiralty jurisdiction, the high seas comprised all oceans, seas, bays, channels, rivers, creeks and waters below low-water mark, and where great ships could go, with the exception only of such parts of such oceans, etc. as were within the body of a country.[130] However, the *Admiralty Court Act* 1861 extended the jurisdiction of the Court of Admiralty to causes of action for damage done by a ship whether or not on the high seas.[131] This extension applies to colonial Courts of Admiralty by virtue of the *Colonial Courts of Admiralty Act* s. 2 (2). Damage done by a ship involves *inter alia*, damage flowing from the negligent operation of gear or negligent navigation which leads to personal injury.[132]

In *Ferguson* v. *Union Steamship Co. Ltd*,[133] the High Court held that its Admiralty jurisdiction covered an injury suffered by a member of a crew of a vessel tied up at the port of Burnie in Tasmania who was injured when a winch operated by another member of the crew was set in motion and caused the plaintiff to lose his footing. The majority of the Court took the view that this was not a case of a tort occurring on the high seas and therefore had to be considered under the extension of jurisdiction effected by the *Admiralty Court Act* 1861 as damage done by a ship,[134] although Barwick C.J. considered that the location of the act was the high seas and not within the body of a county.[135]

The jurisdiction of the High Court of a Colonial Court of Admiralty would appear to be "frozen" as at 1890 and not to encompass later extensions of jurisdiction.[136] Consequently, there are some actions which although occurring on the high seas may not be within the jurisdiction of the High Court as a Colonial Court of Admiralty. In *Parker* v. *Commonwealth*,[137] Windeyer J. considered that actions for loss of life could not be brought in the Admiralty jurisdiction of England (until the law was changed in 1911). Consequently, in respect of a next of kin action for death arising out of a collision on the high seas where the commonwealth was the defendant, Windeyer J. treated the case as arising in the *ordinary* jurisdiction of the High Court.[138]

In so far as the Supreme Courts of the states are also courts of unlimited civil jurisdiction of a British possession, they also are Colonial Courts of Admiralty and may exercise Admiralty jurisdiction as set out in s. 2(2) of the 1890 Act. But s. 39(2) of the *Judiciary Act* invests them with federal jurisdiction in all matters in which the High Court has original jurisdiction or may have original jurisdiction conferred upon it. Under s. 76(iii) of the Constitution the High Court may be invested with federal jurisdiction in matters of admiralty and maritime jurisdiction. Consequently, it would appear that unless s. 109 applies so as to render inoperative the existence of state Admiralty jurisdiction under the *Colonial Courts of Admiralty Act*, state Supreme Courts have a dual jurisdiction derived from Imperial and commonwealth legislation. The jurisdiction derived from the *Judiciary Act* would be more extensive and not confined by the limitations arising under the *Colonial Courts of Admiralty Act*.[139]

Criminal Jurisdiction

Under the interpretation of the external affairs power adopted by the High Court in *New South Wales* v. *Commonwealth*, the commonwealth parliament has full power to define and punish crimes occurring outside territorial limits.[140] It has also a power to punish offences as incidental to the exercise of its legislative power over subject-matter related to the uses of the seas, e.g. fishing and navigation.[141] In the light of the decision of the Court in *Pearce* v. *Florenca*[142] the state parliaments may also, in the absence of commonwealth legislation, punish acts associated with the uses of the seas at least within the three mile limit and possibly outside that limit.

However, the position is complicated by the existence of certain Imperial Statutes conferring Admiralty jurisdiction in criminal matters and by the decision of the High Court in *New South Wales* v. *Commonwealth* (based on *R.* v. *Keyn*) that state boundaries end at the low-water mark. There also dicta of some of the judges of the High Court in *R.* v. *Bull*[143] and the decision of the Privy Council in *R.* v. *Oteri*[144] which indicate that Admiralty jurisdiction and not ordinary state jurisdiction applies to crimes occurring at sea. The legislation which is relevant to jurisdiction of Australian courts in relation to offences at sea are the *Offences at Sea Act* 1799,[145] the *Admiralty Offences (Colonial) Act*, 1849,[146] the *Courts (Colonial) Jurisdiction Act*, 1874[147] the *Merchant Shipping Act*, 1894[148] and the Commonwealth *Navigation Act* 1912.

The *Offences at Sea Act* provides that offences committed on the high seas are offences liable to the same punishment as if they had been offences committed on land.

The *Admiralty Offences Act* confers Admiralty jurisdiction on colonial (and therefore state) courts of criminal justice in respect of offences at sea and in the maritime areas in which the Admiral had jurisdiction, Section 1 of that Act provides:

1. *Trial of Admiralty offences in Colonies*—If any person within any colony shall be charged with the commission of any treason, piracy, felony, robbery, murder, conspiracy, or other offence, of what nature or kind soever, committed upon the sea, or in any haven, river, creek or place where the admiral or admirals have power, authority, or jurisdiction, or if any person charged with the commission of any such offence upon the sea, or in any such haven, river, creek, or place shall be brought for trial to any colony, then and in every such case all magistrates, justices of the peace, public prosecutors, juries, judges, courts, public officers, and officers, and other persons in such colony

141

shall have and exercise the same jurisdiction and authorities for inquiring of, trying, hearing, determining, and adjudging such offences, and they are hereby respectively authorised, empowered, and required to institute and carry on all such proceedings for the bringing of such persons so charged as aforesaid to trial, and for and auxiliary to and consequent upon the trial of any such persons for any such offence wherewith he may be charged as aforesaid, as by the law of such colony would and ought to have been had and exercised or instituted and carried on by them respectively if such offence had been committed, and such person had been charged with having committed the same, upon any waters situate within the limits of any such colony and within the limits of the local jurisdiction of the courts of criminal justice of such colony.

Because of doubts[149] relating to the nature of the punishment which might be imposed in relation to such offences (i.e. whether it should be punishment according to the laws of England, or the laws of the colony), the *Courts (Colonial Jurisdiction) Act* was passed. Section 3 of that Act provided:

> *At trials in any colonial courts by virtue of Imperial Acts, courts empowered to pass sentences as if crimes had been committed in the colony.*
> When by virtue of any Act of Parliament now or hereafter to be passed, a person is tried in a court of any colony for any crime or offence committed upon the high seas or elsewhere out of the territorial limits of such colony and of the local jurisdiction of such court, or if committed within such local jurisdiction made punishable by that Act, such person shall, upon conviction, be liable to such punishment as might have been inflicted upon him if the crime or offence had been committed within the limits of such colony and of the local jurisdiction of the court, and to no other, anything in any Act to the contrary norwithstanding: Provided always, that if the crime or offence is a crime or offence not punishable by the law of the colony in which the trial takes place, the person shall, on conviction, be liable to such punishment (other than capital punishment) as shall seem to the court most nearly to correspond to the punishment to which such person would have been liable in case such crime or offence had been tried in England.

Section 686 of the *Merchant Shipping Act* (1894) deals with offences on board ships. It provides:

> *Jurisdiction in case of offences on board ship—*
> (1) Where any person, being a British subject is charged with having committed any offence on board any British ship on the High seas

or in any foreign port or harbour or on board any foreign ship to which he does not belong, or, not being British subject, is charged with having committed any offence on board any British ship on the high seas, and that person is found within the jurisdiction of any court in Her Majesty's dominions, which would have had cognizance of the offence if it had been committed on board a British ship within the limits of its ordinary jurisdiction, that court shall have jurisdiction to try the offence as if it had been so committed.

(2) Nothing in this section shall affect the *Admiralty Offences (Colonial) Act* 1849.

In *R. v. Bull*[150] Gibbs J. considered that the continuing effect of the *Admiralty Offences (Colonial) Act* and the *Courts (Colonial Jurisdiction) Act* was to give local courts power to try offences committed at sea against local or English law.[151] Menzies J. also was of a similar view.[152] However, the opinion of other members of the Court was that the jurisdiction conferred was a jurisdiction to exercise Admiralty jurisdiction in relation to offences against British law.[153] Barwick C.J. considered that the jurisdiction of the 1849 Act was limited to crimes which the Admiral might try, i.e. Imperial offences, and that the only effect of the 1874 Act was to substitute a local punishment for the Imperial punishment if such existed or "if there should be no like offence under colonial law, the most appropriate English penalty".[154] Of like opinion were Stephen J.[155] and Mason J.[156]

The majority dicta were applied by the Full Court of Western Australia in *R. v. Oteri*[157] where the accused who were Australian citizens normally resident in Western Australia were charged with stealing crayfish pots on a British ship twenty-two miles from the coast "within the jurisdiction of the Admiralty". The Full Court held that the Western Australian District Court has jurisdiction to try the accused by virtue of the *Admiralty Offences (Colonial) Act* 1849 read with the *Courts (Colonial Jurisdiction) Act* 1874 and the *Merchant Shipping Act* 1894. The law to be applied was British law as contained in the *Theft Act* 1968. The decision was upheld on appeal to the Privy Council.[158]

In this context, reference may also be made to the *Territorial Waters Jurisdiction Act* 1878 which confers criminal jurisdiction on colonial courts with respect to acts of foreigners occurring within territorial waters. An "offence" is defined by the Act in terms of English law.[159] The effect of s. 381 of the Commonwealth

Navigation Act 1912 must also be noted in this context. It provides:

> Where any person (a) being an Australian citizen is charged with having committed an offence on board a ship registered in Australia on the high seas or in a foreign port or harbour, or on board a foreign ship to which he does not belong or (b) not being an Australian citizen is charged with having committed an offence, on board a ship registered in Australia on the high seas; and that person is found within the jurisdiction of any Court in Australia which would have had cognizance of the offence if it had been committed on board a ship registered in Australia within the limits of its ordinary jurisdiction, that Court shall have jurisdiction to try the offence as if it had been so committed.

The *Navigation Act* has a more limited operation than the *Merchant Shipping Act* in relation to the British Ships registered in Australia (i.e. Australian ships) as s. 2(1) does not apply to smaller types of vessels unless they are engaged in overseas inter-state or territorial trade and commerce or are on the high seas or in waters which are used by ships engaged in trade or commerce with other countries or any other states.

Moreover s. 381 of the *Navigation Act* only applies to *registered* ships while s. 681 of the *Merchant Shipping Act* applies to British ships whether registered or not. Presumably if the vessel[160] in *R. v. Oteri* had been registered, then s. 381 of the *Navigation Act* would have applied to it as the vessel was on the high seas when the offence occurred.

All this points to an unsatisfactory situation so far as crime on the high seas is concerned. Clearly, as pointed out previously, the commonwealth parliament has full authority after *New South Wales* v. *Commonwealth* to define and punish offences occurring on the seas whether on British ships or not. However, it is also necessary to examine the legislative power of the states to punish crimes in off-shores waters.

It would appear that ordinary state criminal law, unless it is expressly made to operate outside territorial limits, operates only to low-water mark. That would appear to be the effect of *New South Wales* v. *Commonwealth* applying *R. v. Keyn*. Consequently offences at sea or on ships outside territorial limits are within Admiralty jurisdictions.

But the effect of *Pearce* v. *Florenca*[161] is that state law (including, it would appear, criminal law) may be extended at least to the three-mile limit and probably beyond that limit provided that there exists a sufficient nexus with the state. Several states have already extended the operation of their general criminal law to acts committed within two hundred miles of their coastline where the "actor" is a resident of the state or has used state facilities (i.e. port facilities).[162] It is a possible argument that such legislation would be repugnant to English legislation (i.e. the *Admiralty Offences (Colonial) Act* and therefore invalid under s. 2 of the *Colonial Laws Validity Act*, but this would imply an argument based on exclusive British jurisdiction *vis-à-vis* ordinary state jurisdiction in relation to offences at sea. While the matter is not clear, it would appear that exclusive Admiralty jurisdiction is not involved and that state laws may co-exist with the old Admiralty jurisdiction in relation to offences off the Australian coastline.

WRECKS AND SALVAGE

Part VII of the *Navigation Act* is headed "Wrecks and Salvage" and contains rules relating to dealing with wrecks found on or near the Australian coast, and relating to the procedure for claiming salvage reward for services rendered in saving life or property where a ship is wrecked, stranded or in distress at any place on or near the coast of Australia.

In recent decades historic wrecks and articles have been discovered off the Western Australian coast comprising the remains of old Dutch shipwrecks. It was considered that many of the provisions of Part VII were inapplicable to these wrecks and a new act—the *Historic Shipwrecks Act*—was passed in 1976 to deal with them. This Act purports, *inter alia*, to give effect to an Agreement between Australia and the Netherlands concerning old Dutch shipwrecks which was signed in 1972, and to enable arrangements to be made with the Western Australian State Museum for the protection and custody of articles received from these wrecks.

The Act provides protection for historic wrecks and relics by enabling the responsible minister (the minister for administrative services) to make a declaration (by notice) that the remains of a ship, that are situated in Australian waters (defined as territorial waters and the waters on the landward side of such waters) or on the Australian continental shelf, are historic shipwrecks (s. 5(1)) or the articles associated with such a ship are historic relics (s. 5(2)). Protected zones (not exceeding one hundred hectares) may be established around the site of a historic shipwreck or relic for the purpose of affording protection to them (s. 7). Duties are imposed on persons who find or who have possession of an article relating to a historic shipwreck to notify the minister in relation to the article. (s. 9) Discovery of a shipwreck is also to be notified (s. 17). The minister, who has an obligation to keep a Register of Historic Shipwrecks (s. 12), may give directions in relation to the custody of shipwrecks and articles (s. 11). A person may not, except in accordance with a permit, deal with historic shipwrecks or relics (s. 13). Such permits may be granted by the minister on conditions that may be prescribed (s. 15). Rewards may be paid by the minister to persons who notify the minister of the location of remains or articles (s. 18).

A co-operative relationship between federal and state authorities is envisaged by s. 19 of the Act which empowers the governor-general to make arrangements with the governor of a state for the performance of functions by a competent authority of the state in relation to the protection, recovery, preservation and exhibition of historic shipwrecks and historic relics. Section 20 empowers the minister in order to give effect to the Act or the Dutch-Australian Agreement to make a declaration of ownership (including a declaration of ownership that a specified relic is vested in the commonwealth or state or a foreign government). Section 21 deals with the determination of compensation where action taken under the Act may lead to an acquisition by the commonwealth of property under s. 51 (xxxi) of the Constitution which imposes the requirement of "just terms".

Succeeding sections of the Act confer powers of arrest, search and seizure on inspectors appointed under the Act.

MILITARY USES OF THE SEA AND SEABED

Australia is a signatory to the nuclear test-ban treaty[163] and the treaty relating to the placing of weapons of mass destruction on the ocean floor.[164] Under the first of these treaties no testing of nuclear weapons can take place, *inter alia*, over or under water. Under the second treaty, no nuclear weapons can be emplaced or emplanted on the sea-bed *outside* a twelve miles contiguous sea-bed zone extending from the baselines of the territorial sea of coastal states. This does not, of course, prevent the navigation of surface vessels or submarines equipped with nuclear weapons on or under the surface of the sea.

12

Conclusion

Australia has actively participated in the plenary session and committee work of the Third Law of the Sea Conference.[1] Basically, the position of the Australian delegation appears to steer a middle course between the national aspirations of the Third World groupings which favour extensive controls over the economic zone and activities occurring therein and a dominant position for the International Sea Bed Authority in the deep sea-bed area, and on the other hand an unregulated freedom of access approach to resources of the economic zone and deep sea-bed area.

The major points of disagreement which exist at the Conference as this concluding chapter is being written lie in the following areas:

(i)   The question of who should have the right to exploit the resources of the deep sea-bed beyond national jurisdiction and on what terms and conditions.

(ii)   The question of passage through straits used for international navigation.

(iii) The balance of rights and duties in the two hundred miles economic zone with particular reference to living resources, the marine environment, scientific research and freedom of navigation.

(iv)   The rights of the coastal state with respect to the continental shelf.

(v)   The maritime spaces pertaining to islands.

(vi)   The need for an adequate disputes settlement system.

EXPLOITATION OF THE RESOURCES OF THE DEEP SEA-BED

The issue to be resolved here is whether the operating arm of the Deep Sea-bed Authority—the International Enterprise—shall have favoured treatment in undertaking operations of exploitation of the resources of the sea-bed or whether states and the entities (corporations, etc.) acting under national laws should have equal or at least non-discriminatory treatment in terms of access to the area.

Australia favours a position where access is shared. It should be pointed out that Australia has accepted the Moratorium Resolution and has not made any arrangements or enacted any legislation for exploiting the resources of deep sea-bed area until an international regime is agreed upon. It is unlikely that there will be any domestic pressure for legislation (as there has been in the United States) to facilitate access to the area on the part of Australian entities, as the technological expertise and financial commitment to such an enterprise is not at present available in this country.

STRAITS

It is obvious that the rights of navigation through international straits would be affected if the width of territorial waters was extended to twelve miles. Australia favours the concept of freedom of navigation. The doctrine of innocent passage as expressed in the existing Convention on the Territorial Sea and Contiguous Zone is subject to qualification and interpretation by the coastal state, and consequently many of the maritime nations favour a concept of free transit through straits as a *quid pro quo* for the recognition of a twelve mile territorial waters limit.

ACCESS TO THE LIVING RESOURCES OF THE ECONOMIC ZONE

The access of geographically disadvantaged states to the living resources of the sea within a two hundred miles economic zone must be guaranteed in any settlement which recognizes coastal state management or jurisdictional rights over the resources of this zone. Unilateral acts of a number of coastal states including the United States, Russia and member countries of the European Economic Community have led to the creation of two hundred miles national fishing zones which involve claims of jurisdictional rights to determine catch quotas and other matters affecting fishing within the zone and rights to allocate such quotas by a method which will recognize the preferential rights of the coastal state, with foreign vessels having access under licence to those resources which the coastal state is not able to exploit. If these unilateral acts survive challenge then a customary rule may be established within a short period of time justifying such claims. Australia is in favour of coastal state management rights over fisheries within two hundred miles zones,[2] but recognizes that access must be given to geographically disadvantaged nations and other nations which have traditionally fished in the zones.

RESEARCH AND POLLUTION IN THE ECONOMIC ZONE

There is also much disagreement as to the rights of the coastal state to control scientific research and pollution (arising from vessel sources) in the zone. Australia favours a guarantee of freedom of scientific research which does not depend on any consent issuing from the coastal state except where *inter alia* the research bears substantially upon the exploration and exploitation of the resources of the zone or involves drilling on the sea-bed. Also it has supported the proposition that any control of vessels navigating through the nations of the zone should depend not on national but on internationally agreed standards.

RELATIONSHIP OF THE CONTINENTAL SHELF TO THE ECONOMIC ZONE

Discussion has revolved round the question of revenue-sharing rights in the continental shelf where it extends *beyond* the two hundred mile zone. Australia has not agreed to the proposals of revenue-sharing, believing that the rights to the continental shelf resources, whatever the width of the shelf, are guaranteed by existing international law.

ISLANDS

The question of the status of islands and their effect on the delimitation of the economic zones of adjacent or opposite states has generated much controversy. Suggestions have been made that islands which cannot sustain population or economic activity should not have economic zones or only very restricted ones, but Australia has not favoured such a classification.

DISPUTES SETTLEMENT PROCEDURE

A disputes settlement procedure is regarded by Australia as essential both in the context of conflicts of interest in the economic zone and also in respect of the exploitation of the resources of the deep sea-bed area. The nature of such procedures (e.g. whether emphasis should be placed on conciliation, arbitration or judicial settlement or a combination of methods) is under discussion.

DOMESTIC IMPLEMENTATION OF EXTENDED FISHERIES ZONE

If an overall treaty or even a partial Convention is agreed to by the Conference and comes into effect internationally, the commonwealth parliament will have full legislative power to give effect to it under s. 51(xxix). Even in the absence of such a treaty, the scope of the external affairs power is such that the commonwealth could legislate with respect to ocean matters. Certainly, fisheries management powers applied to foreign vessels beyond the twelve mile limit would fall also under s. 51(x) of the Constitution.

Appendix

Seas and Submerged Lands Act 1973

An Act relating to Sovereignty in respect of certain Waters of the Sea and in respect of the Airspace over, and the Sea-bed and Subsoil beneath, those Waters and to Sovereign Rights in respect of the Continental Shelf and relating also to the Recovery of Minerals, other than Petroleum, from the Sea-bed and Subsoil beneath those Waters and from the Continental Shelf.

Preamble.   WHEREAS a belt of sea adjacent to the coast of Australia, known as the territorial sea, and the airspace over the territorial sea and the bed and subsoil of the territorial sea, are within the sovereignty of Australia:

AND WHEREAS Australia is a party to the Convention on the Territorial Sea and the Contiguous Zone a copy of which in the English language is set out in Schedule 1:

AND WHEREAS Australia as a coastal state has sovereign rights in respect of the continental shelf (that is to say, the sea-bed and subsoil of certain submarine areas adjacent to its coast but outside the area of the territorial sea) for the purpose of exploring it and exploiting its natural resources:

AND WHEREAS Australia is a party to the

Convention on the Continental Shelf a copy of which in the English language is set out in Schedule 2:

BE IT THEREFORE ENACTED by the Queen, the Senate and the House of Representatives of Australia, as follows:–

PART I—PRELIMINARY

1. This Act may be cited as the *Seas and Submerged Lands Act* 1973.[1] Short Title.

2. This Act shall come into operation on the day on which it receives the Royal Assent.[1] Commencement.

3. (1) In this Act, unless the contrary intention appears— Interpretation.
"Australia" includes the Territories to which this Act extends;
"continental shelf" has the same meaning as in the Convention on the Continental Shelf.

(2) In this Act, including section 6, a reference to the territorial sea of Australia is a reference to that territorial sea so far as it extends from time to time.

(3) In this Act, including section 11, a reference to the continental shelf of Australia is a reference to that continental shelf so far as it extends from time to time.

(4) Where a Proclamation is in force under section 7, the territorial sea of Australia shall, for all purposes of this Act, be taken to extend to the limits declared by that Proclamation.

(5) Where a Proclamation is in force under section 12, the continental shelf of Australia shall, for all purposes of this Act, be taken to extend to the limits declared by that Proclamation.

4. This Act extends to all the Territories, other than the Territory of Papua and the Territory of New Guinea. Extension to Territories.

PART II—SOVEREIGNTY AND SOVEREIGN RIGHTS

Division 1—The Territorial Sea

Definition.

5. In this Division, "territorial sea" means the territorial sea of Australia.

Sovereignty in respect of territorial sea.

6. It is by this Act declared and enacted that the sovereignty in respect of the territorial sea, and in respect of the airspace over it and in respect of its bed and subsoil, is vested in and exercisable by the Crown in right of the Commonwealth.

Limits of territorial sea.

7. (1) The Governor-General may, from time to time, by Proclamation, declare, not inconsistently with Section II of Part I of the Convention on the Territorial Sea and the Contiguous Zone, the limits of the whole or of any part of the territorial sea.

(2) For the purposes of such a Proclamation, the Governor-General may, in particular, determine either or both of the following:–

(a)   the breadth of the territorial sea;

(b)   the baseline from which the breadth of the territorial sea, or of any part of the territorial sea, is to be measured.

Declaration of historic bays and historic waters.

8. Where the Governor-General is satisfied—

(a)   that a bay is an historic bay, he may, by Proclamation, declare that bay to be an historic bay and shall, by the same or another Proclamation, define the sea-ward limits of that bay; or

(b)   that waters are historic waters, he may, by Proclamation, declare those waters to be historic waters and shall, by the same or another Proclamation, define the limits of those waters.

9. (1) The Minister may cause to be prepared and issued such charts as he thinks fit showing any matter relating to the limits of the territorial sea.

Charts of limits of territorial sea.

(2) In particular, the Minister may cause to be prepared and issued large-scale charts showing the low-water line along the coast and may cause to be shown on such a chart any other matter referred to in sub-section (1).

(3) The mere production of a copy of a paper purporting to be certified by the Minister to be a true copy of a chart prepared under this section is *prima facie* evidence of any matter shown on the chart relating to the limits of the territorial sea.

10. It is by this Act declared and enacted that the sovereignty in respect of the internal waters of Australia (that is to say, any waters of the sea on the landward side of the baseline of the territorial sea) so far as they extend from time to time, and in respect of the airspace over those waters and in respect of the sea-bed and subsoil beneath those waters, is vested in and exercisable by the Crown in right of the Commonwealth.

Sovereignty in respect of internal waters.

Division 2—The Continental Shelf

11. It is by this Act declared and enacted that the sovereign rights of Australia as a coastal State in respect of the continental shelf of Australia, for the purpose of exploring it and exploiting its natural resources, are vested in and exercisable by the Crown in right of the Commonwealth.

Sovereign rights in respect of continental shelf.

12. The Governor-General may, from time to time by Proclamation, declare not inconsistently with the Convention on the Continental Shelf or any relevant international agreement to which Australia is a party, the limits of the whole or any part of the continental shelf of Australia.

Limits of continental shelf.

Charts of limits of continental shelf.

13. (1) The Minister may cause to be prepared and issued such charts as he thinks fit showing any matter relating to the limits of the continental shelf of Australia.

(2) The mere production of a copy of a paper purporting to be certified by the Minister to be a true copy of a chart prepared under this section is *prima facie* evidence of any matter shown on the chart relating to the limits of the continental shelf of Australia.

Division 3—Savings

Part II does not affect waters, &c., within State limits.

14. Nothing in this Part affects sovereignty or sovereign rights in respect of any waters of the sea that are waters of or within any bay, gulf, estuary, river, creek, inlet, port or harbour and—

(a)   were, on 1st January, 1901, within the limits of a State; and

(b)   remain within the limits of the State,

or in respect of the airspace over, or in respect of the sea-bed or subsoil beneath, any such waters.

Certain property not vested in Commonwealth.

15. Nothing in this part shall be taken to vest in the Crown in right of the Commonwealth any wharf, jetty, pier, breakwater, building, platform, pipeline, lighthouse, beacon, navigational aid, buoy, cable or other structure or works.

Saving of other laws

16. The preceding provisions of this Part—

(a)   do not limit or exclude the operation of any law of the Commonwealth or of a Territory in force at the date of commencement of this Act or coming into force after that date; and

(b)   do not limit or exclude the operation of any law of a State in force at the date of commencement of this Act or coming into force after that date, except in so far as the law is expressed to vest or make exercisable any sovereignty or sovereign rights otherwise than as provided by the preceding provisions of this Part.

SCHEDULE 1

CONVENTION ON THE TERRITORIAL SEA AND THE CONTIGUOUS ZONE

The States Parties to this Convention
Have agreed as follows:

PART I

TERRITORIAL SEA

Section I. General

ARTICLE 1

1. The sovereignty of a State extends, beyond its land territory and its internal waters, to a belt of sea adjacent to its coast, described as the territorial sea.

2. This sovereignty is exercised subject to the provisions of these articles and to other rules of international law.

ARTICLE 2

The sovereignty of a coastal State extends to the air space over the territorial sea as well as to its bed and subsoil.

Section II. Limits of the territorial sea

ARTICLE 3

Except where otherwise provided in these articles, the normal baseline for measuring the breadth of the territorial sea is the low-water line along the coast as marked on large-scale charts officially recognized by the coastal State.

ARTICLE 4

1. In localities where the coast line is deeply indented and cut into, or if there is a fringe of islands along the coast in its immediate vicinity, the method of straight baselines joining appropriate points may be employed in drawing the baseline from which the breadth of the territorial sea is measured.

2. The drawing of such baselines must not depart to any appreciable extent from the general direction of the coast, and the sea areas lying within the lines must be sufficiently closely linked to the land domain to be subject to the régime of internal waters.

3. Baselines shall not be drawn to and from low-tide

157

elevations, unless lighthouses or similar installations which are permanently above sea level have been built on them.

4. Where the method of straight baselines is applicable under the provisions of paragraph 1, account may be taken, in determining particular baselines, of economic interests peculiar to the region concerned, the reality and the importance of which are clearly evidenced by a long usage.

5. The system of straight baselines may not be applied by a State in such a manner as to cut off from the high seas the territorial sea of another State.

6. The coastal State must clearly indicate straight baselines on charts, to which due publicity must be given.

ARTICLE 5

1. Waters on the landward side of the baseline of the territorial sea form part of the internal waters of the State.

2. Where the establishment of a straight baseline in accordance with article 4 has the effect of enclosing as internal waters areas which previously had been considered as part of the territorial sea or of the high seas, a right of innocent passage, as provided in articles 14 to 23, shall exist in those waters.

ARTICLE 6

The outer limit of the territorial sea is the line every point of which is at a distance from the nearest point of the baseline equal to the breadth of the territorial sea.

ARTICLE 7

1. This artcle relates only to bays the coasts of which belong to a single State.

2. For the purpose of these articles, a bay is a well-marked indentation whose penetration is is such proportion to the width of its mouth as to contain landlocked waters and constitute more than a mere curvature of the coast. An indentation shall not, however, be regarded as a bay unless its area is as large as, or larger than, that of the semi-circle whose diameter is a line drawn across the mouth of that indentation.

3. For the purpose of measurement, the area of an indentation is that lying between the low-water mark around the shore of the indentation and a line joining the low-water

marks of its natural entrance points. Where, because of the presence of islands, an indentation has more than one mouth, the semi-circle shall be drawn on a line as long as the sum total of the lengths of the lines across the different mouths. Islands within an indentation shall be included as if they were part of the water areas of the indentation.

4. If the distance between the low-water marks of the natural entrance points of a bay does not exceed twenty-four miles, a closing line may be drawn between these two low-water marks, and the waters enclosed thereby shall be considered as internal waters.

5. Where the distance between the low-water marks of the natural entrance points of a bay exceeds twenty-four miles, a straight baseline of twenty-four miles shall be drawn within the bay in such a manner as to enclose the maximum area of water that is possible with a line of that length.

6. The foregoing provisions shall not apply to so-called "historic" bays, or in any case where the straight baseine system provided for in article 4 is applied.

ARTICLE 8

For the purpose of delimiting the territorial sea, the outermost permanent harbour works which form an integral part of the harbour system shall be regarded as forming part of the coast.

ARTICLE 9

Roadsteads which are normally used for the loading, unloading and anchoring of ships, and which would otherwise be situated wholly or partly outside the outer limit of the territorial sea, are included in the territorial sea. The coastal State must clearly demarcate such roadsteads and indicate them on charts together with their boundaries, to which due publicity must be given.

ARTICLE 10

1. An island is a naturally-formed area of land, surrounded by water, which is above water at high-tide.

2. The territorial sea of an island is measured in accordance with the provisions of these articles.

ARTICLE 11

1. A low-tide elevation is a naturally-formed area of land

which is surrounded by and above water at low-tide but submerged at high tide. Where a low-tide elevation is situated wholly or partly at a distance not exceeding the breadth of the territorial sea from the mainland or an island, the low-water line on that elevation may be used as the baseline for measuring the breadth of the territorial sea.

2. Where a low-tide elevation is wholly situated at a distance exceeding the breadth of the territorial sea from the mainland or an island, it has no territorial sea of its own.

ARTICLE 12

1. Where the coasts of two States are opposite or adjacent to each other, neither of the two States is entitled, failing agreement between them to the contrary, to extend its territorial sea beyond the median line every point of which is equidistant from the nearest points on the baselines from which the breadth of the territorial seas of each of the two States is measured. The provisions of this paragraph shall not apply, however, where it is necessary by reason of historic title or other special circumstances to delimit the territorial seas of the two States in a way which is at variance with this provision.

2. The line of delimitation between the territorial seas of two States lying opposite to each other or adjacent to each other shall be marked on large-scale charts officially recognized by the coastal States.

ARTICLE 13

If a river flows directly into the sea, the baseline shall be a straight line across the mouth of the river between points on the low-tide line of its banks.

Section III. Right of innocent passage

Sub-section A. Rules applicable to all ships

ARTICLE 14

1. Subject to the provisions of these articles, ships of all States, whether coastal or not, shall enjoy the right of innocent passage through the territorial sea.

2. Passage means navigation through the territorial sea for the purpose either of traversing that sea without entering internal waters, or of proceeding to internal waters, or of making for the high seas from internal waters.

3. Passage includes stopping and anchoring, but only in so far as the same are identical to ordinary navigation or are rendered necessary by *force majeure* or by distress.

4. Passage is innocent so long as it is not prejudicial to the peace, good order or security of the coastal State. Such passage shall take place in conformity with these articles and with other rules of international law.

5. Passage of foreign fishing vessels shall not be considered innocent if they do not observe such laws and regulations as the coastal State may make and publish in order to prevent these vessels from fishing in the territorial sea.

6. Submarines are required to navigate on the surface and to show their flag.

ARTICLE 15

1. The coastal State must not hamper innocent passage through the territorial sea.

2. The coastal State is required to give appropriate publicity to any dangers to navigation of which it has knowledge, within its territorial sea.

ARTICLE 16

1. The coastal State may take the necessary steps in its territorial sea to prevent passage which is not innocent.

2. In the case of ships proceeding to internal waters, the coastal State shall also have the right to take the necessary steps to prevent any breach of the conditions to which admission of those ships to those waters is subject.

3. Subject to the provisions of paragraph 4, the coastal State may, without discrimination amongst foreign ships, suspend temporarily in specified areas of its territorial sea the innocent passage of foreign ships if such suspension is essential for the protection of its security. Such suspension shall take effect only after having been duly published.

4. There shall be no suspension of the innocent passage of foreign ships through straits which are used for international navigation between one part of the high seas and another part of the high seas or the territorial sea of a foreign State.

ARTICLE 17

Foreign ships exercising the right of innocent passage shall comply with the laws and regulations enacted by the coastal

State in conformity with these articles and other rules of international law and, in particular, with such laws and regulations relating to transport and navigation.

Sub-section B. Rules applicable to merchant ships

ARTICLE 18

1. No charge may be levied upon foreign ships by reason only of their passage through the territorial sea.

2. Charges may be levied upon a foreign ship passing through the territorial sea as payment only for specific services rendered to the ship. These charges shall be levied without discrimination.

ARTICLE 19

1. The criminal jurisdiction of the coastal State should not be exercised on board a foreign ship passing through the territorial sea to arrest any person or to conduct any investigation in connexion with any crime committed on board the ship during its passage, save only in the following cases:

    (a) If the consequences of the crime extend to the coastal State; or

    (b) If the crime is of a kind to disturb the peace of the country or the good order of the territorial sea; or

    (c) If the assistance of the local authorities has been requested by the captain of the ship or by the consul of the country whose flag the ship flies; or

    (d) If it is necessary for the suppression of illicit traffic in narcotic drugs.

2. The above provisions do not affect the right of the coastal State to take any steps authorized by its laws for the purpose of an arrest or investigation on board a foreign ship passing through the territorial sea after leaving internal waters.

3. In the cases provided for in paragraphs 1 and 2 of this article, the coastal State shall, if the captain so requests, advise the consular authority of the flag State before taking any steps, and shall facilitate contact between such authority and the ship's crew. In cases of emergency this notification may be communicated while the measures are being taken.

4. In considering whether or how an arrest should be made, the local authorities shall pay due regard to the interests of navigation.

5. The coastal State may not take any steps on board a

foreign ship passing through the territorial sea to arrest any person or to conduct any investigation in connexion with any crime committed before the ship entered the territorial sea, if the ship, proceeding from a foreign port, is only passing through the territorial sea without entering internal waters.

ARTICLE 20

1. The coastal State should not stop or divert a foreign ship passing through the territorial sea for the purpose of exercising civil jurisdiction in relation to a person on board the ship.

2. The coastal State may not levy execution against or arrest the ship for the purpose of any civil proceedings, save only in respect of obligations or liabilities assumed or incurred by the ship itself in the course or for the purpose of its voyage through the waters of the coastal State.

3. The provisions of the previous paragraph are without prejudice to the right of the coastal State, in accordance with its laws, to levy execution against or to arrest, for the purpose of any civil proceedings, a foreign ship lying in the territorial sea, or passing through the territorial sea after leaving internal waters.

Sub-section C. Rules applicable to government ships other than warships

ARTICLE 21

The rules contained in sub-sections A and B shall also apply to government ships operated for commercial purposes.

ARTICLE 22

1. The rules contained in sub-section A and in article 18 shall apply to government ships operated for non-commercial purposes.

2. With such exceptions as are contained in the provisions referred to in the preceding paragraph, nothing in these articles affects the immunities which such ships enjoy under these articles or other rules of international law.

Sub-section D. Rule applicable to warships

ARTICLE 23

If any warship does not comply with the regulations of the coastal State concerning passage through the territorial sea and disregards any request for compliance which is made to it, the coastal State may require the warship to leave the territorial sea.

PART II
CONTIGUOUS ZONE
ARTICLE 24

1. In a zone of the high seas contiguous to its territorial sea, the coastal State may exercise the control necessary to:
   (a) Prevent infringement of its customs, fiscal, immigration or sanitary regulations within its territory or territorial sea;
   (b) Punish infringement of the above regulations committed within its territory or territorial sea.

2. The contiguous zone may not extend beyond twelve miles from the baseline from which the breadth of the territorial sea is measured.

3. Where the coasts of two States are opposite or adjacent to each other, neither of the two States is entitled, failing agreement between them to the contrary, to extend its contiguous zone beyond the median line every point of which is equidistant from the nearest points on the baselines from which the breadth of the territorial seas of the two States is measured.

PART III
FINAL ARTICLES
ARTICLE 25

The provisions of this Convention shall not affect conventions or other international agreements already in force, as between States Parties to them.

ARTICLE 26

This Convention shall, until 31 October 1958, be open for signature by all States Members of the United Nations or of any of the specialized agencies, and by any other State invited by the General Assembly of the United Nations to become a Party to the Convention.

ARTICLE 27

This Convention is subject to ratification. The instruments of ratification shall be deposited with the Secretary-General of the United Nations.

ARTICLE 28

This Convention shall be open for accession by any States belonging to any of the categories mentioned in article 26. The instruments of accession shall be deposited with the Secretary-General of the United Nations.

ARTICLE 29

1. This Convention shall come into force on the thirtieth day following the date of deposit of the twenty-second instrument of ratification or accession with the Secretary-General of the United Nations.

2. For each State ratifying or acceding to the Convention after the deposit of the twenty-second instrument of ratification or accession, the Convention shall enter into force on the thirtieth day after deposit by such State of its instrument of ratification or accession.

ARTICLE 30

1. After the expiration of a period of five years from the date on which this Convention shall enter into force, a request for the revision of this Convention may be made at any time by any Contracting Party by means of a notification in writing addressed to the Secretary-General of the United Nations.

2. The General Assembly of the United Nations shall decide upon the steps, if any, to be taken in respect of such request.

ARTICLE 31

The Secretary-General of the United Nations shall inform all States Members of the United Nations and the other States referred to in article 26:

(a) Of signatures to this Convention and of the deposit of instruments of ratification or accession, in accordance with articles 26, 27 and 28;

(b) Of the date on which this Convention will come into force, in accordance with article 29;

(c) Of requests for revision in accordance with article 30.

ARTICLE 32

The original of this Convention, of which the Chinese, English, French, Russian and Spanish texts are equally authentic, shall be deposited with the Secretary-General of the United Nations, who shall send certified copies thereof to all States referred to in article 26.

IN WITNESS WHEREOF the undersigned Plenipotentiaries, being duly authorized thereto by their respective Governments, have signed this Convention.

DONE at Geneva, this twenty-ninth day of April one thousand nine hundred and fifty-eight.

(*Here follow the signatures of the plenipotentiaries, including the plenipotentiary of Australia.*)

SCHEDULE 2 Preamble

CONVENTION ON THE CONTINENTAL SHELF

The States Parties to this Convention
Have agreed as follows:

ARTICLE 1

For the purpose of these articles, the term "continental shelf" is used as referring (a) to the seabed and subsoil of the submarine areas adjacent to the coast but outside the area of the territorial sea, to a depth of 200 metres or, beyond that limit, to where the depth of the superjacent waters admits of the exploitation of the natural resources of the said areas; (b) to the seabed and the subsoil of similar submarine areas adjacent to the coasts of islands.

ARTICLE 2

1. The coastal State exercises over the continental shelf sovereign rights for the purpose of exploring it and exploiting its natural resources.

2. The rights referred to in paragraph 1 of this article are exclusive in the sense that if the coastal State does not explore the continental shelf or exploit its natural resources, no one may undertake these activities, or make a claim to the continental shelf, without the express consent of the coastal State.

3. The rights of the coastal State over the continental shelf do not depend on occupation, effective or notional, or on any express proclamation.

4. The natural resources referred to in these articles consist of the mineral and other non-living resources of the seabed and subsoil together with living organisms belonging to sedentary species that is to say, organisms which, at the harvestable stage, either are immobile on or under the seabed

or are unable to move except in constant physical contact with the seabed or the subsoil.

ARTICLE 3

The rights of the coastal State over the continental shelf do not affect the legal status of the superjacent waters as high seas, or that of the airspace above those waters.

ARTICLE 4

Subject to its right to take responsible measures for the exploration of the continental shelf and the exploitation of its natural resources, the coastal State may not impede the laying or maintenance of submarine cables or pipe lines on the continental shelf.

ARTICLE 5

1. The exploration of the continental shelf and the exploitation of its natural resources must not result in any unjustifiable interference with navigation, fishing or the conservation of the living resources of the sea, nor result in any interference with fundamental oceanographic or other scientific research carried out with the intention of open publication.

2. Subject to the provisions of paragraphs 1 and 6 of this article, the coastal State is entitled to construct and maintain or operate on the continental shelf installations and other devices necessary for its exploration and the exploitation of its natural resources, and to establish safety zones around such installations and devices and to take in those zones measures necessary for their protection.

3. The safety zones referred to in paragraph 2 of this article may extend to a distance of 500 metres around the installations and other devices which have been erected, measured from each point of their outer edge. Ships of all nationalities must respect these safety zones.

4. Such installations and devices, though under the jurisdiction of the coastal State, do not possess the status of islands. They have no territorial sea of their own, and their presence does not affect the delimitation of the territorial sea of the coastal State.

5. Due notice must be given of the construction of any such installations, and permanent means for giving warning of their presence must be maintained. Any installations which are abandoned or disused must be entirely removed.

6. Neither the installations or devices, nor the safety zones around them, may be established where interference may be caused to the use of recognized sea lanes essential to international navigation.

7. The coastal State is obliged to undertake, in the safety zones, all appropriate measures for the protection of the living resources of the sea from harmful agents.

8. The consent of the coastal State shall be obtained in respect of any research concerning the continental shelf and undertaken there. Nevertheless, the coastal State shall not normally withhold its consent if the request is submitted by a qualified institution with a view to purely scientific research into the physical or biological characteristics of the continental shelf, subject to the proviso that the coastal State shall have the right, if it so desires, to participate or to be represented in the research, and that in any event the results shall be published.

ARTICLE 6

1. Where the same continental shelf is adjacent to the territories of two or more States whose coasts are opposite each other, the boundary of the continental shelf appertaining to such States shall be determined by agreement between them. In the absence of agreement, and unless another boundary line is justified by special circumstances, the boundary is the median line, every point of which is equidistant from the nearest points of the baselines from which the breadth of the territorial sea of each State is measured.

2. Where the same continental shelf is adjacent to the territories of two adjacent States, the boundary of the continental shelf shall be determined by agreement between them. In the absence of agreement, and unless another boundary line is justified by special circumstances, the boundary shall be determined by application of the principle of equidistance from the nearest points of the baselines from which the breadth of the territorial sea of each State is measured.

3. In delimiting the boundaries of the continental shelf, any lines which are drawn in accordance with the principles set out in paragraphs 1 and 2 of this article should be defined with reference to charts and geographical features as they exist at a particular date, and reference should be made to fixed permanent identifiable points on the land.

ARTICLE 7

The provisions of these articles shall not prejudice the right of the coastal State to exploit the subsoil by means of tunnelling irrespective of the depth of water above the subsoil.

ARTICLE 8

This Convention shall, until 31 October 1958, be open for signature by all States Members of the United Nations or of any of the specialized agencies, and by any other State invited by the General Assembly of the United Nations to become a Party to the Convention.

ARTICLE 9

This Convention is subject to ratification. The instruments of ratification shall be deposited with the Secretary-General of the United Nations.

ARTICLE 10

This Convention shall be open for accession by any States belonging to any of the categories mentioned in article 8. The instruments of accession shall be deposited with the Secretary-General of the United Nations.

ARTICLE 11

1. This Convention shall come into force on the thirtieth day following the date of deposit of the twenty-second instrument of ratification or accession with the Secretary-General of the United Nations.

2. For each State ratifying or acceding to the Convention after the deposit of the twenty-second instrument of ratification or accession, the Convention shall enter into force on the thirtieth day after deposit by such State of its instrument of ratification or accession.

ARTICLE 12

1. At the time of signature, ratification or accession, any State may make reservations to articles of the Convention other than to articles 1 to 3 inclusive.

2. Any Contracting State making a reservation in accordance with the preceding paragraph may at any time withdraw the reservation by a communication to that effect addressed to the Secretary-General of the United Nations.

ARTICLE 13

1. After the expiration of a period of five years from the date on which this Convention shall enter into force, a request for the revision of this Convention may be made at any time by any Contracting Party by means of a notification in writing addressed to the Secretary-General of the United Nations.

2. The General Assembly of the United Nations shall decide upon the steps, if any, to be taken in respect of such request.

ARTICLE 14

The Secretary-General of the United Nations shall inform all States Members of the United Nations and the other States referred to in article 8:

(a) Of signatures to this Convention and of the deposit of instruments of ratification or accession, in accordance with articles 8, 9 and 10;

(b) Of the date on which this Convention will come into force, in accordance with article 11;

(c) Of requests for revision in accordance with article 13;

(d) Of reservations to this Convention, in accordance with article 12.

ARTICLE 15

The original of this Convention, of which the Chinese, English, French, Russian and Spanish texts are equally authentic, shall be deposited with the Secretary-General of the United Nations, who shall send certified copies thereof to all States referred to in article 8.

IN WITNESS WHEREOF, the undersigned Plenipotentiaries, being duly authorized thereto by their respective Governments, have signed this Convention.

DONE at Geneva, this twenty-ninth day of April one thousand nine hundred and fifty-eight.

(*Here follow the signatures of the plenipotentiaries, including the plenipotentiary of Australia.*)

NOTE

1. Act No.161, 1973; assented to 4 December 1973.

Notes to Text

PART 1

1. Introduction

1. See A.G. Lang, *Manual of the Law and Practice of Mining and Exploration in Australia* (Sydney: Butterworths, 1971), ch.4.
2. Ibid., ch.12.
3. See *Halsbury's Laws of England*, vol.1: *Admiralty* (London: Butterworths, 1954) pp. 208 ff.
4. See D.W. Bowett, *The Law of the Sea* (Manchester University Press, 1967). The existence of a preliminary draft from a specialized body differentiates that Conference from the present United Nations Conference on the Law of the Sea (The Third Conference) which commenced its deliberations without the benefit of a draft set of articles from the International Law Commission and only at a later stage was assisted by what became known as a "Single Negotiating Text" prepared by the Chairmen of the Committees. However, it did have before it a report of a United Nations Committee (Committee on the Peaceful Uses of the Sea-Bed) which dealt with some of the issues.
5. Each Convention was expressed to come into effect following the date of deposit of the twenty-second instrument of ratification. All the Conventions came into effect in the 1960s. In the words of Bowett, (writing in 1967), "there are already clear indications that these Conventions have achieved a status as evidence of what present international law is far beyond that what is apparent from the list of formal ratifications"; *The Law of the Sea*, p.4. However the decision of the International Court of Justice in the *North Sea Continental Cases*, [1969] *I.C.J. Reports*, pp.3–54, indicates that certain articles of these conventions do not have the status of customary international law. See below, pp.45–47.
   Copies of the texts of the Conventions are to be found in Bowett, *The Law of the Sea*, Appendix 1–Appendix 4; Lay, Churchill, Nordquist, eds., *New Directions in the Law of the Sea* (Oceania Publications, 1973), vol. 1, documents, pp.1, 101, 257, 353. See also E.D. Brown, *The Legal Regime of Hydrospace* (London: Stevens & Sons, 1971), Appendix 1, for useful information on ratifications.
6. Text in *New Directions in the Law of the Sea*, vol.1, p.101.
7. Ibid., p.257.
8. Ibid., p.1.
9. It is to be noted that the "straight baseline" method for drawing the baseline of the territorial sea which was adopted by the International Court of Justice

in the *Anglo Norwegian Fisheries Case* (1951) is regarded in the Convention as applicable to certain types of coastline.

10. The question of the breadth of the territorial sea which was not successfully negotiated at the First Conference was examined at the Second United Nations Conference on the Law of the Sea held at Geneva in 1960. It ended in failure. See Bowett, *The Law of the Sea*, pp.11–12.

11. Text in *New Directions in the Law of the Sea*, vol.1, p.353.

12. See various declarations of Latin-American and African nations collected in *New Directions in the Law of the Sea*, vol.1, pp.231–356.
    See K.G. Nweihed, "Assessment of the Extension of State Jurisdiction in Terms of the Living Resources of the Sea", *Law of the Sea: The Emerging Regime of the Oceans*, Proceedings of the Law of the Sea Institute, Rhode Island, 1973, p.17ff.

13. This doctrine was formally enshrined in United Nations General Assembly resolutions in 1969 and 1970. See *New Directions in the Law of the Sea*, vol.2, p.737 ff. For an excellent study of possible regimes for the deep sea-bed area see L. Henkin, *Law for the Sea's Mineral Resources* (Institute for the Study of Science in Human Affairs, Columbia University, 1969). See below ch.5.

14. The various Conventions are to be found in *New Directions in the Law of the Sea*, vol.2, p.557 ff. See also Brown, *The Legal Regime of Hydrospace*, Part 3, p.127 ff.

15. [1969] *I.C.J. Reports*, pp.3–59.

16. [1974] *I.C.J. Reports*, pp.3–35.

17. Among the many recent discussions of the work of the Conference, reference may be made to the articles in *8 Case Western Reserve Journal of International Law* (1976), p.5 ff; "Symposium on Law of the Sea and Protection of the Marine Environment", 6 *Georgia Journal of International and Comparative Law*, (1976) p.1 ff. Reference may also be made to the annual issues of the *San Diego Law Review* and the *Proceedings of the Rhode Island Law of the Sea Institute*. National policies are examined in Lay, Churchill, Nordquist, eds, *New Directions in the Law of the Sea* (1973), vol.3.

18. See below, p.92.

19. See in particular D.P. O'Connell, "Australian Coastal Jurisdiction", *International Law in Australia*, ed. D.P. O'Connell (Sydney: Law Book Co, 1966), p.246 ff; D.P. O'Connell, "The Juridical Nature of the Territorial Sea", 45 *British Year Book of International Law* (1971), p.303, 378 ff; L.F.E. Goldie, "Australia's Continental Shelf: Legislation and Proclamations", 3 *International and Comparative Law Quarterly* (1954), p.535; Sir Kenneth Bailey, "Australia and the Geneva Conventions on the Law of the Sea", *International Law in Australia*, ed. D.P. O'Connell (Sydney: Law Book Co., 1966), p.228 ff.; Enid Campbell, "Regulation of Australian Coastal Fisheries", 1 *Tasmanian University Law Review* (1960), p.404; W.R. Edeson, "Australian Bays", *Australian Year Book of International Law* (1968–69), p.5.

20. (1976) 8 A.L.R., p.1.

21. On this question, see A.L. Shalowicz, *Shore and Sea Boundaries* (U.S. Department of Commerce, Washington, 1962); S.W. Boggs, "Delineation of Seaward Areas under National Jurisdiction", 45 *American Journal of International Law* (1951), p.240; A. Guilcher, "Geo-physical characteristics", in *New Directions in the Law of the Sea*, vol.3, p.109 ff.

2. *National Waters and Zones*

1. For an analysis of the doctrine of the territorial sea see D.P. O'Connell, "The Juridical Nature of the Territorial Sea", 45 *British Year Book of International Law* (1971), p.303.
2. See A.H. Dean, "The Second Geneva Conference on the Law of the Sea: The Fight for Freedom of the Seas", 54 *American Journal of International Law* (1960), 751, p.772 ff. Bowett, *The Law of the Sea*, pp. 11–12.
3. Ibid.
4. See the table of claims set out in E.D. Brown "Maritime Zones" ch. 14 in *New Directions in the Law of the Sea*, vol.3, 157, p.161.
5. See judgment of the International Court of Justice in the *Fisheries Jurisdiction Case* (1974), *I.C.J. Reports* 3, p.23. See also R.R. Churchill, "The Fisheries Jurisdiction Case: The Contribution of the International Court of Justice to the Debate on Coastal States Fisheries Rights", 24 International and Comparative Law Quarterly (1975), p.82, 87 ff.
6. Brown, "Maritime Zones", p.162. See also "Table showing Showing Changes in the Breadth of Territorial Sea and Fishing Zones Claimed Between 1958 and 1972" in *New Directions in the Law of the Sea*. vol.2, p.873.
7. Ibid. The Articles relating to innocent passage are Articles 14–23. See Appendix below, pp.160–64.
8. Convention of the Territorial Sea and Contiguous Zone, Article 3.
9. Article 4(1).
10. Article 4(2).
11. Article 4(6).
12. See below pp.14–15, 95–96.
13. Article 4(4).
14. Article 5(1).
15. Article 5(2).
16. Article 6.
17. [1951] *I.C.J. Reports*, p.116.
18. For an excellent discussion of the policy factors involved in a straight baseline system see M.S. McDougal and W.T. Burke, *The Public Order of the Oceans*, (New Haven: Yale University Press, 1962), especially pp. 402–11.
19. Article 7(4).
20. Article 7(5).
21. Article 7(3).
22. Article 7(6).
23. For an analysis of the international law relating to bays see M.P. Strohl, *The International Law of Bays* (The Hague: Martinus Nijhoff, 1963) and L.J. Bouchez *The Regime of Bays in International Law* (Leiden: Sijthoff, 1964).
24. Bouchez, *The Regime of Bays in International Law*, pp.16 ff; Strohl, *The International Law of Bays*, pp.78 ff.
25. On the question of historic bays see Bouchez, *The Regime of Bays*, ch.4, McDougal and Burke, *The Public Order of the Oceans* p.357ff; Pharand, *The Law of the Sea of the Arctic* (University of Ottawa Press, 1973), pp.104–16. See also *United Nations Conference on the Law of the Sea, Official Records,* 1, 1958, p.28 ff.
26. See L.M. Alexander, "Special Circumstances: Semi-enclosed Areas", in *Law*

of the Sea: The Emerging Regime of the Oceans, Proceedings of the Law of the Sea Institute, Rhode Island (1973), 201, pp.212–14.

27. Article 11(1).
28. Ibid.
29. Article 11(2).
30. See below pp.14–15 for the relationship of these provisions.
31. On the applicability of this provision see Strohl, *The International Law of Bays*, pp.60–61.
32. See C.J. Colombos, *International Law of the Sea*, p.126.
33. See O'Connell, "Australian Coastal Jurisdiction", *International Law in Australia*, ed. D.P. O'Connell, p.270.
34. McDougal and Burke, *The Public Order of the Oceans*, p.397.
35. See "Third United Nations Law of the Sea Conference: The Current Status of the 'Informal Single Negotiating Text' ", 8 *Case Western Reserve Journal of International Law* (1976), 33, pp.44–45. See also Hodgson, "Islands: Normal and Special Circumstances", in *Law of the Sea: The Emerging Regime of the Oceans*, p.137.
36. Article 11.
37. Comment by Sir Gerald Fitzmaurice at meeting of I.L.C. Committee. See *Year Book of the International Law Commission* (New York: United Nations, 1955), 1, p.253.
38. See McDougal and Burke, *The Public Order of the Oceans*, pp.391–97.
39. See G. Marston, "Low-Tide Elevations and Straight Baselines", 46 *British Year Book of International Law* (1972–73), p.405.
40. Ibid., p.386.
41. Ibid., p.411 ff.
42. Ibid., p.386.
43. See J. Evenson, "Certain Legal Aspects Concerning the Delimitation of the Territorial Waters of Archipelagos", *United Nations Conference on the Law of the Sea, Official Records*, 1 (1958), Preparatory Documents, pp.289–302. O'Connell, "Mid-Ocean Archipelagos in International Law", 45 *British Year Book of International Law* (1971) p.1.
44. McDougal and Burke, *The Public Order of the Oceans*, p.416.
45. Ibid., p.419.
46. O'Connell, "Mid-Ocean Archipelagos", n.43, pp.75–77. Mochtar Kusumaatmadja, "The Legal Regime of Archipelagos: Problems and Issues", in *The Law of the Sea: Needs and Interests of Developing Countries* (Law of the Sea Institute, 1973), p.166.
47. See "The Third United Nations Law of the Sea Conference: The Caracas Session and its Aftermath", 8 *Case Western Reserve Journal of International Law* (1976), 13, pp.22–23. See also Brown, "Maritime Zones: A Survey of Claims", ch.14 of *New Directions on the Law of the Sea*, vol.3, 157, pp.159–60, Hodgson, "Islands: Normal and Special Circumstances", in *The Law of the Sea: The Emerging Regime of the Oceans* p.155 ff.
48. See generally O'Connell, *International Law*, 2nd end., vol.2 p.639 ff.; L.C. Fell, "Maritime Contiguous Zones" 62 *Michigan Law Review* (1962), p.848.
49. Article 24(1) (b).
50. H.G. Knight, "International Fisheries Management Without Global Agreement: United States Policies and their Impact on the Soviet Union" 6 *Georgia Journal of International and Comparative Law* (1976), p.119;

R.R. Churchill, "The Fisheries Jurisdiction Case: the Contribution of the International Court to the Debate on Coastal States Fisheries Rights", 24 *International and Comparative Law Quarterly* (1975), 82, pp.87–92.

51. [1974] *I.C.J. Reports*, pp.3, 23.
52. See Tables relating to claims in Churchill, "The Fisheries Jurisdiction Case", *op. cit.*, p.89.

3. *The Continental Shelf*

1. See the decision of the International Court of Justice in the *North Sea Continental Shelf Cases*, [1969] *I.C.J. Reports*, 3, p.32–33.
2. Despite the fact that in 1958 in his *Abu Dhabi* arbitral opinion, Lord Asquith had rejected the view that the continental shelf doctrine was part of customary international law. See 1 *International and Comparative Law Quarterly* (1952), p.47.
3. Article 2.
4. [1969] *I.C.J. Reports*, p.3.
5. Ibid., p.22.
6. However the "legal" continental shelf begins at the outer limit of territorial waters. The sea-bed within territorial limits, although geologically part of the shelf, comes under the Convention on the Territorial Sea. The distinction is fundamental as the legal rights exercised over the territorial sea-bed differ from those that may be exercised over the "outer" continental shelf.
7. See A. Guilcher, "Geo-Physical Characteristics", in *New Directions in the Law of the Sea*, vol.3, pp.109–10; K.O. Emery, "Geological Aspects of Sea Floor Sovereignity" in *The Law of the Sea: Offshore Boundaries and Zones*, ed. L.M. Alexander (Rhode Island: 1967), pp.139–60.
8. On the question of the outer boundary of the shelf see R.Y. Jennings, "The Limits of Continental Shelf Jurisdiction: Some Implications of the *North Sea Case* Judgment", 18 *I.C.L.Q*, (1969), p.819; E.D. Brown, "The Outer Limit of the Continental Shelf", *Juridical Review* (1958), p.111; L. Henkin, *Law for the Seas Mineral Resources*, I.S.H.A. Monograph (1968) p.42 ff; L.F. Goldie, "Where is the Continental Shelf's Outer Boundary", 1 *Journal of Maritime Law and Commerce* (1970), p.461, 2 *Journal of Maritime Law and Commerce* (1970), p.173; B. Oxnam, "The Preparation of Article 1 of the Convention on the Continental Shelf", 3 *Journal of Maritime Law and Commerce* (1971–72), pp.245, 445, 683; L.W. Finlay, "The Position of the American Bar Association on the Law of the Sea", 8 *Case Western Reserve Journal of International Law* (1976), p.84.
9. This type of extraction must be distinguished from the taking of test samples which would be considered to be merely part of the process of exploration. See Guilcher, "Geo-Physical Characteristics" pp.7, 114.
10. But see Brown, *The Legal Regime of Hydrospace*, pp.7–8.
11. Provided of course that the limiting criterion of adjacency in Article 1, vague as it is, is adhered to.
12. [1969] *I.C.J. Reports*, pp.3, 22.
13. Jennings, "The Limits of Continental Shelf Jurisdiction" n.8, p.829; Finlay, "The Position of the American Bar Association" n.8, p.91 ff.
14. Oxnam, "The Preparation of Article 1", n.8, pp.715–16. Oxnam suggests

that the inclusion of the "exploitability" criterion was to satisfy those countries (such as the Latin-American countries) with narrow shelves.

15. See *North Sea Continental Shelf Cases*, [1969] *I.C.J. Reports*, p.3, 30.
16. But the position is subject to some uncertainty. See Brown, *The Legal Regime of Hydrospace*, pp.6–7. See also ibid., p.20 (as to United States jurisdiction over Cortes Bank off the coast of California). Norway's rights to the continental shelf which extends beyond the break known as the "Norwegian Trough" has been implicitly recognized in the Anglo-Norwegian Agreement relating to the Continental Shelf (*United Kingdom Treaty Series*, No.71 of 1965).
17. Article 1 provides that "for the purposes of these articles, the term 'continental shelf' is used as referring to ... the seabed and subsoil of similar submarine areas adjacent to islands".
18. On this question see below pp.26, 151. See also R.D. Hodgson, "Islands: Normal and Special Circumstances", in *Law of the Sea: The Emerging Regime of the Oceans* (1973), p.137.
19. See "The Third United Nations Law of the Sea Conference: The Caracas Session and its Aftermath", 8 *Case Western Reserve Journal of International Law* (1976), p.13, 20 ff.
20. See M.S. McDougal and W.T. Burke, *The Public Order of the Oceans* pp.698–99:, (New Haven: Yale University Press, 1962).
21. In fact, it is expressly provided in Article 3 of the Convention that the rights of other countries on the high seas are not affected.
22. However, it has been pointed out that the Convention did not purport to determine other uses (e.g. military) of the shelf. See McDougal and Burke, *The Public Order of the Oceans*, pp.716–17. See now *Treaty on the Prohibition of the Emplacement of Nuclear Weapons and other Weapons of Mass Destruction on the Sea-bed and the Ocean Floor and in the Subsoil thereof* (1971). The Treaty applies to the area of the sea-floor beyond the contiguous zone (i.e. beyond 12 miles from the coastline). See below ch.11, pp.146–47.
23. Article 2(3).
24. Article 2(2).
25. Article 4.
26. Article 5(1).
27. Article 5(7).
28. Article 5(3).
29. Article 5(6).
30. Article 5(5).
31. Article 5(4).
32. If the request is submitted by a qualified institution with a view to purely scientific research into the physical or biological characteristics of the continental shelf: Article 5(8). The coastal state has the right to participate in the research and the results are to be published.
33. Article 2(4).
34. See Goldie, "Some comments on Gidel's views", 3 *University of Western Australia Annual Law Review* (1956), 108, p.110.
35. These come within the phylum of molluscs.
36. These come within the phylum of crustacea.
37. "It is the earnest hope of its draftsmen that it will be found in practice to exclude the shrimp and the sole from the natural resources of the continental shelf just as unequivocally as it includes the mother of pearl

shell, the pearl oyster, the bêche-de-mer, the trochus and the green snail".
K. Bailey "Australia and the Geneva Conventions on the Law of the Sea",
in D.P. O'Connell *International Law in Australia* (Sydney: Law Book Co.,
1966) ch.10, 228, p.236. See also S. Oda, *International Control of Sea
Resources* (Leiden: A.W. Sythoff, 1963), pp.192–93. F.V. Garcia Amador,
The Exploitation and Conservation of the Resources of the Sea (Leiden:
A.W. Sijthoff, 1959) pp.127–28. Recent developments suggest that a number
of states are taking a wider view of "sedentary resources". See Bowett, *Law
of the Sea*, p.37 (lobsters claimed by Brazil to be a continental shelf
resource). H.G. Knight, "International Fisheries Management", *Georgia
Journal of International and Comparative Law*, 6 (1976) 119, p.138, n.85.
(Species of crab designated as shelf resources in agreements between
the U.S.S.R. and U.S.A.) See also *Fisheries Conservation and Management Act* (U.S.A., 1976), s.2 (crabs, lobsters, deemed continental shelf
resources).
38. Article 6(1).
39. Article 6(2).
40. [1969] *I.C.J. Reports*, p.3.
41. Ibid., p.53.
42. Ibid., p.54.
43. For a criticism of the Court's judgment see Brown, *The Legal Regime of
Hydrospace*, esp. pp.70–71.
44. [1969] *I.C.J. Reports*, p.37.
45. *Report of the International Law Commission*, United Nations General
Assembly, Official Records, 11th Session, Supplement No.9 (1956),
p.44.
46. *The Public Order of the Oceans*, p.729.
47. For an excellent discussion see Hodgson "Islands: Normal and Special
Circumstances", p.176 ff.

4. *The High Seas*

1. Text in *New Directions in the Law of the Sea*, vol.1, p.257.
2. Article 6.
3. Article 5.
4. Ibid.
5. Article 10. See "International Regulations for Preventing Collisions at Sea"
(approved by the International Conference on Safety of Life at Sea in 1960)
in *New Directions in the Law of the Sea*, vol.11, p.511. See also "1971
Amendments to the International Convention on the Safety of Life at Sea"
(relating to traffic separation schemes), ibid., p.505.
6. Article 12(1).
7. Article 12(2).
8. Article 23(1).
9. Article 23(2). Other procedures are set out in the sub-paragraphs of the
Article that follow.
10. Controls on nuclear weaponry testing are set out in the *Treaty Banning
Nuclear Weapon Tests in the Atmosphere, in Outer Space and Under Water*
(1963). Text in *New Directions in the Law of the Sea*, vol.2, p.285. See
also *Treaty on the Prohibition of the Emplacement of Nuclear Weapons
and other Weapons of Mass Destruction on the Seabed and Ocean Floor*

and in the Subsoil thereof (1971), ibid., p.288. The area covered is the area outside the 12 mile limit. (See Article 2 of the Convention).

11. For discussions of the relevant Conventions and rules of international law see M. Hardy, "Definition and Forms of Marine Pollution" in *New Directions in the Law of the Sea*, vol.3, p.73 ff. C.A. Fleischer, "Pollution from Seaborne Sources", ibid., p.78, ff. T.A. Mensah, "International Environmental Law: International Conventions concerning Oil Pollution at Sea", 8 *Case Western Reserve Journal of International Law* (1976), p.110; R.E. Stein, "Responsibility and Liability for Harm to the Marine Environment", 6 *Georgia Journal of International and Comparative Law* (1976), p.41; R.A. Frank, "Protection of the Marine Environment from Pollution", ibid., p.73; E.D. Brown, *The Legal Regime of Hydrospace* (1971), Part 3.

12. Text in *New Directions in the Law of the Sea*, vol.2, pp.557, 567.

13. Text, ibid., p.580.

14. The Convention also defines areas of the sea where discharge is prohibited even beyond 50 miles. (See Annex A.) The "nearest land" is defined as the baseline from which the territorial sea of the territory in question is measured in accordance with the Convention on the Territorial Sea.

15. For an analysis of the original Convention and the amendments made see Brown, *The Legal Regime of Hydrospace*, pp.130–139.

16. Text in 12 *International Legal Materials* (1973), p.1319. For a discussion of the provisions see Mensah, "International Environmental Law", p.117 ff.

17. Ibid., pp.119–121.

18. Text in *New Directions in the Law of the Sea*, vol.2, p.592. See Brown, *The Legal Regime of Hydrospace*, p.139 ff.

19. Maritime casualty is defined in Article 11 as a "collision of ships, stranding, or other incident of navigation, or other occurrence on board a ship or external to it resulting in material damage or imminent threat of material damage to a ship or cargo."

20. Article 5.

21. Text in *New Directions in the Law of the Sea*, vol.2, p.602. See Brown, *The Legal Regime of Hydrospace* (1971), p.164 ff.

22. Article 3.

23. Article 5(1).

24. Article 5(2).

25. Text in 11 *International Legal Materials* (1972), p.1291. See Fleischer, "Pollution from Seaborne Sources", *op. cit.,* pp. 86–88.

26. The following definitions are contained in Article 3. "Special permit" means permission granted specifically on application in advance and in accordance with Annex 2 and Annex 3. "General permit" means permission granted in advance and in accordance with Annex 3.

27. See generally, H.G. Knight, ed; *The Future of International Fisheries Management* (St. Paul, Minnesota: West Publishing Co., 1975).

28. For an analysis of the Articles of the Convention see W.W. Bishop, "The 1958 Geneva Convention on Fishing and Conservation of the Living Resources of the High Seas", 62 *Columbia Law Review* (1962), p.1206.

29. Article 2.

30. Article 4(1).

31. Article 4(2).

32. Article 6.

33. A conservation measure may be framed in such a way that, although no discrimination appears on its face, it may nevertheless discriminate against foreign fishermen because of the nature of the circumstances.
34. Article 9.
35. This would appear to mean that they can be effectively observed in the light of existing fishery practices.
36. See Anderson, "The Geneva· Convention: Ten Years Later", *Proceedings of the Third Annual Conference of the Law of the Sea Institute* (1968), pp.77–78.
37. Bishop, "The 1958 Geneva Convention", *op. cit.*, pp.1228–9.
38. See D.M. Johnston, *The International Law of Fisheries: A Framework for Policy-Oriented Inquiries* (New Haven: Yale University Press, 1965), pp.363–65.
39. Ibid., pp.366–69.
40. This Convention is discussed in "North Pacific Fisheries Symposium" 43 *Washington Law Review* (1967), p.1 ff. As contrasted with the other Convention it enshrines the principle as absention. See D.M. Johnston, "The Japanese-U.S. Salmon Conflict", 43 *Washington Law Review* (1967), p.27. Following the adoption of a 200 miles fisheries conservation and management zone, the United States has given notice of withdrawal from the Treaty.
41. International Convention for the Regulation of Whaling (1946) and 1971 Amendments. See *New Directions in the Law of the Sea*, vol.2, pp.418, 425.
42. For a study of difficult control systems see J.E. Carroz and A.G. Roche. "The International Policing of High Seas Fisheries", *Canadian Year Book of International Law* (1968), p.61.
43. Ibid., p.73.
44. See R. Eisenbud, "Understanding the International Fisheries Debate", 4 *Natural Resources Lawyer* (1971), 1, pp.28–30; J.A. Crutchfield, "Natural Quotas for the North Atlantic Fisheries: An Exercise in Second Best", *Proceedings of the Third Annual Conference on the Law Institute* (1968), p.263.
45. Ibid., p.266.
46. Ibid., p.269 ff.
47. *Fisheries Jurisdiction Case*, [1974] *I.C.J. Reports*, p.3, discussed by R.R. Churchill in 24 *International and Comparative Law Quarterly* (1975), p.82. A similar judgment was also handed down in a second case *Federal Republic of Germany v. Iceland* [1974] *I.C.J. Reports*, p.175.
48. [1974] *I.C.J. Reports*, p.34.
49. Ibid., pp.34–35.
50. Ibid., p.23.
51. Ibid., p.25.
52. Ibid., p.26.
53. See H.G. Knight, "International Fisheries Management without Global Agreement: United States Policies and their Impact on the Soviet Union", 6 *Georgia Journal of International and Comparative Law* (1976), p.119; Churchill, 24 *International and Comparative Law Quarterly* (1975), p.98.
54. See 25 *International and Comparative Law Quarterly* (1976), p.685. Exclusive management rights over fishing in a 200 mile zone were claimed by the United States in the *Fishery Conservation and Management Act* (1976).
55. Described as "landlocked and geographically disadvantaged States".

56. See R.A. Frank "Protection of the Marine Environment from Pollution", 6 *Georgia Journal of International and Comparative Law* (1976), p.73.
57. See R.R. Baxter, "The International Law of Scientific Research in the Oceans" ibid., pp.27, 31 ff.
58. But see Knight, "International Fisheries Management" p.142, n.53.

5. *The Deep Sea-bed*

1. See J.M. Murphy, "Deep Ocean Mining: Beginning of a New Era", 8 *Case Western Reserve Journal of International Law* (1976), p.46, 54 ff; L.M. Alexander, "Future Regimes: A Survey of Proposals", in *New Directions in the Law of the Sea*, vol.3, p.119.
2. Murphy, "Deep Ocean Mining", p.54; Alexander, "Future Regimes", p.126.
3. The Resolution is reproduced in *New Direction in the Law of the Sea* vol.2, p.737.
4. Ibid., p.740.
5. Ibid., p.740, para.9 of Resolutions.
6. Ibid., p.738.
7. For a discussion of the issues see T.M. Franck, "An International Regime for the Seabed beyond National Jurisdiction", 6 *Georgia Journal of International and Comparative Law* (1976), p.151.
8. A. Guilcher, "Geo-Physical Characteristics", in *New Directions in the Law of the Sea*, vol.3, p.109; K.O. Emery, "Geological Aspects of Sea-floor Sovereignty" in *The Law of the Sea: Off-Shore Boundaries and Zones*, ed. L.M. Alexander (1967), pp.139–60.
9. Murphy, "Deep Ocean Mining", p.47. See Franck, "An International Regime", p.172 ff., on the economic problems associated with the mining of the nodules.
10. See above, pp.19 et seq.
11. [1969] *I.C.J. Reports*, p.3, 22.
12. R.Y. Jennings, "The Limits of Continental Shelf Jurisdiction", 18 *International and Comparative Law Quarterly* (1969), pp.819, 831–32. But see Alexander, "Future Regimes", *op. cit.*, p.133, n.43.
13. B. Oxnam, "The Preparation of Article 1 of the Convention on the Continental Shelf", 3 *Journal of Maritime Law and Commerce* (1972), 682, p.715.
14. See Franck, "An International Regime", *op. cit.*, p.155, for an analysis of the distribution of minerals in the various zones.
15. See "The Third United Nations Law of the Sea Conference: The Caracas Session and Its Aftermath", 8 *Case Western Reserve Journal of International Law* (1976), 13, pp.20–22.
16. Based, for example, on the value or volume of production by the coastal State in the area.
17. L. Henkin, *Law for the Sea's Mineral Resources*, (Institute for the Study of Science in Human Affairs, Columbia University, 1969), p.59 ff.
18. See Brown, *The Legal Regime of Hydrospace*, pp.115–23.
19. See L.W. Finlay, "Symposium: The Position of the American Bar Association on the Law of the Sea", 8 *Case Western Reserve Journal of International Law* (1976), pp.84, 97–102.
20. Franck, "An International Regime", pp.159–66.
21. Murphy, "Deep Ocean Mining", *op. cit.*, pp.56–57.

PART II

6. The Law of the Sea and Australian Law

1. The following are the dates on which the Conventions entered into force: Convention on the High Seas, 30 Sept. 1962; Convention on the Continental Shelf, 10 June 1964; Convention on the Territorial Sea and Contiguous Zone, 10 Sept. 1964; and the Convention on Fishing and Conservation of the Living Resources of the High Seas, 20 March 1966. An associated agreement, the Optional Protocol of Signature concerning the Compulsory Settlement of Disputes, entered into force on the 30 Sept. 1962.
2. On the 14 May 1963.
3. See "Table of Ratifications", in *New Directions in the Law of the Sea*, vol.2, pp.799–805.
4. See D.P. O'Connell ed., *International Law in Australia* (Sydney: Law Book Co., 1966) vol.1, p.460.
5. See Article 12 of the Convention.
6. Articles 6, 7, 9, 10, 11, 12, 19.
7. Articles 6, 7, 9.
8. O'Connell, *International Law*, vol.1, p.460.
9. Ibid.
10. [1969] *I.C.J. Reports*, 3, p.39.
11. [1969] *I.C.J. Reports*, 3, p.38.
12. See the *Anglo-Icelandic Fisheries Case*, [1974] *I.C.J. Reports* 3, p.24 ff.
13. See R.R. Churchill, "The Fisheries Jurisdiction Case" 24 *International and Comparative Law Quarterly*, (1974), 82, p.96, n.45.
14. See A.D. McNair, *The Law of Treaties* (Oxford: Clarendon Press, 1969) p.81.
15. [1892] A.C. 491.
16. The exercise of certain prerogatives of the Crown may, however, indirectly affect the rights of a citizen. See *Chow Hung Ching v R.* (1949), 77 C.L.R. 449, p.478.
17. J.G. Starke, *Introduction to International Law*, (London: Butterworths, 1972), pp.79–80. See also *New South Wales v. Commonwealth* (1975) 8 A.L.R. 1, p.76, per Stephen J.
18. Starke, *Introduction to International Law*, p.74.
19. [1876], 2 Ex.D., p.63.
20. (1949), 77 C.L.R., p.449.
21. Ibid., pp.462, 472.
22. Ibid., p.471, citing with approval the dictum of the Privy Council in *Chung Chi Cheung v R.* [1939], A.C. 160, pp.167, 168.
23. [1905], 2 K.B. p.391.
24. See C.H. Alexandrowicz, "International Law in the Municipal Sphere According to Australian Decisions", 13 *International and Comparative Law Quarterly* (1964), 78, p.83.
25. Starke, *Introduction to International Law*, p.38.
26. Alexandrowicz, "International Law in the Municipal Sphere", p.83; J. Seidl-Hohenveldern, "Transformation or Adoption of International Law into Municipal Law", 12 *International and Comparative Law Quarterly* (1963), 88, pp.123–24. However, in the recent Court of Appeal decision *Trendtex Trading Corporation v. Central Bank of Nigeria* [1977] 2 W.L.R. 356

pp.364–65 Lord Denning M.R. expressed the view that the doctrine of incorporation was the correct one in that it gave the courts greater leeway in applying changes in international law.

27. Starke, *Introduction to International Law*, p.39.
28. See *Halsbury's Laws of England*, 3rd edn., vol.7 (London: Butterworths, 1954), pp.279–82.
29. Presumably a certificate of the foreign affairs department would be the appropriate method to be adopted by the government in legal proceedings (in which it was a defendant) in claiming that a certain act was an "Act of State". See *Ffrost* v. *Stevenson* (1937), 58 C.L.R. pp.528, 549, 565–66.
30. [1892] A.C., p.491.
31. *Ridge's Constitutional Law* Forrest ed. (London: Stevens, 1950), p.225.
32. State legislative power over fishing within the 3 mile limit has been exercised from an early period. See *Pearce* v. *Florenca* (1976), 9 A.L.R. 289, p.297, per Gibbs J.
33. 51 Vic. No.1.
34. 52 Vic. No.1.
35. No.149.
36. See Act No.116, 1967.
37. See Part 4 of the Act ("Ships and Shipping").
38. See Part 7 A of the Act ("Prevention of Pollution of Oil of Australian Coast, Coastal Waters and Reefs").
39. *Pollution of Sea by Oil Act* 1960–1973, giving effect to 1954 Convention with 1962 amendments. The *Pollution of the Sea by Oil Act* 1972 purports to give effect to the 1969 amendments but the operative sections of the Act have not yet been proclaimed.
40. No.12.
41. No.85.
42. Each state has also enacted legislation under the title of the *Petroleum (Submerged Lands) Act*. Although there are certain differences which take account of individual state circumstances, the basic principles and the mining code are enshrined in all the Acts.
43. No.161.
44. The original Bill contained an extensive mining code to regulate mining for minerals other than petroleum. This part was, however, deleted by the Senate.
45. (1975), 8 A.L.R. 1.
46. Barwick C.J., McTiernan, Mason, Jacobs and Murphy JJ., Gibbs and Stephen JJ. dissenting.
47. A number of the judges considered that at federation proprietary rights were vested in the Imperial Crown. See below, 73 et seq.
48. See below, p.79.
49. See *Pearce* v. *Florenca* (1976), 9 A.L.R. p.289.

7. *Australian Maritime Zones: Territorial Waters*

1. The low-water mark—the outer limit of the foreshore—would be determined by taking the average of the low spring tides.
2. Blackstone, *Commentaries on the Law of England*, 20th edn., pp.1, 317. *Chitty on the Prerogative*, pp.206–8.
3. Commonwealth legislation may also apply in this area, e.g. the *Navigation*

Act 1912. See the excellent discussion of colonial prerogative rights by Stephen J. in *New South Wales* v. *Commonwealth* (1975), 8 A.L.R. 1, pp.66–68.

4. See *Re Dominion Coal Company Limited and County of Cape Breton* 40 D.L.R., 2d, (1963), 593, and the English authorities referred to therein. Colombos, *International Law and the Sea*, pp.182–83.
5. *Lord Fitzhardinge* v. *Purcell* (1908) 2 Ch., 139, p.166, per Parker, J.
6. *New South Wales* v. *Commonwealth* (1975), 8 A.L.R. 1, p.68, per Stephen J. citing the opinion of Evatt J.
7. The Letters Patent were promulgated in 1836. For a discussion of Australian boundaries, see F.W. Cumbrae-Stewart, "Australian Boundaries", 5 *U.Q.L.J.* (1965), p.1.
8. R.D. Lumb, *The Constitutions of the Australian States* (St. Lucia: University of Queensland Press, 1972), 3rd edn., p.74.
9. *Seas and Submerged Lands Act*, 1973, s.10. See below ch.8., for further discussion.
10. A good definition of the term "coastline" is that contained in the United States *Submerged Lands Act*: "the line of ordinary low water along that portion of the coast which is in direct contact with the open sea and the line marking the seaward limit of inland waters".
11. See below, pp.79–81.
12. 1876) 2 Ex.D., p.63. Keyn was charged with manslaughter in the Central Criminal Court as a result of the collision of his vessel with a British vessel resulting in the death of an English passenger on the latter vessel.
13. E. Campbell, "Regulation of Australian Coastal Fisheries", 1 *Tasmania University Law Review* (1960), 404, p.415.
14. V. Windeyer, "The Seabed in Law", 6 *Fed.L.R.*, 1 (1974) 1, p.16. D.P. O'Connell, "Australian Coastal Jurisdiction", in *International Law in Australia*, ed. O'Connell (Sydney: Law Book Co., 1966), 246, p.250. However, O'Connell, in a later essay adopts the narrower ratio, namely, that it merely established jurisdictional limits. See "The Juridical Nature of the Territorial Sea", 45 *British Year Book of International Law* (1971), pp.303, 372, 377.
15. C.H. Alexandrowicz, "International Law in the Municipal Sphere according to Australian decisions", 13 *International and Comparative Law Quarterly* (1964), 78, p.85.
16. Constitution, s.51 (x).
17. Alexandrowicz, "International Law in the Municipal Sphere". p.85. But see *Bonser* v. *La Macchia* discussed below.
18. The American cases span a period from 1947 to 1975. The Canadian decision was handed down in 1967.
19. Campbell, "Regulation of Australian Coastal Fisheries", p.410 ff.
20. Ibid., p.415.
21. *Chitty on the Prerogative*, pp.206–8.
22. *Secretary of State for India* v. *Chelikani Rama Rao* (1916), L.R. *Ind. App.*, p.199.
23. [1941] St.R. Qd., pp.1, 218.
24. Ibid., p.21 (Mansfield, J.), p.220 (Webb, J.).
25. 41 & 42 Vic. c.73.
26. See J.L. Brierly, *The Law of Nations*, 5th edn. (1963), pp.202 ff.
27. See, for example, Lord *Fitzhardinge* v. *Purcell* (1908), 2 Ch.D. 139, p.166 (Parker, J.).

28. In *D* v. *Commissioner of Taxes* (1941), St.R. Qd 1, p.218, doubts felt by some members of the court on the question of state limits revolved around this point.

29. The American critical date is 1776 (time of separation of the thirteen colonies from England); the Canadian date (in relation to British Columbia) was 1871.

30. The prerogatives being exercised by the Colonial Governors (except in relation to these matters reserved to the Monarch) as the Monarch's representatives and advised by Colonial Ministers.

31. See O'Connell, "Australian Coastal Jurisdiction," p.272 ff.

32. (1940), 63 C.L.R., p.278.

33. Ibid., pp.320–21.

34. Ibid., p.322. My italics.

35. Of the other classes of prerogative, the first are, according to Evatt J., exclusively vested in the commonwealth, while the second class are shared by commonwealth and states.

36. In much the same way as authority over aerial navigation within a state's borders is shared by commonwealth (licensing system based on safety and efficiency requirements) and states (licensing of the transportation of goods and passengers by air within state borders). See *Airlines of New South Wales Pty. Ltd.* v. *State of New South Wales*, (No.2) (1964–65) 113 C.L.R. p.54.

37. The term "Tidelands" was originally used in a more popular sense to describe off-shore maritime areas and not in a technical sense as referring only to the foreshore and inland waters. See J.S. Wright, "The Tidelands and Louisiana's Shoreline", in R. Slovenko, ed. *Oil and Gas Operations: Legal Considerations in the Tidelands and on Land* (Baton Rouge: Claitor's Law Books, 1963), p.20.

38. *U.S.* v. *California* (1947) 332 U.S. 19; *U.S.* v. *Louisiana* (1950) 339 U.S. 599; *U.S.* v. *Texas* (1950) 339 U.S. 707.

39. 67 Stat. 29 (1953), 43 U.S.C. 1301–15 (Supp. 1952), 67 Stat. 462 (1953), 43 U.S.C. 1331–43 (Supp. 1952).

40. *Alabama* v. *Texas* (1954) 347 U.S. 272.

41. This litigation started with *U.S.* v. *Louisiana et al.* in 1960 and has continued to *U.S.* v. *Florida* in 1975. The various cases are discussed in the following pages.

42. Decided 23 June 1975.

43. *U.S.* v. *Maine* (1975) 420 U.S. 515.

44. *Pollard's Lessee* v. *Hogan* (1845) 44 U.S. 212.

45. But see the strong dissenting opinion of Frankfurter J. who argued that the majority opinion confused political rights (*imperium*) and proprietary rights (*dominium*).

46. U.S.C. 1301(1).

47. U.S.C. 1301(b).

48. U.S.C. 1312.

49. *Alabama* v. *Texas* (1954) 347 U.S. 272.

50. *Ibid.*, at p.247.

51. *U.S.* v. *Louisiana et al.* (1960) 363 U.S. 1; *U.S.* v. *Florida* (1960) 363 U.S. 121.

52. 363 U.S. p.33.

53. 363 U.S. p.35.

54. 363 U.S. pp.36 ff., 121.

55. Louisiana, Mississippi, Alabama.

56. Subsequent litigation has dealt with the nature of the coastline of these states. In *U.S.* v. *Louisiana et al.* (1967) 389 U.S. 155 the Court held that the natural shoreline as it existed in 1845, when Texas was admitted to the Union, excluding artificial jetties constructed subsequently, was the basis for determining Texas' claim to its submerged lands. In *U.S.* v. *Louisiana et al.* (1969) 394 U.S. 1, it was held that the coastline of Texas was the modern ambulatory coastline based on the definition of coastline formulated in the Convention on the Territorial Sea, even though the coastline of Texas had been affected substantially by erosion occurring since 1845. In *U.S.* v. *Florida* (1975) 420 U.S. 531, a special Master's Report applying the criteria embodied in the Convention on the Territorial Sea to Florida's coastline was substantially accepted by the Court.
57. 363 U.S., p.35.
58. 363 U.S., p.66.
59. 363 U.S. pp.78–79.
60. 381 U.S. 139.
61. 381 U.S., p.169.
62. 381 U.S., p.165.
63. 381 U.S., p.164.
64. 381 U.S., p.164.
65. 381 U.S., p.168.
66. 381 U.S., p.174.
67. 381 U.S., p.175.
68. 381 U.S., pp.175–76. The line of ordinary low water is obtained by taking the average of all the low tides.
69. 394 U.S. 11.
70. 394 U.S., p.35.
71. 394 U.S., pp.35–66.
72. 394 U.S., p.67.
73. 394 U.S., pp.74–78.
74. (1975) 422 U.S. 184.
75. 422 U.S., p.189.
76. 422 U.S., p.198.
77. 420 U.S., p.515.
78. 420 U.S., p.515.
79. (1967), 65 D.L.R., 2d, p.353.
80. (1876), 2 Ex.D., p.63.
81. Ibid., p.373.
82. Ibid., p.375.
83. Ibid., p.380.
84. (1968–69), 122 C.L.R., p.177. Discussed by O'Connell under the title "The Australian Maritime Domain" 44 *A.L.J.* (1970) p.192.
85. S.7.
86. On 30 November 1954; varied on 7 February 1956.
87. In the view of a majority of judges the fisheries power extended to areas of waters beyond the 3 mile limit. See below, ch.9.
88. 122 C.L.R., p.184 ff. (Barwick C.J.), 220 ff. (Windeyer J.).
89. 122 C.L.R., p.202 ff.
90. 122 C.L.R., p.189 (Barwick C.J.), pp.223–24 (Windeyer J.).
91. See *Airlines of New South Wales* v. *State of New South Wales* (No.2), (1964–65) 113 C.L.R., p.54.
92. In its basic features the Bill had been introduced by the Gorton government

some years earlier but had been shelved owing to opposition from the states and differences within the federal coalition parties.

93. (1975), 8 A.L.R. 1.
94. 8 A.L.R., p.10 ff. (Barwick C.J.); 20 ff. (McTiernan J.), 82 ff. (Mason J.); 99 ff. (Jacobs J.); 118 ff. (Murphy J.)
95. (1950) 339 U.S. 707, p.719.
96. 8 A.L.R., p.6.
97. 8 A.L.R., pp.82–84 (Mason J.); 99–103 (Jacobs J.). The one exception was South Australia. The Letters Patent establishing its boundaries included gulfs and bays, See ibid., p.83 (Mason J.). On this question see W.R. Edeson "Australian Bays", *Australian Year Book of International Law*, (1968) pp.1, 14 ff.
98. 8 A.L.R. p.12 (Barwick C.J.); p.85 (Mason J.); p.108 (Jacobs J.). Consequently its ratio was not restricted to the exercise of criminal jurisdiction over foreigners committing acts within territorial waters.
99. 8 A.L.R., p.85. Mason J. was referring to the judgment of Coleridge C.J., Grove and Denman J.J. in *Harris* v. *Owners of Franconia* (1877) 2 *C.P.D.*, pp.173, pp.177–78.
100. [1900], A.C. 48, p.66.
101. [1908], 2 Ch. 139, pp.166–67.
102. (1926), L.R. 43 Ind App., p.192.
103. 8 A.L.R., p.87. He considered however that the decision in *Chelikani's Case* could be supported on the basis of the principle that islands formed within the territorial sea by accretion belonged to the coastal state.
104. 8 A.L.R., p.7.
105. Ibid., pp.7–8.
106. Ibid., pp.85–86. See also ibid., p.110 (Jacobs J.). V. Windeyer, "The Seabed in Law", 6 *Fed. L.R.* (1974), 1 p.16 ff.
107. 8 A.L.R., p.23 ff.
108. Ibid., p.34.
109. Ibid., p.38.
110. Ibid., p.39.
111. Ibid., p.40.
112. 8 A.L.R. p.57 ff. See in particular ibid., p.61.
113. 8 A.L.R., pp.14–15 (Barwick C.J.); 90 (Mason J.); 104, 108–10 (Jacobs J.).
114. *Williams* v. *Attorney-General for New South Wales* (1913), 16 C.L.R., p.404.
115. (1911), 12 C.L.R., pp.667, 710.
116. *Attorney-General for New South Wales* v. *Butterworth and Co. (Aust) Ltd* (1938), 38 S.R., (N.S.W.), p.195.
117. 8 A.L.R. p.67. See also Marston, "Colonial Enactments relating to the Legal Status of Offshore Submerged Lands", 50 A.L.J. (1976), pp.402, 408–9.
118. 8 A.L.R., p.16. But see O'Connell's criticism of this line of reasoning in "The Juridical Nature of the Territorial Sea", 45 *British Year Book of International Law* (1971), 303, pp.308–91.
119. Viz., until at some time *after* the Statute of Westminster.
120. 8 A.L.R., p.90.
121. 8 A.L.R., p.43 (Gibbs J.); p.70 (Stephen J.).
122. "The Commonwealth of Australia Bill" (1900), 16 *L.Q.R.* 35, pp.39–40. G. Sawer, "Australian Constitutional Law in Relation to International Relations and International Law", in *International Law in Australia*, ed.

O'Connell, p.35; J. Starke, "Australia and the International Labour Organisation", ibid., pp.121–23.
123. S.51 (x), for example.
124. *Annotated Constitution of the Commonwealth of Australia*, pp.631–32.
125. See *R* v. *Foster, ex parte Eastern and Australian Steamship Co.* (1958–59), 103 C.L.R., p.256.
126. *R* v. *Burgess ex parte Henry* (1936), 55 C.L.R. p.608.
127. Ibid., p.646 ff.
128. *R* v. *Poole ex parte Henry* (1939), 61 C.L.R. p.634.
129. 55 C.L.R., p.669.
130. Ibid., pp.643–44.
131. Ibid., pp.680–81.
132. Ibid., p.669.
133. Reliance was also placed on S.51(i)—the overseas and interstate trade and commerce power.
134. *Airlines of New South Wales Pty. Ltd* v. *State of New South Wales*, No.2 (1964–65), 113 C.L.R., pp.54, 85–86.
135. Ibid., p.102 ff.
136. Ibid., p.136.
137. See for example, the *Whaling Act* 1960, s.26(2). The *Whaling Act* is partially dependent on the external affairs power (Australia being a party to the International Convention on Whaling).
138. 8 A.L.R. pp.6 (Barwick C.J.); 91 (Mason J.); 12 (Jacobs J.).
139. Ibid., p.118.
140. Ibid., p.6 (Barwick C.J.); 17–18 (McTiernan J.); 91 (Mason J.).
141. Ibid., p.26 (Gibbs J.); 76–77 (Stephen J.).
142. Ibid., p.76.
143. See above ch.2.
144. As reflected in various ministerial statements of government policy.
145. See O'Connell "Australian Coastal Jurisdiction" in *International Law in Australia* 246 p.272 ff.
146. The recognition of this right as a prerogative right is to be found in the action taken in 1964 by the British government in establishing a baseline system by Order in Council pursuant to the Convention of the Territorial Sea and Contiguous Zone. See "Developments in the Law of the Sea 1958–1964" *British Institute of International and Comparative Law*, Special Publication No.6, (1965). See also *Post Office v. Estuary Radio* (1968) 2 Q.B. p.740.
147. See for example, the judgment of Jacobs J: 8 A.L.R., p.109.
148. Ibid., p.89.
149. It will be recalled that no breadth of territorial sea is specified in the *Convention on the Territorial Sea*. See above ch.2.
150. That is, assuming a line of demarcation as distinct from a "joint use" policy is agreed upon by the parties. See below, ch.10, pp.120 et seq.
151. See Lumb, *The Maritime Boundaries of Queensland and New South Wales*, University of Queensland, Faculty of Law Paper (1964).
152. It appears that this issue is related to the drawing of a sea-bed line of demarcation in the Torres Strait. See below, ch.10, pp.120 et seq.
153. See below, ch.10, p.123.
154. (1976) 9 A.L.R. 289.
155. Defined by 3(1) of the *Fisheries Act* 1905–1975 (W.A.) as including the sea from "high water mark to 3 nautical miles from the low water mark."

156. The general test of "peace welfare and good government" was laid down In *Croft* v. *Dunphy* [1933], A.C., 156, p.163. See 9 A.L.R. p.294 ff. (Gibbs J.) for a discussion of the test and its application to legislation applying in off-shore waters.
157. See 16(b) of the Act.
158. 9 A.L.R. p.297.
159. Ibid., p.303.
160. Ibid., p.304.
161. See below, pp.116–18.
162. Note S.15B(4) of the *Acts Interpretation Act* 1976, which defines the coastal sea of Australia as meaning "(i) the territorial sea of Australia; and (ii) the sea on the landward side of the territorial sea of Australia not within the limits of a State or internal territory, and includes the airspace over, and the sea-bed and subsoil beneath, any such sea ...". This section recognizes a composite Australian National Sea comprising the territorial sea and that portion of internal waters which did not inhere in any State at federation.

8. *Internal Waters*

1. For a discussion of Australian law and practice relating to bays see D.P. O'Connell, "Australian Coastal Jurisdiction" in *International Law in Australia* (Sydney: Law Book Co., 1966) 246, p.262 ff; W.R. Edeson, "Australian Bays" in *Australian Year Book of International Law* (1968), p.5; W.R. Edeson, "The Validity of Australia's Possible Maritime Historic Claims in International Law" 48 *Australian Law Journal* (1974), p.295.
2. That is, approval by federal parliament, the state parliament and the electorate of the state concerned. See *New South Wales* v. *Commonwealth* (1975), 8 A.L.R. 1, p.89 (Mason J.).
3. See, for example, *The Fargenes* [1927] P.311.
4. That is until the passage of the *Seas and Submerged Lands Act*, s.7 of which refers to the method of demarcating the baseline of the territorial sea in accordance with the Convention on the Territorial Sea and Contiguous Zone.
5. For example, *Harbours Act* (S.A.) 1936. s.43.
6. "Australian Coastal Jurisdiction", p.266.
7. Ibid.
8. The 1952 *Fisheries Act* was amended in 1967. The 1967 amendment defines the "declared fishing zone" within which foreign fishing is controlled as extending 12 miles from the territorial sea baseline. The outer limits of "Australian waters" are established by proclamations made under the Act.
9. *Territorial Waters Order in Council* (1964). See *Post Office* v. *Estuary Radio* [1968], 2 Q.B. 740.
10. (1918), 25 C.L.R. 32.
11. (1937), 58 C.L.R. p.528, 549.
12. (1949), 77 C.L.R. p.449, 467.
13. (1968–69), 122 C.L.R. pp.117, 193–94 (Barwick C.J.); 208 (Kitto J.); 217 (Windeyer J.).
14. At common law waters within the jaws of the land (*inter fauces terrae*) were treated as internal waters of the realm. See *Bonser* v. *La Macchia* 122 C.L.R. 177, p.233 per Windeyer J. See also Edeson, "Australian Bays" p.18 ff.

15. The *Acts Interpretation Act* 1976, s.4, treats the coastal sea pertaining to Australia as comprising (a) the territorial sea of Australia and (b) the sea on the landward side of the territorial sea and not within the limits of a state or territory.
16. See above, Ch.2.
17. Article 7, par.5.
18. See O'Connell "Australian Coastal Jurisdiction", p.262 ff. Edeson, "Australian Bays", n.1.
19. O'Connell, "Australian Coastal Jurisdiction", p.264.
20. *The Regime of Bays in International Law* (1964), p.101.
21. Strohl, *The International Law of Bays* (1963), pp.253–55.
22. *United Nations Conference on the Law of the Sea, Official Records*, 1, Preparatory Documents, 8–9 (1958).
23. A.H. Charteris, *Chapters on International Law* (1942), p.99.
24. *The International Law of Bays*, p.255.
25. Ibid., p.267.
26. L.J. Bouchez, The Regime of Bays in International Law, p.305. D. Pharand, *The Law of the Sea of the Arctic* (1973), pp.99–116. See also *United Nations Conference on the Law of the Sea, Official Records*, 1, p.28 ff. (1958). See also the American cases cited above, Ch.7, and *Re Dominion Coal Company Limited and County of Cape Breton* (1963), 40 D.L.R. (2d), p.593.
27. O'Connell, "Australian Coastal Jurisdiction", p.246. See also Edeson, "The Validity of Australia's Possible Maritime Historic Claims in International Law" 48 *A.L.J.*, (1974) pp.295, 298–300; as to the status of Van Diemen's Gulf see particularly, pp.303–4.
28. Subject to the conditions of "historic title" being proved: *The International Law of Bays*, p.64. But this is doubtful. See Edeson, "The Validity of Australia's Claims" p.302; Lumb, "Sovereignty and Jurisdiction over Australian Coastal Waters", 43 *A.L.J.* (1969), 421, p.423.
29. Ibid., p.265.
30. Ibid.
31. It is on this ground that Mason J. in *New South Wales* v. *Commonwealth* (1975), 8 A.L.R., 1, p.83 considered that the gulfs were part of South Australia. The High Court has recently held in *Raptis and Son* v. *State of South Australia* that the Gulfs (but not Investigator Strait) are internal waters of South Australia.
32. C.J. Colombos, *The International Law of the Sea*, 6th edn. (1967), p.190.
33. Strohl, *The International Law of Bays*, pp.60–61. See also the application of the Convention to the American coastline in *California II* and *Louisiana II*, above, Ch.7, pp.64 et seq.
34. See Edeson, "The Validity of Australia's Claims" p.303, n.26.
35. Article 4(4).
36. Article 4(3).
37. For an excellent discussion of the policy factors involved in the adoption of a straight baseline system, see M.S. McDougal and W.T. Burke, *The Public Order of the Oceans*, (New Haven: Yale University Press, 1962) pp.402–11.
38. As to the relationship of this provision with Article 11 see below, pp.95 et seq.
39. [1951] *I.C.J. Reports*, p.116. See above ch.2.
40. [1951] *I.C.J. Reports*, p.130.
41. McDougal and Burke, *The Public Order of the Oceans*, p.385.
42. Ibid., pp.386–87.

43. Ibid., p.387.
44. The power of determining such baselines is vested in the governor-general under s.7 of the *Seas and Submerged Lands Act*.
45. See Lumb, "Sovereignty and Jurisdiction over Australian Coastal Waters" (1969) 43 *Australian Law Journal* (1969), 421, p.424. Mr. Justice Mason, ibid., at p.441. Note, however, the seemingly contrary opinion expressed by the Imperial Law Officers in 1875: D.P. O'Connell and A. Riordan, *Opinions on Imperial Constitutional Law*, pp.194–95. Of course, the method of determining internal waters as provided for in the Convention differs from customary international law pre-dating the Convention.
46. See Edeson, "The Validity of Australia's Claims" pp.303–4, n.26.
47. Strohl, *The International Law of Bays*, pp.60–61.
48. "The Geneva Conference on the Law of the Sea: Possible Implications for Australia", 32 *A.L.J.* (1958), pp.134, 135.
49. Strohl, *The International Law of Bays*, p.65. And see Edeson, "The Validity of Australia's Claims", pp.298–300, n.26. See now *Raptis and Son* v. *State of South Australia* referred to in fn. 31.
50. Above, ch.2, p.14. McDougal and Burke, *The Public Order of the Oceans*, p.397.
51. O'Connell, "Australian Coastal Jurisdiction", p.270.
52. Article 11.
53. Above, ch.2, pp.15–16.
54. As in circumstances where the "enclaves" are small in area and entirely surrounded by territorial seas.
55. But see O'Connell, "Mid-Ocean Archipelagos in International Law", 45 *British Yearbook of International Law* (1972), 1 pp.1–4, who refers to nineteenth-century Imperial practice which did not favour such enclosures. But the practice was not uniform. Present international legal opinion is now moving in favour of adopting an archipelagic principle. See the conclusion of O'Connell, ibid., pp.74–78.

9. *Fishery Zones*

1. Introduced by Act No. 116 of 1967. See Lumb "Sovereignty and Jurisdiction over Australian Coastal Waters", 43 *A.L.J.* (1969), 421, p.437.
2. Proclamations of 9 December 1954 and 11 February 1956. See *Bonser* v. *La Macchia* (1968–69), 122 C.L.R. pp.177, 182–83 (Barwick C.J.); 199–200 (Kitto J.).
3. The waters adjacent to a territory and within territorial limits are subject to commonwealth legislative power under s.122 of the Constitution (the territories power).
4. (1968–69), 122 C.L.R. p.177.
5. 122 C.L.R. p. 170 (Barwick C.J.); 198 (McTiernan J.); 202 (Kitto J.); 211 (Menzies J.); 235 (Owen J.); *Contra*, Windeyer J., pp.226–31.
6. 122 *C.L.R.*, pp.190–91.
7. Ibid., p.192.
8. (1975), 8 A.L.R. p.1.
9. *Pearce* v. *Florenca* (1976), 9 A.L.R. 289. See below, ch. 11, p.124.
10. See *Chen Yin Ten* v. *Little* [1976], 11 A.L.R. 353.
11. As contained in the Convention on the Territorial Sea and Contiguous Zone. See *Bonser* v. *La Macchia* (1968–69), 122 C.L.R., 177, p.232 (Windeyer J.).

12. That is, until mid-1974. See *Treaty Series*, 1969, No.22
13. See *Commonwealth of Australia Gazette*, No.8 of 16 February 1956.
14. 122 C.L.R. pp.193–94 (Barwick C.J.); 207–8 (Kitto J.); 217 (Windeyer J.).
15. Ibid., p.208.
16. See above, ch.4, p.36, and below, ch.12, p.151.

10. *The Continental Shelf*

1. A map of the Australian continental shelf is to be found in L.F.E. Goldie, "Australia's Continental Shelf: Legislation and Proclamations", 3 *International and Comparative Law Quarterly* (1954), 535, p.536–37.
2. *Commonwealth of Australia Gazette* (1953), p.2563.
3. The Pearl Fisheries legislation comprised Act No.8 of 1952 and Acts No.4 and 38, 1953. For a discussion of the legislation see Goldie "Australia's Continental Shelf", n.1., and O'Connell, "Sedentary Fisheries and the Australian Continental Shelf", 49 *American Journal of International Law* (1955), p.185.
4. *The Queensland Pearl Shell and Bêche-de-mer Fisheries (Extra-territorial) Act* No. 1 of 1888. *The Western Australian Pearl Shell and Bêche-de-mer Fisheries Act (Extra-territorial) Act* No. 1 of 1889.
5. *Pearl Fisheries Act*, s.8.
6. S.5(1). By proclamation made in 1958 all Australian waters north of the parallel of 27 degrees south latitude (roughly, waters above a line extending from Gantheaume Bay in Western Australia to Moreton Bay in Queensland) were declared proclaimed waters. See *Commonwealth of Australia Gazette* (1958), p.1339.
7. S.5(3).
8. Goldie, "Australia's Continental Shelf: Legislation and Proclamations", pp.538–39.
9. Ibid., p.568.
10. See Lumb, *The Maritime Boundaries of Queensland and New South Wales*, p.9 ff. *Coral Sea Islands Act* 1969.
11. See above, p.115.
12. See W.A. Wynes, *Legislative, Executive and Judicial Powers in Australia*, 3rd edn, p.190, n.19.
13. Below. pp.108 et seq.
14. See L.F. Goldie, "Symposium on the Geneva Conventions", in Alexander, ed, *The Law of the Sea: Off-Shore Boundaries and Zones* pp. 85–90.
15. See Bowett, *The Law of the Sea*, p.36.
16. S. Oda, *International Control of Sea Resources* (Leiden: A.W. Sythoff, 1963), p.193.
17. F.V. Garcia Amador, *The Exploitation and Conservation of the Resources of the Sea* (Leiden: A.W. Sijthoff, 1959), p.128.
18. See the opinions cited in M.M. Whiteman, *Digest of International Law*, vol.4, pp.856 ff.
19. Goldie, "Symposium on the Geneva Conventions", pp.287–88. The King crab (and lobster) are specified as sedentary resources under recent American legislation.
20. See comment by Azzam on the France–Brazil Lobster Dispute 13 *I.C.L. Q.* (1964), p.1453.

21. K. Bailey, "Australia and the Geneva Conventions", in *International Law in Australia* (1966), 228, p.236.
22. 51 Vict. No.1.
23. 52 Vict. No.2.
24. Queensland Act, s.19; Western Australia Act, s.2.
25. S.9.
26. S.10.
27. *Pearl Fisheries Act* No.38 of 1953, s.4 amending s.6 of the principal Act.
28. No. 149.
29. S.5. This arises from the definitions of "continental shelf", "Australian continental shelf" and the "continental shelf of a Territory" in this section. However, the Act makes a distinction between the Australian continental shelf, viz. the shelf of the Commonwealth of Australia (comprising the states and the internal territories) and the continental shelves of the external territories.
30. S.9.
31. S.11.
32. S.12.
33. S.13.
34. *Commonwealth of Australia Gazette* (1970), p.2315. See Lumb, "Australian Legislation on Sedentary Resources of the Continental Shelf", 7 *U.Q.L.J.* (1970), p.111.
35. See below, ch.11, pp.126 et seq.
36. Agreement relating to the Exploration of and the Exploitation of the Petroleum Resources and certain other Resources of the Continental Shelf of Australia and of certain other Submerged Lands (October, 1967), Preamble.
37. See above, ch.7.
38. See *Petroleum (Submerged Lands) Act*, Second Schedule.
39. Agreement, cl.11.
40. Ibid., cl.14.
41. *Annex to the Agreement: Memorandum of Understanding Concerning Trade Between the States and the Territories* (October, 1967).
42. See *Petroleum (Submerged Lands) (Royalty) Act* 1967, s.5.
43. Agreement, cl.19.
44. *Petroleum (Submerged) Lands Act*, s.42.
45. Ibid., s.9.
46. For instance, s.10 of the Act invests the Courts of a state with federal jurisdiction in all matters arising under the applied provisions having effect in the adjacent area.
47. On the "intention" of this section see C.H. Harders, "Australia's Off-Shore Petroleum Legislation: A Survey of its Constitutional Background and its Federal Features", 6 *Melbourne University Law Review* (1968), pp.415, 427.
48. See Hansard, Senate, 1967, First Session (2nd Period), p.2337.
49. *Interim Report of the Senate Select Committee on Off-Shore Petroleum Resources* (September, 1970).
50. Ibid., p.126.
51.(1975), 8 A.L.R. p.1.
52. 1975), 8 A.L.R. 1 p.9. In view of Barwick C.J. the sovereign rights extended down the incline (slope). See 8 A.L.R. p.17.
53. Ibid., p.49.

54. Ibid., p.81.
55. Ibid., p.92.
56. S.16(a).
57. The legislation has been examined by O'Connell, in "Australian Coastal Jurisdiction" in *International Law in Australia* (1966), 246, pp.261–62.
58. (1968–69) 122 C.L.R. p.189.
59. Ibid., p.226.
60. (1975) 8 A.L.R. 1, p.111.
61. (1976), 9 A.L.R. 289, p.298.
62. Ibid., pp.301–2.
63. Most state acts and also the common law apply within territorial limits (i.e. to low-water mark). Consequently, in order for these laws to operate beyond these limits, it will be necessary for the state parliaments to specifically extend their operation where required to off-shore waters. See below ch.11, p.144.
64. This is a requirement of state constitutional law. See *Pearce* v. *Florenca* (1976), 9 A.L.R. 289 pp.294–96 (Gibbs J.).
65. *Seas and Submerged Lands Act*, s.16(b).
66. Constitution, s.109.
67. On the question of state legislation applying beyond the 3 mile limit see O'Connell, "Australian Coastal Jurisdiction", pp.276–79. State legislation is usually based on the connection of residency or use of state-based facilities. See below ch.11, p.145.
68. Ibid.
69. Consequently, it would appear that state mining or resources legislation which vests ownership of minerals *other than* petroleum in the state Crown is invalid.
70. These islands were annexed to the Northern Territory by the *Ashmore and Cartier Islands Acceptance Act* 1933, s.16. See the *Petroleum (Ashmore and Cartier Islands) Act* 1967 as to the operation of the petroleum legislation in this area. See also the *Coral Sea Islands Act* 1969–1973, providing for the government of islands in the Coral Sea.
71. See *Treaty Series*, 1973, No.3, for text.
72. See *Treaty Series*, 1973, No.32, for text.
73. See *Treaty Series*, 1974, No.26, for text.
74. For example the Norwegian Trough in the North Sea. See Brown, *The Legal Regime of the Hydrospace* (1971), p.7, n.15.
75. See "Territorial Boundary between Australia and Indonesia" Ministerial Statement, Hansard, House of Representatives (1972), p.2287. J.R. Prescott, *The Political Geography of Oceans* (Newton Abbott: David & Charles, 1975), p.194, points out that an area of 1,350 sq. miles for which exploration rights had been granted was ceded to Indonesia by Australia. See map of boundaries, ibid., p.193.
76. By amendments to the boundaries delineated in the Second Schedule.
77. *Continental Shelf (Living Natural Resources) Regulations.* See *Statutory Rules* 1974, Nos. 213, 214.
78. [1969] *I.C.J. Reports* p.3.
79. See above ch.3, pp.24 et seq.
80. [1969] *I.C.J. Reports* p.53.
81. Ibid., p.37.
82. R.D. Hodgson, "Islands: Normal and Special Circumstances", in *Law of the Sea: The Emerging Regime of the Oceans*. Proceedings of the Law of

the Sea Institute, Rhode Island (1973), 137, p.176 ff. See also D.J. Padwa, "Submarine Boundaries", 9 *I.C.L.Q.* (1960), 628 p. 649–50. Brown, *The Legal Regime of Hydrospace*, p.64.

83. See Lumb, *The Maritime Boundaries of Queensland and New South Wales* (1964), p.8.

84. Lumb, "The Border Problem between Papua New Guinea and Australia: Legal Issues" 13 *World Review* (1974), 45, p.48.

85. The chronology of the negotiations is set out in 46 *Australian Foreign Affairs Record*, (October 1975), 586, pp.587–88.

86. 47 *Australian Foreign Affairs Record* (June 1976), p.336.

87. *The Torres Strait Boundary: Report by the Sub Committee on Territorial Boundaries* (1976).

88. Approval by the federal parliament, the state parliament and the electorate of the state voting at a referendum.

89. *National Seas Act*, 1977.

11. *Legislation Applying In Australian Off-Shore Waters*

1. Above, ch.7 p.82.

2. *R.* v. *Foster, ex parte Eastern and Australian Steamship Co.* (1958–59) 103 C.L.R. 256. Under s.4 of the *Acts Interpretation Act* 1976, it is provided that, except in so far as a contrary intention appears, the provisions of every Act, whether passed before or after the commencement of the section, shall be taken to have effect in and in relation to the coastal sea of Australia as if the coastal sea were part of Australia.

3. State legislation may also affect operations outside the 3-mile limit by forbidding or regulating the landing or processing in state territory of fish caught outside the 3-mile limit.

4. Above ch.9, pp.98 et seq.

5. S.4.

6. This Act which *inter alia*, gives effect to provisions of the International Whaling Convention, 1946, as amended, applies both to Australian waters and other waters. See s.5.

7. S.13 AB.

8. S.8.

9. S.9.

10. Ibid.

11. S.9A.

12. S.10.

13. Above, ch.10, pp.111–12.

14. S.11.

15. S.12.

16. S.13.

17. S.15.

18. S.14.

19. S.23.

20. Above ch.10, p.112.

21. Contained in Part III of the *Petroleum (Submerged Lands) Act* (Cwth).

22. As provided for in the *Petroleum (Submerged Lands) Act* (Cwth), s.11.

23. *Agreement*, cl.19.

24. As provided for pursuant to ch.9 of the Agreement and ss.14 and 15 of the Act.
25. Agreement, cl.11.
26. Ibid, ch.11(2).
27. Above, pp.75 et seq.
28. Agreement, cl.26.
29. *Petroleum (Submerged Lands) Act*, s.11(2).
30. S.150.
31. S.10.
32. As required by *Judiciary Act*, s.39. See for example, *Petroleum (Submerged Lands) Act* (Vic.) No. 7591 of 1967, s.15(3). Cf.s.10(3) of the Commonwealth Act.
33. S.14 provides: "There shall be, for the purposes of this Act, in respect of each adjacent area, a Designated Authority."
34. S.15(1). Under S.15(4) of the Act.
35. See, for example, *Petroleum (Submerged Lands) Act* (Vic) s.16(1).
36. S.17.
37. *Parliamentary Debates*, H.R., (1967), p.1947 (Second Reading Speech on the Bill).
38. Ibid.
39. S.28.
40. S.29.
41. S.31.
42. S.33.
43. Ss.34, 35.
44. S.36.
45. S.37. No operations for the recovery of petroleum may be carried on without a licence: s.39.
46. S.40. However, it is provided that a permittee may take up a lesser number of blocks than the number to which it is entitled: S.40(2).
47. *Petroleum (Submerged Lands) Royalty Act* (Cwth), s.5(2).
48. S.42.
49. S.52.
50. S.53.
51. See *Parliamentary Debates*, H.R. (1967), p.1958 (Second Reading Speech).
52. S.56.
53. S.58.
54. S.59.
55. S.60. See also *Pipeline Authority Act* 1973, which may impliedly vary these provisions of the Act.
56. S.66.
57. Ss.67, 68.
58. S.72. In this case there is a right of appeal to the Supreme Court of a state.
59. S.73.
60. S.76.
61. S.78.
62. S.83.
63. S.88.
64. That is, to conserve marine resources.
65. S.97.
66. S.107(a).

67. S.107(c).
68. S.119.
69. S.124.
70. *Petroleum (Submerged Lands (Royalty) Act; Petroleum (Submerged Lands) (Exploration Permit Fees) Act; Petroleum (Submerged Lands) (Production Licences) Act; Petroleum (Submerged Lands) (Pipeline Licence Fees) Act; Petroleum (Submerged Lands) (Registration Fees) Act*, all of 1967.
71. Division 8 of the Acts.
72. S.129
73. See Agreement, cl.19(1)(b).
74. Above, ch.4, p.29.
75. S.6(1).
76. S.6(4) and see s.6(2).
77. See s. 7(1)(b).
78. S.2(2). For these amendments see above, Ch.4. It should be noted that an amendment to the Convention was adopted in 1971 to give special protection to the Great Barrier Reef. Under the amendment (which at the time of writing had not entered into force) the outer line of the Great Barrier Reef is designated as the "nearest land" for the purpose of delineating the boundary of the prohibited zone in the Australian region.
79. Above, ch.4, p.29.
80. (1975), 8 A.L.R. p.1.
81. S.329J.
82. S.329R (3)–(8).
83. S.329K(3).
84. S.329K(4).
85. S.329K(5).
86. See Article 5(1) of the Convention.
87. S.101.
88. No.12 of 1975.
89. No.85 of 1975.
90. S.6(1).
91. Such international agreements are specified in a schedule to the Act. Under s.69(1) the governor-general may make regulations to give effect to any of these agreements.
92. S.7(1).
93. S.7(7).
94. S.10(2).
95. See s.10(5), 10(6).
96. S.11.
97. S.12.
98. S.15.
99. S.6.
100. See s.20.
101. S.7.
102. S.30.
103. The Region is defined in s.3 of the Act as meaning (a) the area described in the schedule, and (b) such area (if any) contiguous with the northern boundary of that area as is prescribed, other than any part of such area that is referred to in s.14 of the Seas and *Submerged Lands Act* 1973 or is an island, or a part of an island that forms part of Queensland and is

not owned by Australia. The Schedule lists the northern part of the Region as commencing at the point that is the intersection of the coastline at mean low-water by the parallel of latitude 10°41' south. The area north of this in the Torres Strait *may* be prescribed as part of the Region, by the governor–general.

104. S.31(1).
105. S.31(2).
106. S.32.
107. S.34(2).
108. S.32(7).
109. S.33.
110. S.36.
111. S.38.
112. This definition of the "national estate" is in conformity with the Convention on Natural and Cultural Property to which the Commonwealth is a party. The implementation of the Convention on Wildlife (see above) raises a question of constitutional competence, i.e. whether the external affairs power (s.51 (xxix)) would support such legislation in so far as it operates *within* the territorial limits of Australia. A mere listing of the items of the national estate is within power but any regulatory powers in relation to matters not "indisputably in character" (see Dixon J. in *Burgess Case* (1936), 55 *C.L.R.* 608, p.669) may fall outside power.
113. (1975), 8 A.L.R. 1.
114. See s.478. For a discussion of the earlier cases see W.A. Wynes, *Legislative Executive and Judicial Powers in Australia*, 5th edn. (1976), pp.61–65.
115. See ss.1, 2, 3, 4, 742.
116. See ss.2, 6, 7.
117. *Merchant Shipping Act*, s.2. For exceptions see s.2.
118. *Merchant Shipping Act*, s.1.
119. *Merchant Shipping Act*, s.4.
120. Under amending legislation, the provisions of Part II do not apply to visiting British ships.
121. See *R.* v. *Turner, ex parte Marine Board of Hobart* (1927), 39 C.L.R. p.411.
122. See above, pp.132–33.
123. See above, ch.4, p.28.
124. See s. 187A (definition of "international voyage"), and ss.187D–192C.
125. Under Division 14 of Part 4, obligations are imposed on masters of ships, including foreign ships in certain circumstances, to furnish port officials with sailing plans and position reports while in the prescribed area (which is the area for which Australia has accepted search and rescue responsibility). See clauses 269B–269M of the Navigation Act Amendment Bill 1976. (At the time of writing these amendments had not been proceeded with.)
126. Part 8 entitled Limitation and Exclusion of Shipowners' Liability gives effect to the 1957 Brussels Convention relating to the limitation of liability of sea-going ships. See cl.333 of the Navigation Act Amendment Bill 1976.
127. For an analysis of the development of Admiralty jurisdiction see *R.* v. *Keyn* (1876) L.R. 2 Ex.D. p.63.
128. Previous to the Act, such jurisdiction was exercised by Vice-Admiralty courts in the British possessions.

129. See *Union Steamship Co. of New Zealand Ltd.* v. *Ferguson* (1967–68), 119 C.L.R. p.191, p.198 ff. (Windeyer J.).
130. See *"The Mecca"* (1895), P.95, 107 (Lindley L.J.).
131. S.7.
132. See the cases discussed in *Nagrint* v. *"The Regis"* (1939), 61 C.L.R. p.688. *Union Steamship Co. of New Zealand* v. *Ferguson* (1967–68), 119 C.L.R., 191, pp.202–3 (Windeyer J.).
133. (1967–68), 119 C.L.R. p.191 (Windeyer J.); 204 (on appeal to the Full Court).
134. Kitto, Menzies and Owen J.J.: 119 C.L.R., pp.209–12.
135. Ibid., p.209.
136. See *"The Woron"* [1927], A.C., p.986.
137. (1965), 112 C.L.R., p.295.
138. Ibid., p.298.
139. *McIlwraith McEacharn Ltd.* v. *Shell Co. of Australia Ltd.* (1945), 77 C.L.R., 175, pp.208–9 (Dixon J.). See also Z. Cowen, *Federal Jurisdiction in Australia* (Melbourne: Oxford University Press, 1959), pp.62–65.
140. See above, ch.7, p.78.
141. *Bonser* v. *La Macchia* (1968–69), 122 C.L.R. p.117; *Hume* v. *Palmer* (1926), 38 C.L.R., 441.
142. (1976), 9 A.L.R. p.289.
143. (1974), 3 A.L.R. p.171.
144. (1976), 11 A.L.R. p.142. See also *R.* v. *Robinson* (1976) W.A.R. 155.
145. 30 Geo. 3, c.37.
146. 12 & 13 Vict. c.96.
147. 37 & 38 Vict. c.27.
148. 57 & 58 Vict. c.60.
149. See *R.* v. *Mount* (1875), L.R. 6 P.C., pp.283, 301.
150. (1974), 3 A.L.R. p.171.
151. Ibid., p.217.
152. Ibid., p.205.
153. That is, under the common law or *Imperial* enactments.
154. (1974), 3 A.L.R. p.190.
155. Ibid., p.222.
156. Ibid., p.231.
157. [1975], W.A.R. p.120.
158. (1976), 11 A.L.R. p.142.
159. S.7.
160. The vessel was a vessel "not propelled by oars" and was therefore within the definition of "ship" in s.6 of the Act and it was on the "high seas" (See s.2(1)(b) of the Act.)
161. (1976), 9 A.L.R. p.289.
162. See, for example, the *Criminal Code Amendment Act* (Qld), No. 25 of 1976.
163. *Treaty Banning Nuclear Weapons Tests in the Atmosphere, in Outer Space and under Water* (the "Partial Test Ban Treaty") of 1963. For text see Australian Treaty Series, 1963, No. 26.
164. *Treaty on the Prohibition of the Emplacement of Nuclear Weapons and other Weapons of Mass Destruction on the Sea-bed and the Ocean Floor and in the Subsoil thereof.* For text see *Australian Treaty Series,* 1973, No. 4. Note with respect to the contiguous sea-bed zone that all states *other than* the coastal state are prohibited from emplacing such weapons in the zone of the coastal state (Article 1(2)).

12. *Conclusion*

1. For reports of progress at recent sessions see *Australian Foreign Affairs Record* 47 (1976), pp.331, 648.
2. In the South Pacific Forum, Australia has joined with other South Pacific nations in supporting the concept of a 200 mile resources zone. See "South Pacific Forum Declaration on Law of the Sea Questions", *Commonwealth Record,* 1 (1976), p.1000.

Index

and the Contiguous Zone.
Geographically disadvantaged states.
 See Land-locked States
Great Barrier Reef, 94, 95, 96, 97, 103,
 107, 110, 111, 112, 120, 121, 122,
 123, 135, 136, 196n, 197n
Gulf. *See* Bays
Gulf of Carpentaria, 90, 91
Gulf of Mexico, 60, 61, 62, 63, 64

Harbours, 7, 54, 85, 87
"Heritage of mankind" doctrine, 5, 38,
 39, 42
Hervey Bay, 89
High Seas, 4, 5, 7, 16, 21, 27, 28, 29,
 30, 31, 32, 33, 34, 35, 36, 37, 42, 45,
 46, 47. *See also* Fishing and fisheries;
 Pollution
High-water mark, 6, 10, 13, 14, 15, 54,
 96, 97, 159, 160
Historic wrecks. *See* Wrecks and
 Salvage
Hot pursuit, 28
Hydrocarbons. *See* Continental shelf;
 Territorial sea, resources of;
 Petroleum legislation

Iceland, 34, 35
Indentation. *See* Bays; Territorial
 waters, delimitation of
Indonesia, 119, 120, 193n
Inland waters. *See* Internal waters
Inlet, 87
Innocent passage, 9, 10, 11, 17, 149,
 160, 161, 162, 163, 164
Internal waters
 and bays, 12, 13, 54, 60, 64, 65, 66,
  87, 88, 89, 90, 91, 92 (*See also*
  Bays)
 delimitation of, 10, 11, 12, 13, 14,
  15, 16, 51, 55, 64, 65, 66, 84, 85,
  86, 87, 91, 92, 93, 94, 95, 96, 97,
  188n, 190n
 extent of, 6, 7, 10, 11, 54, 55, 84,
  85, 86, 87
 and islands, 13, 14, 15, 16, 64, 65,
  66, 87, 91, 92, 93, 94, 95, 96, 97
 jurisdiction over, 10, 11, 51, 52, 54,
  55, 84, 85, 86, 87
 nature and status of, 6, 7, 54, 55,
  87
 resources of, 55, 61

International Conventions for the
 Prevention of Pollution of the Sea,
 28, 29, 30, 131, 132, 133, 134
International deep sea-bed authority,
 41, 42, 148
International law and Australian law,
 45, 46, 47, 48, 49, 50, 51, 52, 55, 57,
 58, 69, 70, 71, 72, 73, 76, 77, 78, 79,
 80, 87, 104, 105, 115, 116, 120, 131,
 132, 133, 134, 171n
International Law Commission 15, 16,
 26, 94
International waters. *See* High seas
Investigator Strait, 89, 95, 189n
Islands
 maritime space pertaining to, 14,
  105, 148, 151
 nature of, 11, 13, 14, 15, 16, 95, 96,
  97, 186
 territorial waters of, 11, 13, 14, 15,
  16, 91, 92, 93, 94, 95, 96, 97. *See
  also* Inland waters; Territorial
  waters and islands

Japan, 100
Jurisdictional rights. *See* Continental
 shelf, jurisdiction over; Internal
 waters, jurisdiction over; Territorial
 waters, jurisdiction over

Kangaroo Island, 95

Lacepede Bay, 88
Land-locked states, 36, 150
Law of the Sea Conferences. *See*
 United Nations Conferences on the
 Law of the Sea
Lighthouses, 11, 13, 15
Lobsters, 24, 107, 108, 109
Low-tide elevations, 11, 13, 14, 15, 95,
 96, 97
Low-water mark, 6, 10, 13, 14, 15, 59,
 71, 82, 96, 97, 157, 160. *See also*
 Inland Waters

Manganese modules. *See* Deep sea-bed
Median line. *See* Territorial waters,
 extent of; Continental shelf, extent of
Minerals
 of the sea bed, 23, 40, 112, 193n
 on land, 3. *See also* Continental
  shelf, resources of; Petroleum

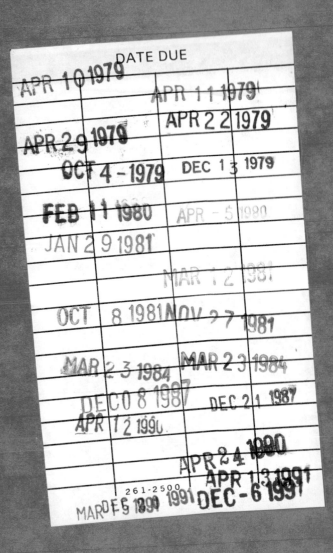